CAMBRIDGE STUDIES IN LINGUISTICS

General Editors · W. SIDNEY ALLEN · EUGENIE J. A. HENDERSON
FRED W. HOUSEHOLDER · JOHN LYONS · R. B. LE PAGE
F. R. PALMER · J. L. M. TRIM

Presupposition and the delimitation of semantics

In this series

Other volumes in preparation

PRESUPPOSITION AND THE DELIMITATION OF SEMANTICS

RUTH M.KEMPSON

Lecturer in Linguistics, University of London

CAMBRIDGE UNIVERSITY PRESS

CAMBRIDGE

LONDON · NEW YORK · MELBOURNE

Published by the Syndics of the Cambridge University Press
The Pitt Building, Trumpington Street, Cambridge CB2 IRP
Bentley House, 200 Euston Road, London NWI 2DB
32 East 57th Street, New York, NY 10022, USA
296 Beaconsfield Parade, Middle Park, Melbourne 3206, Australia

© Cambridge University Press 1975

Library of Congress Catalogue Card Number: 74-25078

ISBN: 0 521 20733 9 (hardcover)
       0 521 09938 2 (paperback)

First published 1975

Printed in Great Britain at the Alden Press, Oxford

P
325
K4
1975

To my father
E. G. H. Kempson

Contents

Preface

The present book originated as a Ph.D. thesis of London University, completed in October 1973. Particular thanks must therefore go to Professor C. Bazell, my thesis supervisor, who with his unique wealth of experience has helped me in countless ways. My gratitude to Professor Randolph Quirk, to whom I shall always be in debt for my introduction to linguistics in the first place, is no less pressing. Without his energy, encouragement, and continuing promotion, I should still be in an administrative job, barely knowing even the meaning of the word *linguistics*.

Perhaps inevitably, the most intangible debt is to one's every-day colleagues, to whom one airs one's views rather before they deserve the light of day. The people to whom such a debt is owing in this instance are Dr Anita Mittwoch, Dr Neil Smith, and Dr Deirdre Wilson, against whose acid criticism I have often had to defend myself—particularly in the early stages of the work for this book. To all of these, and to Professor Y. Bar-Hillel, Peter Cannings, Dr Dick Hudson, Professor Edward Keenan, Professor John Lyons, Professor F. Palmer, and Professor R. Robins, I am extremely grateful for the many and varied comments I received on earlier versions of the book. There remain to be thanked all those who have been my students in the last three years, since the majority of the arguments in this book have at some point been discussed in lectures, seminars and tutorials I have given. Needless to say however, there is unfortunately no one but myself that I can blame for the errors which still remain.

In connection with the preparation of the book for publication, I should like to thank the staff at Cambridge University Press for their unfailingly efficient help. And, on a more personal note, I must not forget to thank my husband, Michael Pinner, who had to show a more than usually generous measure of tolerance during the year in which the book was completed.

School of Oriental and African Studies   R.M.K.
London   July 1974

I Introduction: the linguistic framework

1.1 General conditions on a semantic theory

As an increasingly fashionable subject, semantics has become the light to which, mothlike, linguists are irresistibly drawn. With this sudden increase in popularity it is inevitable that the subject should be interpreted in different ways by different people. But the divergence between the interpretations has become extreme, and – as will shortly become apparent – it is no longer possible to pretend that the alternatives are all terminological variants of one another. In approaching this problem of the delimitation of semantics, one of the first steps must be to extract from the various interpretations the common core of agreement over which there need be no dispute. The extent of the agreement can be quickly listed on one hand. There are four conditions which linguists working within the framework of a formal model of language would agree must be satisfied by a semantic theory (or semantic component of a general theory):

1. It must be able to predict the meaning of any sentence, and it must do so on the basis of the meaning of the lexical items in that sentence and the syntactic relations between those items – i.e. the model must state a systematic relation between the meaning of lexical items and the syntactic structure of the sentence. Moreover, where a sentence has more than one interpretation, the model must predict the appropriate number of interpretations. (How these predictions are carried out will of course vary from theory to theory.)

2. Since the set of sentences for any language constitute an infinite set, the semantic model must be made up of a finite set of predictive rules like its syntactic counterpart: the model cannot merely analyse an arbitrarily selected finite subset of this infinite set.

3. The model must separate the infinite set of semantically non-deviant

sentences from another infinite set – that made up of contradictory or anomalous sentences, such as examples (1)–(8):[1]

(1) John ran but he didn't move.
(2) The man who was running was walking.
(3) The girl is a boy.
(4) Bachelors are married men.
(5) Green ideas sleep furiously.
(6) Ideas ran to catch the train.
(7) Safety likes to be treated gently.
(8) The boulders got married.

4. The model must be able to predict meaning relations between sentences, e.g. entailment (cf. pp. 33–4), contradiction and synonymy (cf. p. 34), since these relations hold by virtue of the meanings of sentences. These four demands are agreed in principle by all linguists.

But there the agreement ends; and the old problem of what constitutes the meaning of sentences raises its ugly head again. There seem to me to be two principal alternatives: either meaning can be defined in terms of conditions for the truth of sentences – i.e. be defined in terms of the relation between sentences (and lexical items) and the external world they describe;[2] or it can be defined in terms of conditions on the use of sentences in communication – i.e. be defined in terms of the relation of sentences to the speech act, the speaker of the sentence, etc. Yet it was on just this question of the definition of meaning that Leech (1969) suggested that there had been 'a movement towards agreement' (p. 4). How is it that Leech's optimistic view is not borne out? The difficulty arose when the notion of presupposition was incorporated into linguistics; because presupposition, like meaning, can be defined in one of two ways – either as a relation between statements (parallel to entailment, synonymy, etc.), or as a property of the speaker's belief in uttering a sentence. And only one of these definitions is compatible with a definition of meaning in terms of truth conditions. Yet if the presuppositions of a sentence are part of its semantic interpretation then by definition they are part of its meaning. Thus if presuppositions in terms of speaker-belief are considered to be part of the semantic interpretation

---

[1] Whether or not the model should treat contradictory and anomalous sentences as ungrammatical (i.e. not well-formed) is not generally agreed upon. For conflicting views, cf. Katz 1972, Jackendoff 1972, McCawley 1971, G. N. Lakoff 1971b.

[2] I shall argue in chapter 2 that Katz' and Bierwisch's positions are not genuine alternatives to this.

of sentences, then it seems that the meaning of sentences must be in terms of speaker-hearer relations and not, or not solely, in terms of the relation between a symbol or set of symbols and the object or state described. The status of speaker-hearer relations in a semantic theory is not however the only problem which presupposition raises. The logical concept of presupposition is defined within a three-valued logic, and if semantics has to include such a concept then it follows that the logic of natural language is not the familiar two-valued logic but a presuppositional, three-valued logic. So both characterisations of presupposition present a theoretical problem for linguistics of no mean significance.

What I shall argue during the course of this book is that all the problems raised by presupposition are in fact pseudo-problems for semantics, since no concept of presupposition has any place within the semantics of natural language. Accordingly, I shall be arguing for a truth-conditional semantics based on a two-valued logic. But in order to maintain such a position, I rely on a pragmatic account of many phenomena generally thought to be semantic. In the final part of the book, I therefore turn to two major problems (*a*) the problem of giving detailed substance to the presently alarmingly insubstantial pragmatic wastepaper basket, (*b*) the question of the status of pragmatics within an over-all theory of language. So, in general terms, this book can be seen as simultaneously an exercise in a linguistic truth-based semantics and a plea to linguists to give up the widely accepted conflation of semantics and pragmatics.

1.2 The relation between syntax and semantics

From a methodological point of view, one of the most important current problems is that semantic arguments are often not sufficiently rigorous to deserve serious theoretical evaluation: there is no agreed formalism in which predictions can be precisely formulated, nor is there even agreement as to what constitutes a semantic argument. In an attempt to combat this failing, I shall present the solution to each problem considered in a formal semantic representation, which will in every case have a precisely stateable set of consequences by which the solution can be tested.

As a preliminary, I must now make clear the assumptions about the interdependence of syntax and semantics which I shall be drawing on throughout the book, and give a more detailed specification of the semantic component to be adopted. On the basis of arguments presented in Chomsky 1969, 1971, 1972; Fodor 1970; Hall-Partee 1970, and elsewhere, I shall accept as currently the most explanatorily adequate theory a (transformational) grammar in which the syntactic component has the generative power, the semantic component being interpretive. That is to say, I shall be taking for granted: (i) that syntactic behaviour of a sentence or structure is not, or not necessarily, determined by its semantic properties, (ii) that the contraints imposed by syntactic structure are not co-extensive with those of semantics, and (iii) that semantic generalisations should not therefore be captured by the same formal means as syntactic generalisations. This stand leads to two consequent assumptions which provide the background to all the arguments to be presented in the course of this book: (*a*) syntactic constructs in general must be defined and justified without reference to semantics, and (*b*) the semantic analysis of a sentence does not automatically lead to a reflex in the syntactic structure of that sentence. I shall not give justification of this position here, as it has been much debated in the literature,[1] but the analysis of the semantics of negation to be presented later in this chapter (1.3.3) gives confirmation of the independent nature of syntactic and semantic constructs, since it constitutes an example of a semantic rule of interpretation which cannot be captured, in any natural way, by the formal apparatus of the syntactic component.

In addition to an interpretive semantic framework, I shall take as familiar the now widely accepted position that selectional restrictions are not a syntactic constraint (cf. McCawley 1968a, 1971). It is not however obvious that they should be analysed as a semantic constraint either. Much of the evidence which shows that a syntactic blocking mechanism of the kind outlined in *Aspects* (whereby the insertion of verbs is dependent on features of the surrounding nouns) cannot be correct also casts doubt on the Katz–Bierwisch formulation, in which the operation of semantic projection rules depends on a prior matching between selectional specification of the modifier and inherent specification of the head. Consider the three following problems.

1. When embedded as a complement to verbs such as *say*, selectional restrictions can be broken without deviance:

[1] Cf. McCawley 1968a, 1968b, 1971, G. N. Lakoff 1970a, 1971a, Ross 1969, 1972, Chomsky 1969, 1971, 1972, Fodor 1970, Katz 1970, Hall-Partee 1970, Jackendoff 1972.

(9) John said that rocks get diabetes.

(10) John claimed that men get pregnant.

(11) Our five-year-old son told Mary that stones have babies.

2. In certain negative environments, selectional restrictions can also be broken without causing deviance:

(12) A rock doesn't get diabetes.

(13) Worms don't worry about money.

(14) Men don't get pregnant.

(15) It's not true that a rock gets tired.

3. Where a verb or adjective has a particular selectional restriction and the noun it modifies is unmarked for that specification, the resulting phrase is interpreted as having that specification as part of its meaning:

(16) John hit it.

(17) That person is pregnant.[1]

(18) Those that get pregnant sometimes regret it.

Thus the last example is interpreted as having a subject which is female, human, and adult, and this interpretation is due to the selectional specification of *pregnant* that its subject be female and adult (but not necessarily human) and the selectional specification of *regret* that its subject be human. In the first two cases, a Chomskian blocking mechanism on lexical insertion has to be prevented from applying; and no explanation of the third set can be provided at all since on this view selectional constraints are syntactic and do not operate in the semantic interpretation of a sentence – they are merely a condition on lexical insertion. More interestingly, both Bierwisch's and Katz' formulation of selectional restrictions as a semantic constraint on the operation of the semantic interpretation rules (cf. Bierwisch 1969, p. 164; Katz 1964, pp. 526–7) meet similar problems. *Ad hoc* and different caveats have to be added for each of these cases, to prevent anomalous predictions such as the synonymy of examples (12)–(15).

On the other hand, if selectional specifications are analysed as a semantic property of the verb in question no different in kind from its inherent properties, then there is a natural solution to all the sentences given above. *Our male cousin became pregnant* will be predicted to be a

---

[1] With *pregnant* we enter the problematic realm of what constitutes knowledge of the language (viz. the meaning of *pregnant*) and what merely knowledge of the world (viz. our knowledge of which sex gives birth to children). For present purposes, however, I am simply assuming that it is part of the lexical specification of *pregnant* that it apply to females.

contradiction by virtue of the joint specification of the subject as male and female (cf. pp. 8–9 for an explicit formulation of contextual specication in terms of semantic components); *John said that rocks get diabetes* will not be predicted to be contradictory by virtue of the semantic property of the verb *say*;[1] *Worms don't worry about money* will not be predicted to be contradictory since the specification of 'human' on the subject of *worry* is interpreted as falling within the scope of negation (cf. *John isn't a woman*) (cf. 1.3.3 for a discussion of negation); and the interpretation of sentences such as *Those that get pregnant sometimes regret it* follows as an automatic consequence since the specification of the subject as human, female, and adult, simply is part of the meaning of the lexical items and hence of the sentence itself.[2] Furthermore, this analysis of selectional specification of lexical items as a part of their meaning makes an important and correct prediction (another piece of evidence that selectional restrictions are semantic in nature): all synonymous lexical items will have identical selectional restrictions (even when they are syntactically distinct – viz. singular *versus* plural), and hence all synonymous sentences will have the same commutation potential:

(19) John used a knife to cut the cake.
(20) ?John used milk to cut the cake.[3]
(21) John cut the cake with a knife.
(22) ?John cut the cake with milk.
(23) The mother of John...
(24) ?The mother of dust...
(25) The woman who gave birth to John...
(26) ?The woman who gave birth to dust...
(27) John killed Mary.
(28) ?John killed milk.
(29) John caused Mary to die.
(30) ?John caused milk to die.

On the basis of this evidence I shall assume that so-called 'selectional restrictions' are neither syntactic restrictions nor semantic restrictions

---

[1] Verbs such as *dream* and *believe* with the same property are discussed on pp. 71–2, 90, 105–9.
[2] It follows from this that there is no longer any distinction in kind between anomaly and contradiction. Cf. Bierwisch 1969 fn. 13 for a critical assessment of this distinction.
[3] I shall consistently depict contradictions with '?', since I argue on p. 11 that these are semantically well-formed, and only deviant on a pragmatic level.

but simply a property of meaning of the item in question. We shall see shortly how this is naturally stateable within a semantic representation.

1.3 On the nature of semantic features and the semantic component

While the nature of syntactic representations is fairly clear, even if their justification is not, the nature of semantic representation is unhappily not at all clear. However this problem is not one with which I wish to deal in any detail. I shall merely assume that semantic specification operates largely along the lines suggested by Bierwisch (1969, 1971) (though cf. 2.3.1 below for a brief defence of semantic representations of this type). In essence, Bierwisch's formulation gives as a semantic representation a fully specified logical form but this level is not that of the syntactically justified deep structure. In this formulation, the rules of the semantic component are interpretive in that they are dependent on a semantic specification of lexical items in the lexicon and the syntactic information provided by the underlying structure of a sentence (in this respect like Katz).

1.3.1 On the form of semantic features.
One important respect in which Bierwisch differs from Chomsky (1965) and Katz (1964, 1966a, 1972) is in the form of the minimal semantic unit. Bierwisch formulates semantic components along the lines defined by predicate calculus, and not in a different way as do Katz and Leech. One of the chief reasons for not using predicate calculus as the basis for description seems to have been the common assumption that the semantic properties of lexical items, like their phonological and syntactic properties, could be formulated in terms of binary features (whether implicitly, like Katz, or explicitly, like Leech). However it is apparent that binary features must be inadequate for analysing terms such as transitive verbs which express a relation between two objects, e.g. *kill*, *chase*, etc., since such features are equivalent to a one-place predicate and hence are not a suitable means of formalising two-place relations. Thus [MALE]X, [HUMAN]X, [ADULT]X,[1] can be rewritten as the binary feature complex +MALE, +HUMAN, +ADULT, but [CAUSE]X_1 ([DIE]X_2) cannot be reformulated in binary features in any transparent

---

[1] I adopt here the format of Bierwisch. A predicate is thus listed first in sequence, followed by its argument(s). Propositional arguments are enclosed in round brackets.

way. The nearest equivalent is perhaps +CAUSATIVE, +RELA-
TIONAL, +DEATH, which is obviously unsatisfactory. Moreover
both Katz' (cf. Katz 1966a, 1967) and Leech's attempts to overcome
this deficiency necessitate dubious additions to the semantic metalanguage, which to the extent that they are adequately justified are
terminological variants of predicate calculus formulations (cf. Bierwisch
1969 for detailed criticisms of Katz' extended component system).[1]
I shall therefore – like Bierwisch (cf. also Weinreich 1962, Bendix
1966) – assume that semantic properties of lexical items can most
appropriately be described by the formulae of predicate calculus,
construing features as predicates with unbound variables indexed for
subject and object (and indirect object in the case of three-place predicates such as *give*). There are however several respects in which the
semantic apparatus differs from that of predicate calculus. One of these
is the need to have propositions functioning as arguments. Thus for
example the lexical entry for *kill* would be:

$$kill: +[V]$$
$$+[—NP]$$
$$[CAUSE]X_{NP,S}([BECOME](NOT[ALIVE]X_{NP,VP}))$$
$$[ANIMATE]X_{NP,VP}$$

In each case the variable X is given a syntactic index. In the first component above, X and the proposition ([BECOME](NOT[ALIVE]X))
function as arguments of the predicate [CAUSE], the proposition
(NOT[ALIVE]X) is the argument of the one-place predicate [BE-
COME], and [ALIVE] has X as argument. Implicit in this formulation
is the assumption that the semantic properties of lexical items are
expressed in terms of the contribution the items make to the meaning
of a sentence.

A further complication of predicate calculus is the need to have
predicates as arguments for predicates. This is necessary in order to
make explicit the meaning of for example *rush* as (approximately)

$$rush: [[FAST]MOTION]X_{NP,S} .$$
$$[[PHYSICAL]ACTIVITY]X_{NP,S} . [ANIMATE]X_{NP,S}{}^{2}$$

In addition to predicative features, there must also be delimiting features
parallel to the quantifiers of predicate calculus to give a semantic

---

[1] The revision of Katz' system in Katz 1972 is not substantially different from earlier
versions and is therefore open to the same criticisms.
[2] I am assuming the standard definition of '.' as *and*.

representation of determiners, numerals, and quantifiers. The exact nature of these I will leave until after a discussion of determiners in chapter 6. The only substantial difference between the formulation used here and that of Bierwisch is on the question of selectional properties, which I have argued are identical to the inherent properties of a lexical item (cf. 1.2).

Each of the lexical entries given here depends on some form of redundancy rule completing the specification of its meaning. For example:

[HUMAN]X⟶[ANIMATE]X
[ANIMATE]X⟶[CONCRETE]X

In fact the lexical entry for *rush* given above could be simplified if the following redundancy rule was taken into account:

[ACTIVITY . MOTION]X⟶[[PHYSICAL]ACTIVITY]X[1]

The need for these rules is very generally recognised. However their complexity has been discussed in detail only by Bierwisch (1969), who points out that many redundancy rules must be of a form

[M]⟶[[M]N]

rather than a mere addition of features. Thus for example a full specification of *woman* would not be in the form:

[FEMALE]X . [HUMAN]X . [ANIMATE]X .
　[CONCRETE]X . [ADULT]X

but rather in the more complex hierarchical form:

[[[FEMALE . HUMAN . ADULT]ANIMATE]CONCRETE]X

since the minimal entry [FEMALE]X . [HUMAN]X . [ADULT]X would be subject to redundancy rules:

[FEMALE]X⟶[[FEMALE]ANIMATE]X
[HUMAN]X⟶[[HUMAN]ANIMATE]X
[ADULT]X⟶[[ADULT]ANIMATE]X
[ANIMATE]X⟶[[ANIMATE]CONCRETE]X[2]

This hierarchy is not only needed to account for relations of inclusion between properties but also to account for the behaviour of semantic complexes under negation (cf. 1.3.3 below).

---

[1] Cf. Bierwisch 1969, pp. 170–1.
[2] Bierwisch's formulation is:
[[RED]*] v [[BLUE]*] v [[GREEN]*] v ... → [COLOUR]
but the difference is not substantive ('*' is interpreted as a place-holder for the more inclusive term). I have preferred the simpler formulation for purposes of clarity.

1.3.2 On the nature of the projection rules. The rules providing the semantic interpretation of a sentence are dependent on this semantic specification of the lexical items as fully interpreted by the redundancy rules, and their syntactic relations as defined by the deep structure phrase-marker. In addition, Bierwisch's system of interpretive rules depends on all noun phrases having a reference index as part of their deep-structure specification.[1] These reference indices are substituted for the grammatical index specified in the lexical entry and all the

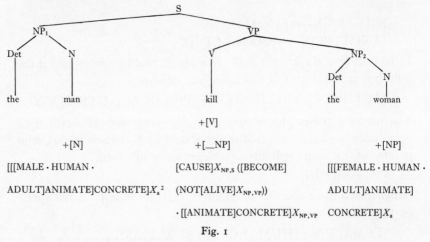

Fig. 1

components are combined to form an unordered conjoint set (i.e. joined by '.'). These so-called projection rules are constrained by the syntactic indices on the lexical items. These must match the noun phrase whose referential index is to be substituted (in the case of a noun, the grammatical index must match the noun phrase immediately dominating it). Thus for example the phrase marker in Fig. 1 is interpreted as:

[[[MALE . HUMAN . ADULT]ANIMATE]CONCRETE]X_1 .
[[[FEMALE . HUMAN .
    ADULT]ANIMATE]CONCRETE]X_2 .
[CAUSE]X_1([BECOME](NOT[ALIVE]X_2)) .
    [[ANIMATE]CONCRETE]X_2[3]

---

[1] Cf. 2.3.2 below for an independent justification of this position. Exceptions to this general statement are considered on p. 111.

[2] a = [NP,S] v [NP,VP] v [NP,PP], where 'v' here and in all subsequent formulations corresponds to logically inclusive *or*.

[3] I ignore here the problem of the definite article. For a more detailed analysis see chapters 5–6.

Any specification which is given twice is then deleted, thus avoiding redundancy (in this case [[ANIMATE]CONCRETE]X₂).[1]

In connection with the prediction of the set of contradictory sentences, there are two possible analyses within this framework. On the one hand they can be said to be semantically deviant and hence excluded by well-formedness conditions. This account of contradictions is adopted by Katz, Bierwisch, and Jackendoff (who makes crucial use of this device (1972) to exclude sentences such as *Themselves were odd* and even *John of the was running*, both normally excluded by a syntactic device). However a plausible and independently motivated alternative would be to demand that the semantic component merely has to characterise them as a natural set, by predicting for example that they be necessarily false, rather than exclude them as not well-formed. Evidence in support of this view is provided by the necessity of a pragmatic maxim (cf. chapter 7) that speakers tell the truth. The deviance of contradictions is thus captured by rules of communication. The problem is on this view parallel to self-embedded constructions whose deviance is explained by some theory of memory rather than by the specifically linguistic competence model.[2] Since this problem is not central to my arguments, I shall leave the question open.

1.3.3 Negation. The semantic rules of interpretation are not exhausted by the projection rules of substitution. Additional rules are needed to interpret negative sentences, and there are special problems over these which constitute the core of the disagreement over presupposition. The problems I shall consider later (chapters 4–6). Here I merely wish to set up a formal means of describing the interpretation of negative sentences. A detailed formulation was set up for negative sentences first by Katz (1964), and this was improved and generalised by Bierwisch to cover all types of sentences and all types of semantic marker, simple and complex. I shall assume here that the latter is the more sophisticated and I shall not deal with Katz' (1964) formulation (it has three caveats which both reduce its over-all generality and detract from its initial plausibility). In both Katz' and Bierwisch's formulation the rule is, in essence, a strict translation into componential terms of the logical equivalence defined by de Morgan. This states that for any conjoint

[1] For further details, cf. Bierwisch 1969.
[2] If this analysis is correct, the plausibility of Jackendoff's characterisation of a large proportion of linguistic deviance is correspondingly reduced.

set of items (whether they be properties, objects or statements), the negation of that conjoint set is equivalent to the disjunct set of the negation of each member of that set, viz:

$$-(P \cdot Q) \equiv -P \text{ v} -Q$$

Thus to take a simple example in componential terms, *It was a girl* has the interpretation that the object described was female *and* young *and* human *and* animate etc. but *It wasn't a girl* then has the interpretation that the object described was either not female *or* not young *or* not human *or* not animate.

There are several complications to this statement. Both Katz and Bierwisch analyse negation in terms of an 'antonymy operator'. This is defined as follows:

For any antonymous set of components $M_1 M_2 \ldots M_n$ the antonymy operator (A/M_i) of some arbitrary component M_i is $(M_1 \text{ v } M_2 \ldots M_{i-1} \text{ v } M_{i+1} \ldots M_n)$.

For those cases such as [ANIMATE] which are sole members of their set:

$$A/M \equiv -M \tag{i}$$

It follows from these definitions that $A/A/M_i = M_i$. Bierwisch extends this to complex markers such that for any markers M and N (either simple or complex):

$$A/[M \cdot N] \equiv [A/M \text{ v } A/N] \tag{ii}$$

(equivalent exactly to de Morgan's law)

$$A/[[M]N] \equiv [[A/M]N \text{ v } A/N] \tag{iii}$$

(deducible from de Morgan's equivalences – cf. Bierwisch 1969, p. 173). The interpretation of a negative sentence is then derived as follows (ignoring for the moment problems of scope). Given Neg S where S is interpreted as a conjoint set of semantic components $(P_1 \cdot P_2 \cdot P_3 \ldots P_n)$ either simple or complex, Neg S is replaced by A/S.

$$A/S \equiv A/P_1 \text{ v } A/P_2 \text{ v } A/P_3 \text{ v } \ldots \text{ v } A/P_n$$

By this rule the interpretation of *It wasn't a woman* is predictable in the following way.[1] The semantic specification of *woman* was given earlier as:

---

[1] I here assume the incorrect simplification that negating a sentence is equivalent to negating its predicate. Cf. chapter 5 for further instances which demonstrate this to be false.

[[[FEMALE . HUMAN . ADULT]ANIMATE]CONCRETE]X

Thus NEG [[[FEMALE . HUMAN . ADULT]ANIMATE]CON-
CRETE]X is replaced by

A/[[[FEMALE . HUMAN .
 ADULT]ANIMATE]CONCRETE]X
≡ (by iii)[A/[[FEMALE . HUMAN .
 ADULT]ANIMATE]CONCRETE v A/CONCRETE]X[1]
≡ (by iii)[[A/[FEMALE . HUMAN .
 ADULT]ANIMATE]CONCRETE v
 [A/ANIMATE]CONCRETE v A/CONCRETE]X[2]
≡ (by ii)[[[A/FEMALE v A/HUMAN v
 A/ADULT]ANIMATE]CONCRETE v
 [A/ANIMATE]CONCRETE v A/CONCRETE]X
≡ (by i)[[[MALE v −HUMAN v
    a   *b*
 −ADULT]ANIMATE]CONCRETE]X v
    c
 [[−ANIMATE]CONCRETE]X v [−CONCRETE]X
    d   *e*

(The *or* in each case is the logically inclusive *or*.) Informally what the
rules states in this example is that the set of components specified by
the statement *It was a woman* does not correspond to the state of affairs
being described. This failure of correspondence may have one of several
causes: either the object described is not female (though human) as in
(*a*), or it is not human (*b*), or it is not adult (*c*), or it is not animate at
all (*d*), or it is not even a concrete object (*e*). Which of these is the cause
of the lack of correspondence is not specified by the sentence, but is
left vague. All the sentence states is that there is not a correspondence
between the statement *It was a woman* and the situation in question.
The context (linguistic or non-linguistic) may however clarify which of
these four possible specifications is the basis of a speaker's asserting
It wasn't a woman – viz:

    (A) P "Was that a woman knocking on the door?"
        Q "No. It wasn't a woman. (It was a man.)"

[1] In this application of (iii), M = [[FEMALE . HUMAN . ADULT]ANIMATE]
                    N = [CONCRETE]
[2] In this application of (iii), M = [FEMALE . HUMAN . ADULT]
                    N = [ANIMATE]

(B) P "Was that a woman knocking on the door?"

Q "No. It wasn't a woman. (It was my dog.)"

(C) P "Was that a woman knocking on the door?"

Q "No. It wasn't a woman. (It was my daughter.)"

(D) P "Was that a woman knocking on the door?"

Q "No. It wasn't a woman. (It was my dustbin leaning up against it.)"

(E) P "Was it a woman that annoyed you?"

Q "No. It wasn't a woman. (It was my own incompetence.)"

In fact, as (A) demonstrates, the possibilities are yet more varied, as the complex (*a*)–(*c*) allows for any combination of [MALE] or [−MALE] with [HUMAN] or [−HUMAN] and with [ADULT] or [−ADULT] – except [−MALE . HUMAN . ADULT]. The sentence is in fact applied in (A) to describe a situation in which a combination of [MALE . HUMAN . ADULT] are involved. Notice that if the redundancy rules had been, as traditionally formulated:

$$[\text{HUMAN}]X \longrightarrow [\text{ANIMATE}]X$$
$$[\text{ANIMATE}]X \longrightarrow [\text{CONCRETE}]X$$

the wrong predictions would have been made: the possible interpretations of *It wasn't a woman* would have been given as

$$-([\text{FEMALE}]X . [\text{HUMAN}]X . [\text{ADULT}]X .$$
$$[\text{ANIMATE}]X . [\text{CONCRETE}]X)$$
$$\equiv A/([\text{FEMALE}]X . [\text{HUMAN}]X . [\text{ADULT}]X .$$
$$[\text{ANIMATE}]X . [\text{CONCRETE}]X)$$
$$\equiv [A/\text{FEMALE}]X \text{ v } [A/\text{HUMAN}]X \text{ v } [A/\text{ADULT}]X \text{ v}$$
$$[A/\text{ANIMATE}]X \text{ v } [A/\text{CONCRETE}]X$$
$$\equiv [\text{MALE}]X \text{ v } [-\text{HUMAN}]X \text{ v } [-\text{ADULT}]X \text{ v}$$
$$[-\text{ANIMATE}]X \text{ v } [-\text{CONCRETE}]X$$

Here the five contextualisations (A)–(E) are predicted, but there is no means of blocking the combination of [−CONCRETE] and [MALE], [−ANIMATE] and [MALE], etc.: i.e. there is no way of capturing the intuition that if animacy or concreteness are negated, then sex human-ness or adult-ness must also be negated.

The fact that there are at least the five different contextualisations (A)–(E) of *It wasn't a woman* does not demonstrate that the sentence is five-ways ambiguous. What the disjunct reading states is that there is one interpretation of this sentence but that there are (at least) five ways of meeting the conditions set by this interpretation. This constitutes vagueness, not ambiguity. This can be shown by considering well-attested cases of vagueness.[1] There is but one interpretation of *neighbour* but more than one way of meeting this interpretation. It is met both by female humans and by male humans. If negative sentences were said to be ambiguous by virtue of their disjunct reading, then every example of vagueness could be shown to be ambiguous. *Neighbour* for example would be shown (falsely) to be an ambiguous lexical item, since it can be used to describe quite different types of object, male humans and female humans. This is clearly incorrect. There is a syntactic test for distinguishing vagueness from ambiguity, which confirms this analysis of negation.[2] If a sentence is ambiguous, then in order for verb-phrase pronominalisation to take place in a conjoined structure containing that sentence, the two conjuncts must agree in their interpretation of the ambiguous sentence. Thus (31) is ambiguous two ways and not four:

(31) John likes visiting relatives and Harry does too.

This cannot be followed by the contextualisation *John likes going to see relatives, and Harry for them to come and see him*. If a sentence is vague in some part of its semantic interpretation, the interpretation of the pronominalised conjunct need not agree with the first conjunct:

(32) John likes music and Harry does too: John likes pop and Harry classical.
(33) John paid a lot for his car, and Harry did too: John paid 3,000 pounds and Harry 6,000 pounds.
(34) John has one neighbour and Mary has one too: John's neighbour is a spinster, and Mary's is a widower.

In all these cases – unlike (31) – the further specification of the conjuncts can vary independently. Now just as the specification of sex in some contextualised use of *neighbour* can vary independently across a verb-phrase pronominalisation of this type, so can the interpretation of negative sentences:

(35) John didn't run away and Harry didn't either: John walked slowly off and Harry stayed stock still.

---

[1] I am using vagueness here and throughout as interchangeable with unspecified. It is arguable that there is a second kind of vagueness which is in principle unspecifiable. An example is *You are the winner*, which may be vague as to whether or not it is being used performatively.
[2] Cf. G. N. Lakoff 1970c.

(36) John doesn't seduce women and Harry doesn't either: John seduces young girls and Harry seduces boys.

(37) On the first day, it wasn't a woman and it wasn't on the second day either: first it was a man and then it was a young girl.

In each of these, the verb phrase of the second conjunct can be prono-minalised (deleted in the case of the copula) by virtue of the two conjunctions sharing an identical negated verb phrase. This does not however constrain the specification of which conditions are interpreted as not being met, i.e. to what components of the sentence the negation applies. On this test therefore, the interpretation of the scope of the negation is vague, not ambiguous.

Furthermore, the two semantic concepts of vagueness and ambiguity are theoretically distinguished. An ambiguous sentence is formulated as having two quite separate structures, whereas a vague sentence is one which is characterised semantically by a disjunction. Thus *neighbour* will have a lexical entry which is unspecified for sex and which will therefore be specified redundantly as [MALE v FEMALE]. Similarly a negative sentence has one underlying structure (given that it is not ambiguous for independent reasons) and is interpreted as vague in its interpretation by a semantic rule which predicts a disjunct set of possible readings.

The basis of the vagueness (non-ambiguity) of negative sentences is not hard to find. Recall that the rule of negation reflects directly the de Morgan equivalence,

$$-(P \cdot Q) \equiv -P \ v \ -Q$$

and that the five different contextualisation (A)–(E) of *It wasn't a woman* depend on this equivalence. Thus anyone wishing to claim that negative sentences are ambiguous according as one interpretation was predominant in a context must also be committed to claiming that the formula $-P \ v \ -Q$ is itself ambiguous. But it is not. The connective *or* (inclusive) has one interpretation: that any statement *P or Q* is true under a disjunction of three independent sets of conditions (*P* true, *Q* true, or *P* and *Q* true). So despite the fact that any statement *P or Q* is true under three separate sets of conditions, *or* itself is not ambiguous – it is characterised by a single disjunct interpretation. And as with *or*, so with negative sentences.

1.3.4 The scope of negation. So far I have referred only in passing to the so-called scope of negation with an implicit assumption of its being understood. It must however be more rigorously defined. In the case of negation, the scope of negation constitutes those semantic components which are altered by the rule of negation. Thus for some conjoint set of semantic components $[e_1 . e_2 . e_3]$ the negation of that set is equivalent to:

$$[A/e_1 \text{ v } A/e_2 \text{ v } A/e_3]$$

and this formulation by definition allows any of the following combinations:[1]

$[A/e_1 . A/e_2 . A/e_3]$	(i)
$[A/e_1 . A/e_2 . e_3]$	(ii)
$[A/e_1 . e_2 . A/e_3]$	(iii)
$[e_1 . A/e_2 . A/e_3]$	(iv)
$[A/e_1 . e_2 . e_3]$	(v)
$[e_1 . e_2 . A/e_3]$	(vi)
$[e_1 . A/e_2 . e_3]$	(vii)

Now in each of these specified cases, the scope of negation differs: it includes all three components in (i), e_1 and e_2 in (ii), e_1 and e_3 in (iii), e_2 and e_3 in (iv) etc. This may seem to stand in contradiction to my statement that the rule applied to a whole sentence reading, with the single disjunct output. But it is not. The specification of $\text{Neg}(e_1 . e_2 . e_3)$ allows for each of these seven possibilities and the scope of negation is indeterminate. Thus *It wasn't a woman* in my example on pp. 12–14 does not specify that the object described was a boy, or that it was a girl, or even that it was the dustbin leaning against the door, etc., but merely states that the object described was not male, human and adult, a specification which covers and is neutral between each of these possibilities. So the scope of negation is indeterminate in this case.

Notice that this accords with our definition of the distinction between ambiguity and vagueness, since *It wasn't a woman* is given a single (disjunct) reading. If negative sentences were ambiguous according as their scope differed, then this sentence (and all other negative sentences) would be described as having the requisite number of different underlying structures with the scope stated specifically for each interpretation.

1.3.5 Rules of semantic interpretation operating on surface structures. The inherent vagueness of negative sentences has not been

---

[1] The only option excluded is $[e_1 . e_2 . e_3]$, since this would correspond to the assertion of such a statement, not its denial.

widely recognised among linguists. In fact attempts have been made
to predict a fully specified scope of negation, and these attempts have
led to a proposed revision of the standard (1965) theory's claim that
the input to the semantic component is the set of deep-structure phrase
markers. There are three chief protagonists in this issue – G. N. Lakoff
(1970b), Jackendoff (1969), and Chomsky (1971), of whom two (Lakoff
and Jackendoff) base their arguments on the mistaken assumption that
negative sentences are fully determinate in their meaning and scope-
specification, and that they are therefore frequently ambiguous.[1] The

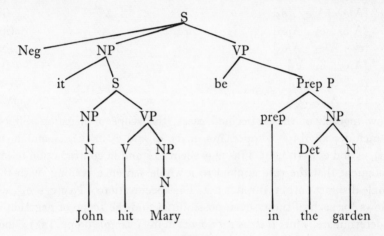

Fig. 2

point at issue is this: are deep-structure phrase markers a sufficient
input for the semantic component to be able to predict the interpretations of sentences, or should this claim be dropped in favour of a weaker
claim that information from both deep structure and surface structure is
necessary in order to predict the meanings of sentences?

Lakoff argued that scope of negation could be predicted at underlying

[1] They are not alone in this mistake. In a comparable analysis of *even*, Fraser (1971)
mistakenly assumes that sentences containing *even* are ambiguous as to its scope and
on the basis of this, he claims to provide a deciding case for the deep-structure
semantics *v.* surface-structure semantics issue. However each of his crucial examples,
e.g. *The statue was even photographed by the king*, *That man is even easy to please* –
which if they allow a verb-phrase-scope reading can only be naturally described in
terms of derived constituent structure – are necessarily vague in scope. Thus any
possibility for verb-phrase-scope interpretation is indistinguishable from and only
one of a disjunct set of readings of a sentence-scope reading. The putative test cases
thus fall to the ground, since a deep-structure specification of scope naturally
predicts a sentence-scope reading.

structure. His argument stemmed from the claim that *John didn't hit Mary in the garden* is synonymous to its cleft congener *It is not in the garden that John hit Mary*, and that a natural explanation of this would be provided if both were derived from the underlying structure corresponding to the cleft construction as shown in Fig. 2. This was generalised to all adverbials so that for every case, the adverbial was analysed as the scope of negation; and the scope of negation was invariably expressed in terms of a cleft-type structure. That which was interpreted as falling within the scope of negation was analysed as the superordinate predicate and that which was not understood as negated was analysed as the subordinate. Even in its own terms this analysis can be shown to be insufficient for a general account of negation. First of all, as both Heidolph (1970) and Chomsky (1971) have pointed out, the scope of negation may be restricted to an item which is not a deep structure constituent,

(38) John didn't run in front of the house, but behind it.
(39) John isn't easy to please or eager to please: he's just a fussy, idle old man.

In (38), the focus of negation is not a constituent at all, and in (39), it is a derived constituent but not a deep-structure constituent. Secondly, an analysis which makes the focus of negation the superordinate term leads to a syntactic contradiction in examples such as:

(40) John isn't a bright boy.

In (40), as the sole item in the scope of negation, *bright* should by definition be superordinate to *boy*, but its syntactic relation to *boy* demands that it be subordinate to *boy*. There is in any case no cleft for (40) to be parallel to. There is no **It isn't bright that John is a boy*. Moreover the argument stems from an incorrect analysis of *John didn't hit Mary in the garden*. It is not obvious that this sentence is synonymous with *It is not in the garden that John hit Mary*, since it stands in a comparable relation to a whole set of cleft sentences:

(41) It is not John that hit Mary in the garden.
(42) It is not Mary that John hit in the garden.
(43) It is not in the garden that John hit Mary.
(44) What John did not do to Mary was hit her in the garden.
(45) What John did not do was hit Mary in the garden.
(46) What John did not do to Mary in the garden was hit her.

There is thus no reason to isolate any single cleft structure as the underlying structure for the corresponding simple negative.

A very similar mistake is made in Jackendoff's attempt to provide an alternative interpretive position. Jackendoff purports to show that some negative sentences are unambiguous as to scope and of these there is a set of sentences in which an active-passive pair are not synonymous since they differ in their scope specification. If the grammar is to maintain the active-passive relation and yet predict this difference, the rule determining scope specification must be carried out after the passive rule has taken place – i.e. at the surface structure. The following sets of data are central to his argument:

(47) (i)   It is not so that many of the arrows hit the target.
      (ii)   Many of the arrows didn't hit the target.
      (iii) Not many of the arrows hit the target.
      (iv)   The target wasn't hit by many of the arrows.
      (iia) Many of the arrows didn't hit the target, but many of them did hit it.
      (iiia) *Not many of the arrows hit the target, but many of them did hit it.
      (iva) *The target wasn't hit by many of the arrows, but it was hit by many of them.

(48) (i)   It is not so that many of the demonstrators were arrested by the police.
      (ii)   Many of the demonstrators weren't arrested by the police.
      (iii) Not many of the demonstrators were arrested by the police.
      (iv)   The police didn't arrest many of the demonstrators.
      (iia) Many of the demonstrators weren't arrested by the police but many were.
      (iiia) *Not many of the demonstrators were arrested by the police but many were.
      (iva) *The police didn't arrest many of the demonstrators, but they did arrest many of them.

The argument proceeds identically for both sets of data:

(*a*) (i) is the characteristic paraphrase of sentence negation.
(*b*) (i) is unambiguous and synonymous with (iii) but not with (ii). Therefore (ii) is not an example of sentence negation, but verb-phrase negation.

(c) (ii) can be denied without forming a contradiction, as in (iia), but (iii) cannot, giving confirmation that (ii) must be an instance of verb-phrase negation, not sentence negation.

(d) (iv) is unambiguous and synonymous with (iii) and not with (ii) its syntactic congener. This is said to be demonstrated by the contradiction in (iiia) and (iva) which is not present in (iia).

(e) Therefore, since (iv) and (ii) are not synonymous, the passive transformation must take place before the specification of scope is predicted – i.e. at surface structure.

Steps (b), (c) and (d) are incorrect and unjustified. Moreover they lead to a contradiction. (b) is wrong in the same way that Lakoff was wrong. *It is not so that many arrows hit the target* covers both *Many arrows didn't hit the target* and *Not many arrows hit the target* since it is neutral as to scope specification. There is thus no evidence so far that either of these is not an instance of sentence negation. Step (c) is incorrect because (iia) is not an example of a negative sentence plus its positive counterpart, despite appearances. The fact which Jackendoff overlooked is that (iia) is only non-contradictory if the *many* in the first conjunct is not coreferential with the *many* in the second conjunct. But on this reading the two conjuncts are thus not identical and do not provide evidence of the scope of negation in the first conjunct. It is this part of the analysis which leads directly to a contradiction. Sentence (iia) on the relevant reading is parallel to *John$_i$ didn't hit the target but John$_j$ did*. Therefore, if Jackendoff's argument concerning (iia) is correct, it also follows that *John$_i$ didn't hit the target* is an instance of verb-phrase negation. But *John$_i$ didn't hit the target* is synonymous with *It is not so that John$_i$ hit the target*. Therefore *John$_i$ didn't hit the target* is an instance of sentence negation. Thus *John$_i$ didn't hit the target* is necessarily both an instance of sentence negation and not an instance of sentence negation. Furthermore step (d) is wrong: (iv) is not synonymous with (iii) but is vague in its specification as between (ii) and (iii). This can be shown by contextualisations of sentences of type (iv):

(49) The doctors didn't treat many of the patients at all. They just sent them away with worthless prescriptions.

(50) The police were persuaded not to arrest many of the demonstrators, who then hung around being a nuisance.

(51) John wasn't treated by many of the specialists, who just said he was imagining things.

In each of these cases *many* is interpreted as not falling within the scope of negation, and corresponds therefore to the natural interpretation of *many* when it is to the left of the negative particle – i.e. to sentence type (ii) in the paradigm. It thus follows that sentences of the type *The target wasn't hit by many of the arrows* must allow at least the two possible scope interpretations claimed of (ii) and (iii) in order to predict the interpretations as in (49)–(51) above. It is thus not obvious that the passive transformation does change meaning, and it does not follow that semantic rules must take surface structure into account.[1]

Chomsky's argument for a semantic rule of negation operating on surface structures is the only argument of the three which predicts an indeterminacy in the interpretation of scope in negative sentences. His argument concerns the interdependence of stress assignment and the interpretation of the scope of negation (and question). It is very generally known that contrastive stress alters the interpretation of negative sentences, as in:

(52a) JOHN didn't hit Mary in the garden.[2]
(52b) John didn't HIT Mary in the garden.
(52c) John didn't hit MARY in the garden.
(52d) John didn't hit Mary in the GARDEN.

I shall return to this problem of the predictability of contrastive stress and the consequent interpretations in chapter 8. However Chomsky seeks to extend this interdependence of stress and scope specification to normal stress assignment and the scope of negation. He suggests that scope (*focus* in his terms) of negation can be determined as restricted to any phrase containing the intonation centre. Thus in *John didn't give away a house in Barnes* with normal final stress assignment, *in Barnes, a house in Barnes, give away a house in Barnes,* or the whole sentence, can constitute the scope of negation, since each contains *Barnes*, the intonation centre. This definition of scope explicitly excludes the possibility of the scope being restricted to the verb only, the subject only, or *a house*, since none of these constitutes a phrase containing the intonation

---

[1] What remains a puzzle for any analysis is the difference between (iiia) and (iva) on the one hand, and (iia). Though (iia) is the odd one out here, it constitutes less of a problem than (iiia) and (iva). It is predictable that two lexically identical sentences containing *many* should not be coreferential. This follows from the conditions for pronominalisation. Any noun phrase which is lexically identical to an antecedent noun phrase and which is not pronominalised is predictably interpreted as not coreferential with its antecedent. What is odd is that *many* in (iiia) and (iva) cannot be interpreted in this way. I have no explanation for this.

[2] Here and elsewhere in the text, words in capital letters indicate contrastive stress.

centre. Furthermore it predicts that the smallest domain of scope is the lexical item. Both of these constraints are unjustified. Each of the following is a possible scope of negation, given unmarked stress assignment:

(53a) John didn't give away a house in Barnes – it was in Wimbledon. (scope = adverbial noun phrase.)

(53b) John didn't give away a house in Barnes – it was only a garage. (scope = object noun phrase.)

(53c) John didn't give away a house in Barnes but he sold it at a fairly low price. (scope = verb.)

(53d) John didn't give away a house in Barnes – it was Bill who did. (scope = subject noun phrase.)

(53e) John didn't give away a house in Barnes – he was arranging for an auction. (scope = verb phrase.)

(53f) John didn't give away a house in Barnes – there hasn't been any property changing hands recently. (scope = sentence.)

(54a) John wasn't running – he was quite still.

(54b) John wasn't running – he was walking.

In (53), the scope can include only the verb, only the object noun phrase, and only the subject, as well as the possibilities predicted by Chomsky's formulation. In (54) the scope can not only include the lexical item *run* but it can be restricted to just one of its components, the specification of the type of motion – namely running. The component of motion is unaffected. So it appears that the scope of negation is not definable either in terms of syntactic units (lexical items) or in terms of syntactic constituents, or in terms of stress placement. Consideration of arguments such as these therefore suggest that scope of negation is not dependent on either syntax or phonology (with the exception of contrastive stress). There is thus so far no evidence of the necessity for rules of semantic interpretation operating on surface structures.

Perhaps the strongest argument for surface-structure interpretation rules is given by Hall-Partee (1970) in connection with conjunction reduction.[1] This transformation relates

(55a) Edward is touchy and Edward is difficult to please.

(55b) Edward is touchy and difficult to please.

(56a) Bill is popular and Bill is likely to succeed.

(56b) Bill is popular and likely to succeed.

---

[1] Some further arguments are provided by Hasegawa (1972) but I shall not take them into account here since Hasegawa's account, involving complements of *think*, crucially confuses ambiguity and vagueness. Cf. 1.3.3 above.

As these pairs demonstrate, the rule is generally meaning-preserving. However, it no longer preserves meaning when the subject[1] includes a quantifier such as numerals, *many, some, few*, or is modified by *only*. Thus the following pairs are not synonymous:

(57a) Few rules are explicit and few rules are easy to read.

(57b) Few rules are explicit and easy to read.

(58a) Some women are married and some women are happy.

(58b) Some women are married and happy.

(59a) Three rules on this page are explicit and three rules on this page are easy to read.

(59b) Three rules on this page are explicit and easy to read.

(60a) Only the three rules on this page are explicit, and only the three rules on this page are easy to read.

(60b) Only the three rules on this page are explicit and easy to read.

Since the verb phrases may be derived constituents, as in all the examples except (58), the scope of the quantifier cannot be stated at the level of underlying structure, because the constituents involved are not necessarily constituents at that level. Thus Hall-Partee suggests the interpretation of scope must be stated at surface structure, after the transformation has taken place. In his reply (1970a), G. N. Lakoff suggested that this conclusion was not inevitable since there was a naturally stateable constraint preventing the derivation of the (b) sentence of each pair from its (a) counterpart, namely the constraint that conjunction reduction can only take place if the subject noun phrases are coreferential. Since the (a) members of each pair are understood to be non-coreferential, it would follow that the (b) member would never be derived from the structure underlying the (a) member. This explanation is not however adequate. Compare (59) with (61).

(61) Three rules on this page are explicit and they are easy to read. By Lakoff's constraint, (61), which clearly involves coreferential subjects, should be synonymous with (59b), but it is not. Moreover, the noun phrases in (60a) are (pace Lakoff) also coreferential, and yet (60a) is not synonymous with (60b). His constraint on conjunction reduction does not therefore handle these cases, and a separate *ad hoc* condition would have to be added to exclude them. Moreover it provides no explanation at all as to why (61) and (59b) do not mean the same. If on the other hand we conclude with Hall-Partee that conjunction reduction

[1] The problem is more complicated than this but the additional complexity does not affect the argument.

applies blind with the interpretation of the conjoined verb phrase as falling within the scope of the subject quantifier being predicted from surface structure, then these examples provide no problem. On this evidence it seems that the only natural solution is to allow rules of semantic interpretation operating on surface structures.

What is more relevant for our immediate concern is that the Hall-Partee argument appears at first glance to carry over directly to scope of negation: the pairs (62) and (63) are clearly not synonymous.

(62a) John isn't ambitious and John isn't eager to become President.
(62b) John isn't ambitious and eager to become President.
(63a) John isn't ambitious or John isn't eager to become President.
(63b) John isn't ambitious or eager to become President.

(62a) denies both propositions, whereas (62b) denies only the combination of ambition and eagerness to become President: (63a) allows for one of the propositions to be true whereas (63b) denies both. (62a) is thus logically equivalent not to (62b) but to (63b), (62b) being equivalent to (63a). If the Hall-Partee argument concerning quantifiers is correct, it would seem natural to allow conjunction reduction also to apply blind in these cases, deriving the (b) sentence from its (a) counterpart with an interpretation of the sentence being read off from the surface-structure configuration. In this case, the rule interpreting negative sentences would operate on the interpretation of surface structure phrase markers.

Notice first of all, that whatever the input to the projection rules (i.e. the main core of the interpretation rules), the formulation of the rule of negation will not be affected. We have already seen how it operates when the input to the projection rules is the set of deep structure phrase markers. Suppose however the set of projection rules operated on surface-structure phrase markers. In this case, as G. N. Lakoff has pointed out (1970a), there would have to be rules of interpretation creating structure as it were, interpreting for example gapped structures such as *John tried to date many rich girls and Bill many poor girls* in a way essentially corresponding to the reverse of gapping.[1] Semantic rules of interpretation of this type would be required wherever the derived structure differs from the underlying structure (whether by virtue of deletion or permutation).[2] The rule of negation would only

---

[1] Called by Lakoff 'anti-gapping' (1970a, p. 421).
[2] Cf. Jackendoff's rule of negation which interprets the negative element generated

operate on the output of these structure-creating rules and it would thus not differ in formulation from that given earlier (pp. 12–13).

Furthermore, it is not obvious that (62b) and (63b) should be derived from (62a) and (63a) respectively, despite their parallel to the quantifier examples. Equally plausible deep structures are shown in Figs. 3 and 4,

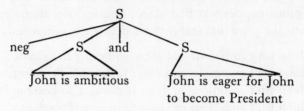

Fig. 3

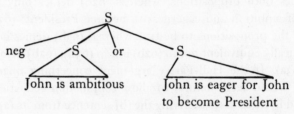

Fig. 4

and these phrase markers are reflexes of the semantic interpretation required for their respective surface sentences. If these phrase markers are syntactically justified, the rules of interpretation can operate on the (fully specified) deep-structure phrase markers. Arguments for having the scope of negation be interpreted from surface-structure configurations are thus logically independent of the Hall-Partee arguments concerning quantifiers.

In any case, her argument is not as water-tight as the data she considered suggest. Both she and Lakoff assumed that when a quantifier was in surface subject position and modified by a co-ordinate verb phrase, it must be non-synonymous with its expanded counterpart. But this is not so. Consider (64) and (65).

(64) Many questions were answered by Richard and Alice.

(65) Five questions must be attempted by each candidate.

Under Hall-Partee's analysis (64), derived by conjunction reduction (and

in the auxiliary position as raised to the S node, essentially the inverse of Neg-Placement (cf. Klima 1964).

passive) from *Richard answered many questions and Alice many questions*, must imply that Richard and Alice answered the same questions. But this is not so, just as in (65) the implication is clearly not that all candidates should attempt the same questions as each other. However under the interpretation that Richard and Alice did not necessarily answer the same questions, (64) is synonymous both with its active counterpart and with the sentence corresponding to its deep structure: there is thus no need to set up a rule of semantic interpretation from surface structure. This creates an anomaly. How can we allow sentences containing quantified subjects to change meaning over conjunction reduction only some of the time? Compare (64) with (66).

(66) Many buildings are guarded by dogs and night watchmen.

There is nothing structually to distinguish these two sentences, and yet only the latter is not synonymous with its expanded counterpart, *Many buildings are guarded by dogs and many buildings are guarded by night watchmen*. The only distinction seems to be the likelihood of a joint reading on the subject – more so in (66), less so in (64). This would imply that in both cases, both readings were possible, the prevalence of one or the other being a non-linguistic matter. The question then arises as to whether this semantic vagueness, though pragmatically resolved, should be extended to the entire range of conjunction reduction examples. This being so, synonymy would be preserved between deep structure and surface structure. A decision on these questions would require another book, and for the moment I shall merely assume that the question of surface-structure rules of semantic interpretation remains an open one.[1] In any case my main concern in chapters 4–6 will be not with the general principle of surface-structure rules of interpretation but with the specific problem of negation. And since the arguments concerning the prediction of negation scope from surface structure are on the one hand not strong and on the other hand do not affect the formulation I have adopted here, I shall assume that negative sentences are given a semantic interpretation from a fully specified deep-structure phrase marker.

---

[1] Since the semantic specification of adverbs is still quite uncertain (cf. Stalnaker and Thomason 1973, Heny 1973), I shall not take into account here the considerable body of arguments concerning adverbials presented in Jackendoff 1972. In any case, if such non-equivalent pairs as *James didn't go to town very often* / *Very often James didn't go to town* indicate the need for a surface-structure semantic rule of negation, then, as in the case of conjunction reduction, the form of the rule will nevertheless be as stated here.

1.4 Summary

The formal framework which I shall be assuming in the central arguments of the book is now more or less complete. This presents the claim that syntax and semantics are two separate though related components, and that any constructs in either of these components must be justified solely in terms of that component. So arguments for deep structure must be based on syntactic evidence, and not semantic evidence. Conversely, arguments concerning the semantic structure of sentences – for example negative sentences – will not be taken as evidence for the deep structure of those sentences. In particular, I argued that so-called selectional restrictions are not in fact a constraint mechanism but rather part of the meaning of lexical items, no different in kind from the inherent meaning of lexical items.

With respect to semantic structure, I argued that all components of meaning forming the meaning of lexical items should be expressed in terms of a predicate and its arguments, closely analogous to the formulation of predicate calculus. Furthermore the rules of the semantic component constitute (i) a set of interpretive projection rules which operate on a deep-structure input and which replace the syntactic indices of the lexical items by referring indices on the noun phrases to give a sentence reading; and (ii) rules such as that for negation which operate on the output of the projection rules.

With respect to negation itself, I argued that in general negative sentences are not ambiguous as to scope, but rather vague (or unspecified), and hence they allow a range of possible interpretations. This range appears to be constrained by the semantic components of the sentence in question and is not stateable in terms of syntactic or phonological constraints. Further evidence of the independent non-syntactic nature of the negation rule is provided by examples such as the following:

(67) The prisoner had not escaped from Dartmoor and Brixton – he had only escaped from Brixton.

Here the domain of the scope allows for a specification in which one part of a conjoint noun phrase, *Dartmoor*, is isolated as the scope of negation. This isolation of one noun phrase from a conjoint noun phrase structure constitutes a flouting of the Co-ordinate Structure Constraint which operates as a general constraint on syntactic processes preventing processes applying to one part of a conjoint noun phrase (cf. Ross 1967). If the domain of the scope of negation is to be explained in syntactic terms, the example above must be stated as an exception to this widely attested constraint. If however the delimitation of scope is explained in terms independent of syntax, then the anomaly disappears. However in so stating the interpretation of negative sentences, one is forced into formulating a rule (with a conjoint input and disjunct output) which has no parallel in the transformational processes of syntax. The rule of negation thus provides a further piece of evidence that constraints on semantic structure are different in kind from those of syntax,[1] a difference which can only be naturally captured in a framework containing two separate components of syntax and semantics.

[1] The evidence is not in fact entirely clear-cut: there is opposing evidence (cf. Lasnik 1972) that the rule of negation shares at least some constraints with syntactic processes.

2 The basis of semantics: a definition of meaning

2.1 On Katz' and Bierwisch's definition of semantic marker

The semantic framework I presented in chapter 1 can be attacked in at least two ways. (*a*) It is not obvious how concepts of speech-act semantics can be incorporated into this system, and in particular it gives no account of the distinction between assertions, questions, and imperatives, and their relation to illocutionary force. (*b*) The entire system is vacuous. The first criticism is merely an observation of the limitations of the theory and it will shortly become obvious that in my view this exclusion of speech-act constructs is not in fact a limitation, but rather correctly a delimitation of pragmatic factors from semantic ones.

The second criticism is much more severe. It is an attack commonly made by philosophers against linguistic semantics (cf. Vermazen 1966; Lewis 1972), who claim that the account which such representations give is circular. In particular, Vermazen argued that if word meaning in terms of semantic features is set up on the basis of entailments, then a definition of entailment in terms of semantic features which such a system would make available is of no explanatory interest whatever. In the face of such attacks, both Katz and Bierwisch retort that semantic features, on which the theoretical definitions of synonymy, sentence-meaning, entailment, etc., are based are not themselves defined in terms of entailment, nor even in terms of 'physical properties and relations outside the human organism' but rather they are symbols 'for the internal mechanisms by means of which such phenomena are perceived and conceptualised' (Bierwisch 1970, p. 181). As an attempt to consider the consequences of universal linguistic constructs for psychology, this statement may be irreproachable, but as a theoretical definition it is untenable. It has the immediate consequence that the status of any semantic component(s) is in principle untestable since there is no means of testing a so-called perceptual construct. By general principles of the philosophy of science, any such definition is vacuous.

2.2 Meaning and reference

The core of the problem is the definition of meaning. In the framework given above, the semantic components are mere artefacts which churn out appropriate artefacts as meanings of sentences. There is no direct attempt to explain the relation between the abstract symbols of language and the external world those symbols describe. Yet this is surely the goal of semantic theory, and any semantic mechanism which does not attempt to explain this relation is merely playing academic parlour games.

The standard defence of this separation in linguistics of the semantics of a language and the world the language describes is given by pointing out that words like *unicorn* have meaning no different in kind from *horse* despite their lack of referent, and perhaps also by pointing out that there are many words which do not obviously refer to anything outside the language (such as *intelligence, goodness*). The conclusion is then drawn that the explanation of problems of reference need not be the linguist's concern. Though these arguments have not I think been clearly formulated in print, their tacit acceptance has been widespread. Almost without exception,[1] linguistic descriptions assume that semantics involves only intra-theoretical statements and therefore does not include any predictions about the relation between words and their referents. In order finally to lay this kind of argument to rest, let me briefly consider why it should ever have been aired.

The assumption behind this argument is that reference is a relation which holds between a symbol of the language and the objects of the world as we know it. Now clearly what the language describes (given that the language – and hence the meaning of the words – is constant) is not merely this 'real' world, but also 2000 BC, AD 2000, the world of one's expectations, the world of one's dreams, etc. It is quite irrelevant to semantics that *the first man to land on the moon* has a specific object to refer to in 1975, but *the first woman to land on the moon* does not. This must be so, since if in 1976 a woman should land on the moon it would not follow that the phrase *the first woman to land on the moon* would have a different meaning. Thus if reference has to be restricted to the world as we know it, then the general assumption that linguistic semantics is not concerned with problems of reference seems to be correct.

[1] For arguments making this assumption, either implicitly or explicitly, cf. Postal 1971b, Bierwisch 1969, Katz 1966b.

However there is an alternative. The concept of reference could be generalised to encompass different worlds, or rather different states of affairs, in the following way. If we conceive of the world and the changing events in the world as a series of states of affairs such that at time$_1$ one state of affairs holds, at time$_2$ another state of affairs holds, etc., then the real world of 'now' in which unicorns do not exist but horses do is just one possible state of affairs.[1] In each of these states of affairs, there will be a set of objects to which the symbols of the language stand in a relation of reference. In the light of this, the relation between meaning and reference could be reformulated: the meaning, or 'sense', of a symbol could be defined as a statement of the conditions necessary and sufficient for a relation of reference to hold in some state of affairs. Thus in talking about meaning, one is not talking about reference itself, but about the (necessary and sufficient) conditions for reference. So the meaning of *unicorn* can be formulated in terms of conditions for reference no different in kind from the specification of *horse*, and it becomes merely a matter of contingent fact that there are no unicorns at the moment.

2.3 Sentence meaning and truth

If meaning were so defined in terms of reference conditions, sentence meaning could then be described interpretively by a set of projection rules. There are however several problems over equating meaning and conditions for reference. First there is the problem that the relation of reference must incorporate abstract concepts such as properties, actions, etc., since the problems of coreference implicit in transformational accounts of pronominalisation, relativisation, etc., hold equally for objects, properties, and actions, as for example in *The happiness that I felt yesterday was overwhelming*. The second and more important problem is that the connectives *and*, *or* and *if-then* will not be characterised as having meaning, since they clearly do not refer.

[1] This philosophical concept of 'possible worlds' is most clearly explained by Hintikka (1969): 'It would be more natural to speak of different possibilities concerning our 'actual' world than to speak of several possible worlds...In our sense, whoever has made preparations for more than one course of events has dealt with several "possible courses of events" or "possible worlds". Of course, the possible courses of events he considered were from his point of view so many alternative courses he considered events might take. However, only one such course of events (at most) become actual. Hence there is a sense in which the others were merely "possible courses of events"' (pp. 90–1). The concept is defined more formally by Prior 1962.

This problem does not arise if instead of defining sentence meaning in terms of word meaning, we take the converse step: that is to take sentence meaning as the basic term and define word meaning in terms of the systematic contribution a word makes to the interpretation of all sentences in which it occurs. Sentence meaning can then be independently characterised for any sentence S_n as a statement of the necessary and sufficient conditions for that S_n to be true. For those to whom such a definition is unfamiliar, consider a statement of the meaning of the sentence *The boy ran to his mother*. This is, approximately, that a male, non-adult, human moved to a female, adult, human who is his parent, with a particular fast motion that we call running. But this specification is also a statement of the necessary and sufficient conditions for the truth of that sentence.[1] So, more generally, we can say that a statement of meaning in a natural language is a statement of the truth conditions of the sentences of that language. Just as with referential conditions, it is important to note again that it is no more relevant to a statement of sentence meaning whether or not a sentence is actually true in any arbitrary state of affairs than it was to a statement of word meaning that the item actually bear a referent. One is not concerned with contingent truth-value assignments – only with the necessary and sufficient conditions for the truth of sentences. Thus the meaning of *I saw a unicorn* is no different in kind from *I saw a horse*. In both cases, the statement of meaning merely gives the conditions under which that sentence would be true. Furthermore this definition of meaning naturally includes the definitions of the connectives, since truth-tables are a statement of truth conditions.

How does this definition of meaning match up to the conditions on a semantic theory given earlier (1.1) – viz. the ability to isolate the infinite set of contradictory sentences and the ability to predict entailment, synonymy, contradiction, etc? The prediction of inter-sentence relations follows as an automatic consequence of the definition of meaning. That is, if all the conditions hold that make true *John killed an actress last night*, then it must be the case that both *An actress died last night* and *A woman died last night* are of necessity true, since each of these constitutes a subset of the conditions specified by *John killed an actress last night*. But this is the logical definition of entailment – that one sentence entails the second if the truth of the second necessarily follows from the

---

[1] Cf. 2.4.1 below for a discussion of the validity of assigning truth values to sentences.

truth of the first.[1] Similarly synonymy. Synonymy is defined logically as mutual entailment, and this too is predicted naturally if the meaning of a sentence is a set of truth conditions: if two sentences mean the same, then they will have the same set of truth conditions; thus whenever one is true the other will be. Moreover both will also be false under the same conditions, a second characteristic of mutually entailing sentences. More interesting is the delimitation of the set of contradictory sentences. If meaning is defined as a statement of the conditions under which a sentence will be true, the oddity of contradictions is also automatically captured. What contradictory sentences have in common, and in contrast to all other sentences, is that (given that the meanings of words remain constant, and are not interpreted metaphorically) they can never be true: there is no possible state of affairs that they describe. They are therefore unlike other sentences, since the assignment of the value false is not a matter of contingent fact. Their separation from other sentences as a natural class is thus automatically predicted.

That the prediction of entailment, contradiction, etc., is an automatic consequence of defining meaning in terms of truth conditions is powerful support for the theory, since these predictions were stated earlier (1.1) as a necessary condition on the adequacy of a semantic theory. However these are only two of the conditions I set up for semantic theories to be judged against. In addition, a theory must (*a*) be recursive and (*b*) state a systematic relation between the syntactic structure of a sentence and its lexical items. But these two additional requirements are met by the model of semantic representations given by Bierwisch. And since his model appears non-distinct from a truth-conditional semantics except in the non-truth-based definition of the term *semantic marker*, a formulation of truth conditions in the format of Bierwisch's semantic markers seems quite legitimate. For example, his rule of negation is naturally interpretable as a rule involving truth conditions. Thus while *A boy ran to his mother* is true if and only if the state of affairs described is such that a male, non-adult human went with a fast motion to someone who was female, adult, and a parent of his, the negation of that sentence is true just in case any one or more of those conditions fails to hold in the world described. That is to say, a negative sentence is used to assert that the corresponding positive sentence is false. But *A boy ran to his mother* can be false for any one of several reasons – either someone ran to their mother, but not a boy, or a boy went to his mother but did not

[1] Cf. chapter 3 for a more detailed definition of entailment.

run, or a boy did something but not run anywhere, let alone to his mother, etc., etc. And this interpretation matches the output of Bierwisch's rule of negation. Thus what the negation rule states is all the possible ways in which the corresponding positive sentence could be false. And just as it is irrelevant in stating the meaning of a sentence to specify whether it is actually true or false for any given state of affairs, so it is irrelevant in stating the meaning of a negative sentence to specify which of the conditions of the corresponding positive sentence may have failed in any utterance of that sentence. I shall therefore assume that linguistic semantics, more specifically semantics as formulated by Bierwisch, has been implicitly a truth-conditional semantics. If this is so, it provides a natural explanation of both the descriptive adequacy of predicate calculus for describing the semantic structure of sentences and also the notational equivalence of de Morgan's law and Bierwisch's rule of negation, since both predicate calculus and de Morgan's laws are defined within a truth-based system.

2.3.1 Component-based semantics and model-theoretic semantics: a linguist's defence.
Before turning to the problems which confront all truth-based semantics, whether Tarskian or truth-conditional, there is one more specific objection which all component- or feature-based semantics have to face, even if the attack of circularity (cf. p. 30) is adequately answered. It has been argued by logicians such as Montague (1970), Lewis (1972), and Bartsch and Vennemann (1972), that semantic models such as Bierwisch's, which present an abstract semantic representation as an interpretation of syntactic structures, do not provide interpretations at all. They merely present the syntax of yet another metalanguage into which the syntactic constructs of the theory are translated. This is in contrast to the formalisation of these logicians themselves whose semantics is interpretive in the stricter sense of defining a function which maps sentences, or the logical form of sentences, into a model. Now it may well be that semantics should have two parts: (*a*) a statement of the logical form of sentences and (*b*) a definition of a function (or functions) mapping logical forms into models. But what a so-called interpretive componential semantics claims, in contrast to generative semantics (and in contrast to those logicians who turn to generative semantics as presenting a theory most closely allied to their own interests), is that the level at which a fully specified logical form – i.e. the level of semantic representation – is given, is not the syntactically

defined level of deep structure, and moreover is not subject to the same constraints as that level. Thus what such a formalism denies is that a logical form of any sort provides a level at which syntactic generalisations about natural language can be made. To put it in another light, what a Bierwisch type of semantics provides (in contrast to logicians' semantics of parts of natural language) is an explicit translation procedure from the sentences of natural language into a fully specified logical form. It might thus be seen as providing the first of two essential steps in a formalisation of semantics while a model-theoretic approach provides the second. So though the semantic formalisation given in this book may not be interpretive in the sense of model-theoretic semantics, it nevertheless makes explicit a necessary step in the statement of meaning for natural languages which logicians characteristically ignore.

For these reasons, it seems to me as unwise for logicians to sneer at linguists' attempts at semantic representation as it is reprehensible for linguists to ignore logicians'. And in this spirit, I shall assume that at least Bierwisch's formalism of semantics is *not* shown obviously to be false by the much greater sophistication of model-theoretic semantics.

2.3.2 Reference and lexical entries. As a final point of exposition, let me tidy up one apparent internal contradiction in my assumption that Bierwisch's formulation of the semantic component can be used to capture the concepts of truth condition and reference condition as I have used them. I referred earlier to conditions of reference in talking of the semantic properties of words. Yet in my original presentation of Bierwisch's model (1.3.2) I stated that reference indices were generated by the base structure as a property not of the lexical item but of the noun-phrase node immediately dominating it. This represents a claim that reference is not a property of lexical items in isolation but only within a syntactic structure. This claim appears to be correct. As Alston pointed out (1964, pp. 15–16) it is by no means clear that *pencil* of itself refers to anything. If I wish to refer to the class of pencils, or a single object which is a pencil, the item *pencil* is insufficient: it only becomes a referring expression when it is part of a noun phrase – i.e. *a pencil, the pencils*, etc.[1] This seems to indicate that the lexical item itself does not refer at all. As a reformulation, let us suggest that every sentence is made up of lexical items in a certain relation (defined syntactically),

---

[1] For an independent justification of this extension of the concept of reference to include indefinite noun phrases, cf. chapters 5–6.

and these items and relations together specify a set of conditions which constitute the meaning of that sentence (a set of truth conditions). A part of these conditions is that there be objects of whom the properties in question are predicated of. But it is a part of the conditions set by the meaning of the sentence, not by the individual items. The items themselves specify descriptive conditions and, in the formulation given here, the dominating node (NP) is interpreted as providing the conditions of reference. That is to say, an implication of reference to some object is a consequence of a lexical item's entering a syntactic construction. The specification of that object or action is provided by the lexical item. It follows automatically that what are entered in the lexicon are the senses of lexical items and not reference relations. As a lexical item in isolation they do not refer. Bierwisch's formulation thus captures the observation made informally by Alston.

2.4 The limitation of a truth-based theory of semantics: a criticism and a defence

I have so far defended an interpretive semantic component operating on syntactic deep structures and I have claimed that this formalism presents us with a fully-fledged truth-conditional semantics. Yet there are many possible forms of attack on a truth-based semantics.

2.4.1 The relation between *sentence* and *statement*. The major criticism of all truth-based theories of semantics as theories of natural-language semantics is that such a theory must be restricted to statements, since it is only these which have the property of being true or false. And since not all sentences can be used to make statements, a theory which is restricted to analysing statements is not giving a complete account of meaning for natural languages. There are three common analyses of the relation between sentences and statements. In all three, this relation is defined in such a way that questions and imperatives are excluded (since they are said to be incapable of being true or false), together with some indicative sentences, e.g. Austin's performatives (*I promise to go home*, *I apologise*, etc.) which are said by Austin to lack a truth value and therefore also cannot be statements. The least restrictive view excludes only these sentences from the set of sentences which can constitute statements. There is a stricter view which by virtue of defining statements as having just one truth-value assignment, true or false, excludes

all sentences containing deictic elements from the set of sentences which can constitute statements – e.g. *You are ill*, *He came here* – since it is characteristic of such sentences that they change their truth value according as the referents (i.e. the speaker and hearer) change. But this relative rather than absolute truth-value assignment is a general property of natural language sentences, since tense is speaker-relative. Thus in order to constitute a statement under this view, a sentence must be phrased in such a way that it will have one and only one possible truth-value assignment: for example *Ruth Kempson of 19 King Henry's Road London is tired on 10 August 1973 at 3 pm* (cf. for example Quine 1966 and elsewhere). The most stringent view, that of Strawson (1950, 1952) is that the semantic analysis of sentences cannot in principle be reduced to the concept of truth, since truth and falsity are not properties of sentences at all, but only of statements.

The two most restrictive views can, I think, be side-stepped if we agree with Lemmon (1966), Lewis (1972) and Davidson (1967) that sentences do have a truth value relative to some context of utterance.[1] Thus deictic and all indexical sentences will have a truth value relative to a person (the speaker), a place and a time. Yet this claim need not lead us into defining the full range of contexts for each and every person in each and every possible state of affairs. The statement of the truth conditions of indexical sentences need be no different in kind from other sentences. The theory is not aiming to predict truth-value assignments of particular utterances, but merely, for every sentence in the language, the necessary and sufficient conditions for its truth. The actual value a sentence may have relative to any specific context is irrelevant. Accordingly I shall assume that predicting conditions on the truth of sentences is not illegitimate and that the problem of handling the truth conditions of deixis can be overcome (cf. Davidson 1967 and Lewis 1972 for more detailed analyses).

2.4.2 Performative verbs, imperatives, and questions – a suggested solution. Two chief apparent limitations of a truth-based semantics remain:[2] performatives, and the non-indicatives – imperative and ques-

---

[1] Cf. 3.3 for a further discussion of statement and sentence, with respect to the logical definition of presupposition.

[2] The claim, widespread among logicians (cf. Strawson 1952, chapter 3 section II), that the logical connectives '.', 'v' and '⊃' do not correspond to their natural-language counterparts *and*, *or* and *if-then*, I have not considered here since I shall consider arguments relating to *and* and *or* in chapter 4, in connection with presupposition. The

tion. It has been claimed by Austin (and others after him) that performative utterances have no truth value (asserted by Austin in 1962 to be obvious and not in need of argument). This purported property of performative utterances is especially important since it seems to have been the major motivation for seeking an alternative speech-act semantics for natural language. Those verbs which can be used to make explicitly performative utterances all have two properties: (i) they describe an act which can only be carried out by speaking (or some other form of communication), (ii) in the first person present tense, the action depicted by the speaker is not so much described by his statement as carried out by that statement. Thus *I promise to go* is not a description of a promise but will itself constitute a promise when it is uttered. The class of verbs is a fairly clear one: what is less convincing is Austin's claim that they cannot be either true or false because they are actions, and not descriptions.[1]

The main argument presented in support of the isolation of performatives as non-statements is the contrast between the simple present and the progressive tense (*I warn you that Edward will leave I am warning you that Edward will leave*), a contrast which is said to be explained by the contrast between performative and constative utterances. But this use of the simple present is not restricted to verbs capable of being performatives. Most verbs of thinking and judgement have a present tense which is neither the generic nor the so-called historic present:

(1) I regret that we went to Turkey.
(2) I believe that capitalism is an unavoidable evil.
(3) I suspect that Margo will fail.
(4) I think I'm right.

Moreover some verbs have precisely the same contrast as performatives and yet are clearly not themselves performative verbs, and would not be excluded from a truth-conditional account:

(5) I wonder whether we should go home.
(6) I am wondering whether we should go home.

relation between '⊃' and *if-then* has been discussed extensively by philosophers. Grice (cf. chapter 7 below) argued in lectures in 1967–8 that the difference between the two was solely pragmatic (though his arguments are disputed by Cohen 1971). For an argument that they must be semantically identical, cf. Clark 1971 (with a counter-argument by Young 1972).

[1] At several points, Austin more or less withdraws this claim. Cf. 1962, lecture XI, particularly pp. 134–5, 144–5. (I am grateful to Deirdre Wilson for pointing this out to me.)

(7) Mike considers that Evelyn should sell her house.

(8) Mike is considering whether Evelyn should sell her house.

The contrast in time specification in the pairs of sentences (5)–(6) (7)–(8) is between a single point in time and over a period of time (in the second sentence of each pair, the mental action in question being not completed). However this difference is specified, it will also automatically explain the contrast between *I promise that we will be there* and *I am promising that we will be there*.

In any case, the performative use of a verb is notably restricted to first person, simple present. In every other case, a truth-conditional analysis is straightforward and unexceptional. As an example, take promises. *John promised to go* will be true if the action described constitutes an undertaking (either verbal or written) made by John sometime in the past to carry out some action in the future, namely going,[1] and these conditions constitute the meaning of the sentence. If these conditions are not met (because John's statement did not constitute such a commitment, because John made no statement at all, etc.), then – just as a truth-based semantic analysis predicts – the sentence is false. Now in the case of an utterance of *I promise to go*, one of the conditions for the truth of the sentence is automatically guaranteed by the utterance itself. And if in addition the speaker is indeed committing himself to an undertaking, it is arguable that the utterance of *I promise to go* constitutes a true statement. Under this analysis, performative utterances can and do carry a truth value: what is odd about them is that the mere fact of their utterance guarantees the fulfilment of at least part of the conditions for the truth of the proposition conveyed.[2] With the verb *say* itself we have the limiting case where the very act of uttering *I say that he is sick* guarantees the truth of the statement. As Lewis points out (1972), to utter *I am speaking* is not only to speak but it is also to speak the truth. The idiosyncratic feature of performative statements is therefore not that they have no truth value but rather that their truth value is at least partially determined by their very utterance.[3] If this is correct, then this class of verbs is not excluded from a truth-based semantics, and so a major motivation for seeking an alternative to such a semantics disappears.[4]

[1] For a more detailed analysis of promises, cf. Searle 1969, chapter 3.

[2] Cf. Lemmon 1962 for a further example and discussion of self-verifying sentences.

[3] It follows from this argument that it is not a necessary condition of a sentence's being a true statement that it constitute a description.

[4] This view has been put forward by a number of people. Cf. in particular Lewis

There remains the problem of imperative and question. How can they be handled within a formal semantic theory? If as is almost universally assumed,[1] they cannot have a truth value, then they constitute exceptions to a theory of truth conditions. What consequences does this have for a theory of semantics in which meaning is so defined? There are five possibilities.

1. The theory should be rejected, since these demonstrate it to be false. Such an out-and-out rejection of a theory would demand the substitution of an alternative more explanatory theory. There are two possibilities: (*a*) since the interpretation of questions, commands, and indeed assertions, appears to depend on some concept of illocutionary force, a general theory of speech acts should constitute the basis of natural language semantics; (*b*) since questions and commands undeniably involve the interaction of speaker and hearer, we might attempt to define meaning in these terms rather than in terms of truth conditions. The second alternative I shall discuss (and reject) in detail in chapter 7, so I shall not consider it here. The first alternative is based on a misconception. The existence of questions and commands does not provide any evidence that concepts relating to the speech act such as illocutionary force need to be incorporated into natural language semantics; for interrogative and imperative forms are not themselves indicators of illocutionary force. Questions and commands are open to as many interpretations as statements. Thus a question such as *Are they thinking of leaving soon?* is no more explicit as to its illocutionary force than is the statement *They are thinking of leaving soon.* It can be used either as an implicit command (if for example said by a bored emperor to his officer in front of some subordinates whom he wishes to get rid of), an implicit threat (if the same emperor intends to suggest that if the people in question *did* leave, they would lose their jobs),[2] or an implicit statement (if the implication is simply one of boredom on the part of the emperor), etc., etc. Furthermore, as these examples demonstrate, the identification of illocutionary force is just as indeterminate with non-statements as with statements. In short, there seems no reason to

1972, pp. 209–12, who presents the most detailed account. Cf. also Wiggins 1971, p. 21 fn. *b*, Landesman 1972, pp. 31–2.
[1] One exception is Lewis 1972.
[2] It has been suggested that these are examples of different intended perlocutionary effect rather than differing illocutionary forces. But this is not so. In these two situations, the intended perlocutionary effect would be to get 'them' to leave and to get 'them' to stay respectively.

suppose any one-to-one correspondence between the operators assertion, question, and command, and concepts such as illocutionary force.
I therefore take it that the existence of questions and commands does
not in itself provide any evidence for a theory of meaning based on speech
acts.[1] Moreover the linguistic evidence purporting to show a syntactic
reflex of implied illocutionary force I find extremely weak. For example,
Sadock's evidence (1970) that constraints on the occurrence of *please*
depend on a distinction between an implicit and overt request (only the
latter – i.e. imperatives and a subset of modal questions – allowing
sentence-final *please*) seems factually incorrect in view of the following:

(9) Is it Daddy's turn to read to us please Mummy?
(10) I've finished my book please sir.
(11) Johnny's finished now please Granny.

Moreover the explanation why *please* of this type is more likely to occur
sentence-initially seems clearly non-linguistic. Its function as a call for
attention demands under normal circumstances that it be sentence-
initial. Sadock's account of so-called 'queclaratives' (1971) is no
stronger. In any case, all arguments of this kind depend on the false
assumption that anything which affects the distribution of items in a
sentence is by definition a phenomenon to be explained linguistically.[2]

2. The second possibility is that the theory of truth-conditional
semantics should be maintained rigorously with no interpretation of any
non-truth-conditional elements. This would exclude any interpretation
of the syntactic markers Q and Imp on the grounds that these are
pragmatic operators (cf. pp. 147–8). This would have the disastrous consequence that *Are you quiet?*, *You are quiet* and *Be quiet* would be predicted
to be synonymous, since with no interpretation of Q and Imp, the three
sentences would have an identical set of truth conditions.

3. One possible way of incorporating questions and imperatives into
a truth-based semantics is to analyse them as having a semantic representation identical to their corresponding performative statement. As
such they would (if we assume that performative utterances are truth-
bearing statements) not only have a truth value on every utterance, but
they would correspond to statements which are very generally true.[3]
Thus for example (12) would have a semantic representation identical to

---

1 For a discussion of illocutionary force within a pragmatic framework, cf. 8.9 below.
2 Cf. Katz and Bever 1974 for a clear account of why this assumption is unfounded.
3 Since they would be of the type whose truth was guaranteed by its utterance.

that of (13), and similarly (14) and (15) would share a semantic representation.

(12) Get out.
(13) I order you to get out.
(14) Is John in the bathroom?
(15) I ask you to tell me whether John is in the bathroom.

However this solution is based on the assumption that the paired sentences (12)–(13) and (14)–(15) are synonymous. Yet there are good reasons for thinking that pairs involving an assertion and its corresponding performative statement (e.g. *John is sick, I tell you that John is sick*) are not synonymous: they have different truth conditions. And since one's intuitions about meaning judgements are even less clear on pairs such as (12)–(13) and (14)–(15), there is little justification for claiming synonymy in the cases of commands and questions and their corresponding performative statements if this parallel does not carry over to assertions. Moreover this equation of all sentences with a performative statement meets the same problems as the first alternative: there are an indeterminate number of speech acts which can be performed with any sentence, and a reduction of every sentence to some explicit performative would have the consequence that all sentences would be multiply ambiguous. For these reasons, this solution too must be rejected.

4. A further alternative is to predict truth conditions as a property of the common content of a sentence, question and imperative (a so-called 'sentence-radical') rather than on sentences themselves. This is the analysis proposed by Stenius (1967). He suggests that every sentence be analysed as containing a sentence-radical and a modal element, the former signifying the descriptive content of the sentence and the latter its mood. Thus *You be quiet, Are you quiet?* and *You are quiet* all share the same sentence-radical but have different moods. A sentence-radical is further described as true if what it describes is the case, and false otherwise – irrespective of mood. Mood itself is defined in terms of separate semantic rules as follows:

Indicative rule: Produce a sentence in the indicative mood only if its sentence-radical is true.
Imperative rule: React to a sentence in the imperative mood by making the sentence-radical true.

Interrogative rule: Answer the question by 'yes' or 'no', according as its sentence-radical is true or false (cf. Stenius 1967, pp. 268, 273).

While an explanation along these lines seems intuitively sound, there are in fact considerable difficulties. Firstly, imperatives will under all normal circumstances be false since truth value is assigned to the radical. Second, and more important, is the problem that if the rules given above are semantic rules, then it becomes semantically deviant to tell a lie, and similarly deviant to answer anything other than *yes* to a question such as *Are bachelors unmarried?* Yet it is clearly irrelevant to a semantic statement whether or not speakers tell the truth. Though Stenius attempts to argue against such criticisms, his rebuffs are not I think entirely just and the criticisms remain. A more exact statement of the indicative rule would surely include a weakening to 'only if there are good reasons for believing the sentence-radical is true'. Now I think there are important reasons (which will emerge in chapter 4) why any semantic theory which introduces the concept of speaker's belief becomes in principle incapable of fulfilling quite basic conditions on linguistic theories, and as such is untenable. For the moment, I merely enter this reservation together with the previous criticisms as justification for not accepting this alternative.

5. The final alternative is to have a truth-conditional semantics which gives no account of questions or imperatives except that they are defined, together with the assertion sign, as semantic primitives, not capable of being assessed as true or false. In this formulation, the relationship between *Be late* and *I order you to be late* or between *Am I wrong?* and *I ask you to tell me whether I am wrong* is captured indirectly, by defining *ask* and *order* in terms of the primitives Q and Imp respectively and stating that *ask* is followed by embedded question, and *order* by embedded imperatives.[1] This alternative differs only from Stenius' suggestion in the definition of the symbols 'ʇ', '?', '!'. Effectively, this framework also separates a sentence-radical on which truth conditions are stated, from a modal element comprising one of the pragmatic mood operators 'ʇ', '?', '!'. Thus the meaning of a *yes-no* question for example is defined by stating the truth conditions of the proposition being questioned and prefixing the semantic primitive '?'. While the treatment of the actual operators 'ʇ', '?' and '!' is admittedly *ad hoc*,

[1] Cf. Stockwell, Schachter and Hall-Partee 1973, who argue (p. 543) that complements of *ask* and *order* are questions and imperatives respectively for syntactic reasons.

there is strong evidence to suggest that whatever solution is adopted for the interpretation of Q and Imp themselves, the semantic analysis of questions in particular must be in terms relating to truth conditions. The evidence concerns the constraints on *or* conjunction in questions. As is well-known, *or* is defined truth-functionally in two ways:

Inclusive *or*			Exclusive *or*	
$P\ Q$	$P\ v\ Q$		$P\ Q$	$P\ v\ Q$
T T	T		T T	F
T F	T		T F	T
F T	T		F T	T
F F	F		F F	F

Now since, when *or* is exclusive, P *or* Q cannot be true if P and Q do not differ in their truth-value assignment, it follows that where there is a truth dependence between conjuncts, the sentence as a whole will be contradictory. That is, there will be no state of affairs in which either P will be true and Q false, or *vice versa*; so P and Q in these cases will never jointly fulfil the necessary conditions specified by *or*. This prediction appears to be correct:

(16) ?Either John left or Bill noticed.

(17) ?Either John was ill or he wasn't well.

(18) ?Either Mary is dead or John killed her.

(19) ?Either John's theorem was right or Bill proved that it was right.

(20) ?Either Edward pretended to be sick or he wasn't sick.

(21) ?Either there was an exhibition or the mayor went to the exhibition.

In every case, the sentence is contradictory if *or* is interpreted exclusively and in every case there is a relation of dependence between the conjuncts. Exactly the same range of contradictions occurs in questions, where the *or* appears to be invariably exclusive:

(22) ?Did John leave or did Bill notice?[1]

(23) ?Are you going to stay here or are you not going to leave?

---

[1] This example is taken from R. Lakoff 1971, and is one of a set of examples that she uses to demonstrate the necessity for a performative analysis of questions. The above argument however shows that there is a natural means of predicting this deviance without the need of underlying higher verbs.

(24) ?Was John's theorem right or did Bill prove that it was?
(25) ?Was there an exhibition or did the mayor go to the exhibition?
(26) ?Did Edward pretend to be sick or wasn't he sick?
(27) ?Is Mary dead or did John kill her?

This contradiction is predicted only if the *or* in questions is given a truth-functional definition. Constraints on conjunction in questions can then be given a natural explanation. It follows that, whatever particular solution is adopted for interpreting the syntactic marker *Q* itself, the constituents of questions must be interpreted in terms of truth conditions.

In summary, I have argued that meaning for natural languages can be defined in terms of conditions on the truth of sentences, and that such a definition need not in principle exclude an analysis of performatives, questions or imperatives. Performative uses of a verb, I have analysed as no different from the remainder of the verb's paradigm. Questions and imperatives I argue must be entered as unanalysed semantic primitives. I cannot and would not wish to pretend that either of these arguments is conclusive. For my purposes however, it has been sufficient to show that an analysis of meaning in terms of truth conditions is not ruled out of court by the mere existence of performatives, imperatives, and questions.

More generally in these first two chapters, I have suggested that an interpretive semantic component along the lines envisaged by Bierwisch provides a formal description by recursive procedure of the truth conditions of the sentences of a language. In presenting this specification, I have assumed that the logic on which it is based contains the two values true and false. In the following chapters, we shall see how this analysis competes with two other analyses: (*a*) one in which the meaning of sentences includes reference to the beliefs of speakers, (*b*) one in which the logic on which the semantic mechanism depends is not two-valued but three-valued, containing the extra value neither true nor false.

3 Presupposition: two definitions

So far I have outlined a truth-conditional theory of meaning, and have shown how it is naturally compatible with the formulation of the semantic component in Bierwisch 1969, 1971. In 1.1, I argued that presupposition constituted a possible falsification of this claim. In this chapter I shall give an account of two ways in which presupposition has been defined, in preparation for considering what issues these definitions raise.

Presupposition was defined by Strawson in an attempt to explain the relation between a definite referring noun phrase and its referent.[1] It was specifically intended as a refutation of Russell's analysis. Russell (1905) made, *inter alia*, two claims: that *The King of France is bald* is logically made up of two assertions (i) *There is one and only one King of France*, (ii) *Whoever is the King of France is bald*; and that the relation between *The King of France is bald* and *There is a King of France* is one of entailment. Strawson on the other hand claimed (1950, 1952, 1964a) that *The King of France is bald* is logically made up of a presupposition that there is a King of France and an assertion that he is bald; and that the relation between the two statements *The King of France is bald* and *There is a King of France* is one of presupposition. Presupposition therefore stands in direct contrast both to assertion and entailment. It is these two contrasts which lead to the two non-equivalent characterisations of presupposition. While Strawson talks informally of what a speaker assumes in using sentences containing definite descriptions as opposed to what he actually states (1950), the formal definition of presupposition is in terms of the relation between two statements. By definition then, the concept of presupposition contrasts with entailment.

[1] The term *presupposition* was first used by Frege 1892, whose account largely agrees with that of Strawson. I shall restrict myself to Strawson's account as it was this that attacked Russell's analysis.

3.1 Entailment *v.* presupposition

Entailment I defined earlier (pp. 33–4) as a relation between sentences such that the truth of the second necessarily follows from the truth of the first. Thus any statement S_1 will entail a statement S_2[1] if when S_1 is true, S_2 must also be true. It is therefore not possible to assert the truth of S_1 and deny the truth of S_2. A different formulation of this same relation is to say that the truth of S_2 is a necessary but not sufficient condition for the truth of S_1; whereas the truth of S_1 is a sufficient but not necessary condition for the truth of S_2. For example, the statement made by uttering *That person is a bachelor* (S_1) entails the statement made by uttering *That person is a man* (S_2) since if S_1 is true, S_2 must be (demonstrating the sufficiency of the truth of S_1 for the truth of S_2). On the other hand, S_2 must be true if S_1 is to be, though this does not itself guarantee the truth of S_1 (demonstrating the necessity of the truth of S_2 for the truth of S_1). It follows from this set of defining conditions that if S_2 is false, then S_1 must also be false. However if S_1 is false, nothing follows – S_2 can be either true or false.

Presupposition differs from entailment in only two ways: the consequence of S_1 being false, and the consequence of S_2 being false. For S_1 to presuppose S_2, the truth of S_2 must follow from the truth of S_1, but if S_2 is false then S_1 will have no truth value, i.e. will be neither true nor false, or it will not constitute a statement at all.[2] It follows from this that if S_1 is false, S_2 must be true. Like entailment then, for a presupposition relation to hold between two statements the truth of S_2 must be a necessary condition on the truth of S_1 and conversely the truth of S_1 must be a sufficient condition on the truth of S_2. But in addition, the truth of S_2 must also be a necessary condition of the falsity of S_1, and conversely the falsity of S_1 must be a sufficient condition for the truth of S_2. The original example *The King of France is bald* is thus said to presuppose *There is a King of France* since, as Strawson argues, one judges the truth or falsity of this statement by assuming the existence

---

[1] I am deliberately using *statement* here and not *sentence* in accordance with the logical definitions. Cf. chapter 2 for a discussion of truth as a property of sentences, and 3.3 below for the justification of ascribing presuppositions to sentences.

[2] It is not clear whether the difference between these two consequences is other than terminological. Lemmon 1966 (p. 98) assumes that they are, but Strawson seems normally to accept the former (1964a, p. 106). If we accept the former we have to allow a definition of statement which does not demand the property of being either true or false. Since I shall be talking about presuppositions on sentences, the question of whether a statement can have no truth value will not concern me. I shall adopt the former alternative.

of the King of France and by assessing on the basis of this assumption
whether or not he actually is bald. If there is no King of France, then
the statement *The King of France is bald* is neither true nor false. It
follows from this that *The King of France is not bald* (which asserts the
falsity of *The King of France is bald*) is also said to be either true or
false only if there is a King of France. If there is no King of France it is
said to be just as odd to say *The King of France is not bald* as it is to say
The King of France is bald. As Strawson would have it, the question
of whether these statements are true or false simply does not arise if
there is no such person as the King of France.[1] This characteristic is
translated into a linguistic criterion for presupposition that a purported
presupposition must be a necessary implication of the positive and the
corresponding negative sentence.[2] The difference between entailment
and presupposition is summarised in table 1:

TABLE 1

Entailment	Presupposition
S_1 S_2	S_1 S_2
T →T	T →T
F ←F	−(T v F)←F
F →T v F	F →T

3.2 Speaker-presuppositions: presupposition *v.* assertion

The definition of presupposition just given is of course entirely consistent with a truth-conditional semantics. It is the contrast between
presupposition and assertion which causes trouble for a truth-based
semantics. Strawson's informal discussion of what is stated as opposed
to what is assumed led to a characterisation of presupposition in terms
of beliefs on the part of the speaker in making a statement. This re-
interpretation of the term was first explicitly given by Sellars (1954) who
infers from Strawson's initial account[3] that what is presupposed in some
utterance of *The King of France is bald* is that the speaker believes that

[1] Cf. Strawson 1950, section III.
[2] It appears to have been doubted whether this negation test is equivalent to the logical
definition since Katz 1973 takes the trouble to argue what should have been obvious
all along that these are equivalent characterisations.
[3] Strawson 1950 is in fact indeterminate as between a truth-based characterisation of
presupposition and a pragmatic one.

there is a King of France and moreover that the hearer does so also. Presupposition is here opposed by definition to what a speaker would assert in uttering a given sentence. This concept is radically different from the logical definition since the defining criterion of presupposition yields quite different results. In Sellars' case presupposition bears no relation to truth conditions but relates rather to conditions for successful communication. Thus if the presupposition fails to hold, the speaker has in some sense spoken incorrectly. But as Strawson points out in his reply to Sellars (1954), this concept is neither incompatible nor compatible with his own definition – it is merely different. Correct and incorrect usage are not co-extensive with the assignment of the truth values true and false to statements. In fact, it has been suggested (by Garner 1971) that anyone wishing to use Sellars' concept of presupposition should scrap the term *presupposition*.

However Sellars' misinterpretation of Strawson is not wholly unjustified, and it is not I think the sole or even the chief source of the widespread conflation of speaker-presupposition and statement-presupposition. There is a very general tendency in describing presupposition to talk about what a speaker would be presupposing in using a particular sentence to make a statement as opposed to what he would actually be asserting. The dangers of this are hinted at by Garner (1971) who separates the various different uses of the term by philosophers and linguists.[1] Yet even he claims that 'we could always rephrase what I have said [about statements] by talking explicitly about what, as a performer of an act of a certain kind, or as a producer of an object of a certain kind, a speaker does (or would) presuppose' (p. 27). But this is to fall into the very trap he is warning other people of. This rephrasing by Garner is only not a danger if it is recognised as a (non-logical) consequence of the logical definition of presupposition, and not part of the definition itself. If however, it is taken as a characterisation of presupposition, then it invites conflation with a subtly different use of presupposition, where all that a speaker assumes his hearer knows constitutes his presuppositions and this stands in contrast with what that speaker is informing his hearer of (asserting). Thus the utterance of *JOHN seduced Mary*, with contrastive stress on *John*, could be said to presuppose not only that there is a man called John but also that someone called Mary was seduced, and to assert that it was John that did it.[2]

---

[1] He draws attention to this conflation in a footnote (p. 227 fn. 5) as a 'potential source of trouble'.   [2] Cf. Chomsky 1971, and 8.6 below.

In a similar way both *John SEDUCED Mary* and *John seduced MARY* would have a different set of presuppositions. Now it is fairly certain that the very great majority of philosophers arguing for the application of a three-valued logic to natural language would not wish to conflate these two uses of presupposition, since the latter is not susceptible to any standard truth-based definition.[1] Indeed, it is essentially equivalent to presupposition in terms of speaker-belief. But it is not clear how this use can be excluded by a characterisation of presupposition in terms of what the speaker presupposes in making such a statement. If therefore the logical definition of presupposition is to be kept distinct from presupposition defined in terms of speaker belief or assumption, the former must not be discussed in terms of what a speaker would do in saying a sentence. I shall therefore assume (*a*) that the logically defined presupposition is a relation defined only between two statements,[2] and (*b*) that it stands in contrast to a pragmatically defined speaker-presupposition, which is defined in terms of what the speaker assumes in saying particular utterances.[3]

3.3 Presuppositions of statements and sentences

Before we can assess how or whether either of these concepts should be incorporated into a formal model of language, there remain two problems: (1) What is meant by *statement?*, (2) Can we justifiably speak of sentences bearing presuppositions? We have already seen in chapter 2 that statements are generally defined as abstract entities which are either true or false with respect to some context of utterance (with the possible caveat of p. 48, fn. 2 above). It is necessary to maintain a distinction between this definition of statement and the illocutionary act definition of statement. The importance of the distinction rests in the fact that the illocutionary act of stating stands in contrast to the illocutionary acts of promising, warning, boasting, etc. The logically defined statement does not. Now it is clear that whatever the presuppositions of the logical statement made by *The King of France visited the exhibition*, we would not want these to stand in potential contrast to those of utterances where the same sentence is used as a boast, a warning, or a threat. The essential feature of the logically defined statement is that whatever act is purported to have taken place, the statement itself and

---

[1] Strawson himself appears to fluctuate between a position keeping these two separate (cf. p. 50 and Strawson 1954) and a position implicitly conflating them (cf. 5.1 below and Strawson 1964a).
[2] This will be extended shortly to include sentences.   [3] Cf. however 5.1 below.

hence its presuppositions remain constant. The presuppositions of a logically defined statement are thus independent of the illocutionary force associated with it. On the contrary however, the presuppositions of the illocutionary act of stating need not in principle hold for other illocutionary acts.

While this distinction is maintained by Strawson, this is not the case with some of his interpreters, for example Garner (1971). Indeed conflation of these two types of statement leads Garner (*ibid.*) to characterise presupposition failure (when S_2 is false) as a failure to constitute a statement (rather than guaranteeing that the statement in question be neither true nor false) on the grounds that it 'allows a natural generalisation to speech acts of other kinds and their objects, since it seems desirable to speak of the presuppositions of promises, commands, questions, bets, warnings, and so on as well as those of statements' (p. 31). He then goes on from this to characterise presupposition in terms of presuppositions on the part of a speaker 'in the performance of an illocutionary act (or the purported performance of one)' (p. 42). His failure to distinguish the illocutionary act of stating from the logically defined statement thus leads directly to a conflation of the two different concepts of presupposition which he initially sought to separate.[1]

More important perhaps for our purposes is that Garner, like Strawson, condemns discussions of the presuppositions of sentences (pp. 38, 42) and he does so on the basis of this conflation of the two uses of the term *statement*. His reason for not allowing presuppositions to be a property of sentences is significantly different from Strawson's. Strawson restricts presupposition to statements because it is only these he says which are true or false, not sentences. Garner however seems to exclude all presuppositions as a property of sentences on the grounds that 'the same sentence...can be used, on different occasions, to perform different kinds of illocutionary acts' (p. 38). But if, as I suggest, presupposition is a property of the logically defined statement, then the question of varying illocutionary act potential does not arise. Moreover if, as Lemmon suggests (1966, p. 91), it is legitimate to speak of sentences as true or false relative to some context of utterance, an extension implicit in all analyses of meaning as conditions on the truth of sentences (cf. 2.3), then it follows that to speak of presuppositions (and entailments) of sentences is not illegitimate either.

[1] Cf. his comments on Sellars, referred to on p. 50.

3.4 Summary

I have now outlined two definitions of presupposition, one in terms of a relation between statements or sentences (by definition in contrast to entailment), the other in terms of what a speaker must assume in saying a given sentence (by definition in contrast to assertion).[1] Neither concept is catered for in the linguistic framework I outlined in chapters 1–2. Of the two concepts, logical presupposition possibly presents the lesser difficulty for this framework. The semantic components set up in chapter 1 were largely justified by their predictive power – viz. the predicting of entailments and contradictions. If now logical presupposition has to be predicted, the logic underlying these predictions will have to be altered to include three values (true, false, and neither true nor false) and this will have to be reflected in either the formalisation of the components themselves or in the formalisation of the projection rules predicting the interpretations of sentences (cf. p. 10). Such a change would for example affect the interpretive rule of negation outlined in chapter 1 (as we shall see in chapters 4–5) since this is based on the de Morgan equivalence

$$-(P \cdot Q) \equiv -P \vee -Q$$

which need not hold in a three-valued logic. However the underlying assumptions about the nature of semantic representation would not be altered with such a revision. In contrast to this, speaker-presuppositions appear to give the lie to the whole framework. If it can be shown that presupposition so defined must be stated as part of the semantic representation, the meaning, of a sentence, then it would appear that meaning itself can no longer be defined in terms of truth conditions. Two issues thus emerge:

1. Should the formalism of the semantic component reflect a three-valued logic rather than a two-valued logic?
2. Is the whole framework outlined in chapters 1–2 in principle based on the wrong premises – i.e. should meaning be defined in some other way, for example in terms of speaker-hearer relations? With these issues in mind, I shall now consider the various ways in which presupposition has been used (or misused) by linguists.

---

[1] There are several problems in the definition of assertion which I shall return to in detail. Cf. 5.3 and 8.6 below.

4 Presupposition: its use by linguists

One of the problems in assessing the nature of presupposition in linguistics is that the separation of the semantic and pragmatic concepts is rarely honoured. Indeed, on the contrary, as an extremely fashionable term, presupposition has been used quite indiscriminately to apply to almost every conceivable relation – either semantic or pragmatic. For example it has been used to cover entailment (Fillmore 1969, 1971; Keenan 1971, 1972; Kiparsky and Kiparsky 1970; G. N. Lakoff 1971a, 1972a), logical presupposition (Keenan *ibid.*), Austin's implication and happiness conditions (Fillmore *ibid.*; Lakoff *ibid.*), Grice's conventional and non-conventional implicature (Lakoff 1971b, 1971c; Gordon and Lakoff 1971; R. Lakoff 1971; Horn 1969; Chomsky 1971), and also lexical presupposition (Fillmore *ibid.*). These distinctions are not always recognised by the writers themselves (even when they are, as in Karttunen 1973, they may be ignored), and presupposition is very generally defined as that which the speaker assumes to be true as opposed to what he asserts to be true. Given such widespread application, it is hardly surprising that presupposition has been thought to have considerable explanatory validity.

Among these various uses two types of application can be separated as influential. On the one hand presupposition, together with assertion, though defined in terms of speakers, is not discussed in relation to utterances as the definition implies, but in relation to sentences and lexical items. This use corresponds directly – as we shall see – to the opposition between presupposition and entailment; and was introduced by Fillmore and the Kiparskys. It is now widely accepted by all breeds of linguist – generative semanticist, interpretivist, and sceptic. Contrasting with this, though often confused with it, is the presupposition which a speaker may have on uttering a sentence which does not follow from the inherent content of the sentence. It is therefore essentially a property only of the utterance. The attempt to incorporate this type

54

of presupposition into linguistic theory (made by the Lakoffs: cf. G. N. Lakoff 1971b, 1972a; R. Lakoff 1971; Gordon and Lakoff 1971) is of more dramatic consequence since in conflating sentence properties and utterance properties, it assumes a conflation of semantics and pragmatics. My most immediate concern will therefore be with the Lakoffs.

4.1 A pragmatic concept of presupposition: the Lakoffs

In an article on conjunction (1971), Robin Lakoff made two claims which have remained influential: (*a*) that there is evidence that the conjunctions *and*, *or* and *but* have, as a semantic property, two senses which differ only in presuppositions which speakers attach to them; (*b*) that there is evidence of a constraint on co-ordination which can only be explained in terms of presuppositions on the part of the speaker and deductions that he might make upon those presuppositions. If either of these claims is correct, a semantic theory based exclusively on truth conditions must be inadequate because, by excluding in principle properties relating to speakers of the language, it will be unable to capture the facts of the language.

First let us consider her arguments for attributing to the conjunctions *and*, *or* and *but* properties which the logical connectives '.' and 'v' do not have. With *and* she brings up an old claim that *and* has two senses, one symmetrical, reversible and equivalent to the logical connective, the second implying a sequence of tense. This second *and* she claims is asymmetrical, non-reversible, and has as a defining property the implication that the first conjunct is presupposed. This is simply false. Her examples are (37) *What a night we had last night: the fuzz came in during the party, and the cat kept dropping the kittens into the punch bowl, and Mary screamed when Bill tried to abduct her, and the strobe light never did arrive,* and (38) *Well, the story is as follows: the police came in, and everyone swallowed their cigarettes, and Bill choked on his, and they had to take him to the hospital, and his mother just about went frantic when she heard, and I had to placate her by lending her my copy of Portnoy's Complaint.* What she claims is that if the first (or any non-final) conjunct in (38) is denied 'the result is bizarre, and renders the whole discourse somehow nonsensical, the usual result of denying a presupposition' (p. 128). But compare the following as responses to (38):

(1a) No, that's not true: the police didn't come in. Mary suggested
we try a new way of taking pot, and everyone swallowed their
cigarettes. Otherwise the story's correct.

(1b) No, that's not true: Bill didn't choke on his cigarette – he
wasn't even smoking. He'd swallowed a fly just as the police
came in, and they had to take him to the hospital. Otherwise
the story's correct.

(1c) No, that's not true: Bill's mother wasn't frantic. She was
amused and said it sounded like an Ed McBain novel.

Thus the entire statement is false if any one conjunct is false, as the
truth-functional definition of *and* predicts. The interpretation of *and*
as having temporal sequence therefore does not rest on the notion of
presupposition, given any standard definition of that term. Moreover
it is not clear that sequence of time is part of the meaning of *and* at all,
since the same implication occurs when there is no *and*:[1]

(2a) The Lone Ranger mounted his horse and rode off into the
sunset.

(2b) ?The Lone Ranger rode off into the sunset and mounted his
horse.

(3a) The Lone Ranger mounted his horse. He rode off into the
sunset.

(3b) ?The Lone Ranger rode off into the sunset. He mounted his
horse.

So however, the implication is achieved, it is not due to the presence of
a particular sense of *and*, unless a fullstop is also given a semantic
characterisation of this kind! It seems therefore that the interpretation
of time sequence between sentences, whether conjoined or not, is a
property of discourse interpretation and not a semantic property of the
conjunction itself.[2]

But, which is traditionally considered a point of divergence between
logic and natural language (cf. Strawson 1952, chapter 3, section II,
she analyses as either presupposing between the conjuncts some contrast which can be lexically specified ('semantic opposition *but*') or as
presupposing an expectation on the part of the speaker of the opposite
of the second conjunct ('contrary-to-expectation *but*') (p. 133), and her
claim is that *but* is ambiguous between these interpretations. Her
examples are (57) *John is tall but Bill is short* and (60) *John hates ice-*

[1] This observation is due to Deirdre Wilson.
[2] Cf. 8.7 below for a pragmatic characterisation of this implication.

cream, but so do I. There are several problems here. She herself discusses
counter-examples which necessitate envisaging at least two additional
meanings for *but* (pp. 136–42). In general though, for those cases where
there is no lexical opposition, she sets up this second 'contrary-to-
expectation' sense of *but.* So she analyses (60) as having the interpretation 'one would not expect that I would hate icecream'. But parallel
examples need not have this interpretation: consider the utterance of
John wants an icecream, but so do I in a situation where there is not
enough money to buy us both icecreams, so neither of us can have one.
It is (*a*) not obvious how her analysis of *but* can handle this case,
and (*b*) how it would predict that these two examples apparently involve
a different sense of *but.* More generally, if there is a semantic component of contrastiveness in *but,* then this should automatically enable
one to predict a set of environments in which *but* may not occur, by
virtue of there being no requisite contrast (analogous to *That man is
pregnant* where the environment does not meet the condition specified
by *pregnant*). The above examples should be *prima facie* cases; but they
are not. And to retreat to a different *but* merely makes the original claim
untestable. Moreover this account of *but* should in addition predict that
examples such as *John is rich but John is poor* are non-contradictory
because they meet the requisite condition of contrastiveness. There is
no obvious way to prevent such a prediction, as Robin Lakoff herself
points out (pp. 134–5). It thus seems doubtful whether a semantic
analysis can predict any contrast in meaning between *but* and *and.* (Their
synonymy is of course what is predicted by a truth-functional analysis.)[1]

Her claim about *or* is that, unlike in logic, it has solely an exclusive
interpretation. This too is false. In analysing *or,* she sets up two uses of
exclusive *or* one of which is asymmetric, e.g. *Either little Seymour eats
his dinner or his mother complains to the neighbours.* This she states makes
no implication that if Seymour eats his dinner his mother will not still
complain; i.e. both conjuncts can be true – by definition, inclusive *or.*
So much for its non-existence in natural language.[2] Thus her discussion
of the conjunctions *and, or* and *but* does not, as she hoped to show,
demonstrate a divergence from the logical connectives in any way which
can be captured within a theory which seeks to make testable claims
about its lexical representations.

[1] Cf. pp. 174–5 for a pragmatic account of *but* and chapter 9 for a discussion of the
problem this account raises for the delimitation of the over-all linguistic theory.
[2] For an argument supporting the opposite claim, that exclusive *or* does not constitute
a separate use of *or,* cf. Barrett and Stenner 1971.

The second of her main claims, about co-ordination and its analysis in terms of presupposition, is based on the premise that *My grandmother wrote me a letter yesterday and six men can fit in the back seat of a Ford* is very odd and should be excluded by the grammar. In order to explain this apparent constraint, she suggests the following solution. If two sentences are to be conjoined, they must share a common relevance or topic. This may be self-evident (and lexically definable) as in *John's a bore and Harry's not very interesting* but may not be, as in

(4) John wants to make Peking Duck and I know that the A and P is having a sale on hoisin sauce.

(5) Edward has a yacht and Michael has a lovely house in Knights-bridge.

In this latter type of case, she argues, one may need to know pre-suppositions with respect to either conjunct in order to deduce a common topic: in the first example that hoisin sauce is the accompaniment to Peking Duck, that a sale is a good time to buy things, and that 'now' would therefore be a good time to make Peking Duck, 'making Peking Duck' thus being the common topic; and in the second that both possession of a yacht and possession of a house in Knightsbridge indicate wealth, and hence a common topic of wealth is deducible. By this means, she claims, one can assess the relative grammaticality of a sentence. The harder and more culturally specific the presuppositions, the more likely a speaker is to reject it, and if there are no available presuppositions, the sentence will be ungrammatical. More generally, in every case of co-ordination, the meaning of the conjuncts, their common topic, and hence the assessment of grammaticality are dependent on what information the sentence is intended to convey. Since this involves the presuppositions of a given sentence, the presuppositions must be part of its underlying semantic representation.

In this form, the argument is extremely easy to attack: first, on the grounds that every sentence she cites as ungrammatical, odd or un-acceptable (the terms are used interchangeably) can be contextualised as a perfectly appropriate utterance, and so as a constraint on gram-maticality the construct of common topic only applies vacuously; and secondly, on the grounds that her position demands that meanings of sentences are unpredictable independent of the actual speech act and hence the grammar itself is non-predictive. Consider the following:

(6) We've been wondering how many people can get into the back

seat of a Ford and my grandmother decided to try the experiment. She tried it two days ago and she wrote me a letter yesterday and six men can fit in the back seat of a Ford.

(7) I'm going to tell you two very peculiar facts. Some people eat thistles and yesterday Mary killed a python with a stone.

One might add as a *reductio-ad-absurdum* example:

(8) I'm going to tell you two quite unrelated facts: the Academic Board has vetoed the recent suggestion that all colleges should have course unit degrees, and I think I'm pregnant.

As these examples show, the purported grammaticality constraint of common topic excludes nothing and hence is not a necessary construct in the grammar. This being so, the concept of common topic provides no evidence that the concept of presupposition on which it depends should be part of a linguistic theory.

This argument is weak in being negative. A consideration of the consequences of a direct representation of such presuppositions within the theory is much stronger: indeed it shows the impossibility of such a position. Robin Lakoff herself points out one consequence: namely that sentences which under all traditional analyses of ambiguity would be unambiguous may have different presuppositions, reflected in different semantic representations, and are therefore by definition ambiguous. This new type of ambiguity she calls 'contextual' (p. 121). It arises because if presupposition is defined as broadly as she allows, no sentence will have a unique set of presuppositions. She suggests that ambiguity of this type only arises in border-line cases: the worse the sentence is, the more interpretations people will strain to produce (pp. 121–2). The example she demonstrates this with is *John wants to make Peking Duck and I know that the A and P is having a sale on hoisin sauce*, which can be interpreted with more than one set of presuppositions leading to different common topics. But this possibility is not restricted to the border-line cases. It is merely that if there is a common interpretation, people will not naturally seek an uncommon one. A sentence like example (5), said to have the presuppositions that owning a yacht and a lovely house in Knightsbridge are examples of 'conspicuous consumption', can be interpreted in many other ways. Imagine a conversation between two extremely rich, flashy people who divide their lives between Switzerland, Bermuda and Hollywood, or a conversation deploring the fact that yachting has been made illegal and that

Knightsbridge has long been a slum area, or a conversation in which Edward's yacht and Michael's house are both known to be extremely small and their owners not well-off, etc., etc. Would we want to say that the meaning of *Michael has a lovely house in Knightsbridge* is different in each of these cases? It is clear that in principle every sentence can be analysed with at least as many different sets of presuppositions as these contextualisations involve, and if furthermore the sentence were used with an illocutionary force other than that of statement, e.g. promise, boast, etc., the sets of presuppositions fast become indeterminate.

This is not the only problem. In characterising presupposition as part of the underlying semantic representation, if presuppositions are not stated as part of the meaning of lexical items, one must give up the standard claim that the meaning of a sentence is a function of the meaning of its constituent parts. Though she is not explicit on this point, it would seem that she is relinquishing this claim, since presuppositions are not claimed to be a property of the lexical item. But if the interpretation of presuppositions is not related to the lexical items, how are they to be derived? They are presumably part of the beliefs of the speaker, or derive from his knowledge about the situation. But if this is so, the meanings of sentences cannot be determined independent of the speaker of a sentence in a particular speech-act situation.[1] One is thus faced with an analysis of meaning which claims that every sentence has an indeterminate number of indeterminable meaning representations. And if the meanings of sentences are indeterminable, then meaning relations between sentences such as entailment, contradiction, by definition cannot be predicted. Moreover, in her terms, it would follow that the grammaticality of sentences cannot be determined either, independent of the situation in which they are uttered. But this has the immediate consequence that one's grammar would not be predictive. We are thus faced with the conclusion that a theory which incorporates a speaker relative concept of presupposition as part of its semantic representation is in principle unable to fulfil any of the four conditions[2] I set up initially (1.1) as a prerequisite for any semantic theory and therefore must be relinquished.

[1] Similar consequences follow from describing the requisite presupposition as a property of the lexical item in question.

[2] Namely (*a*) the ability to predict sentence meaning, (*b*) the ability to predict the set of grammatical sentences, and (*c*) the ability to predict entailments, etc., by (*d*) a finite set of rules.

Some of these consequences however G. N. Lakoff himself claims to avoid since, as he argues (1971b), a sentence will not have presuppositions as part of the underlying semantic representation as such. Rather the task of the grammar is to generate sentence and presupposition pairs: the judgement of whether or not a sentence is grammatical is thus he claims not context or speaker relative but merely relative to a particular presupposition which is, like the sentence itself, a construct of the competence model. On this basis he claims to explain why *JOHN called Mary a LEXICALIST and then SHE insulted HIM* has the interpretation that to call someone a lexicalist is to insult them. But this attempt to avoid the consequence of non-predictability is not successful. Consider the power of such a grammar in connection with Robin Lakoff's data. It has to generate pairs, or n-tuples, such as:

John wants to make Peking Duck and I know that the A and P is having a sale on hoisin sauce.
Peking Duck is an item of Chinese cookery.
Hoisin sauce is used for cooking Peking Duck.

from which the common topic of 'cooking Peking Duck' can by some extra mechanism be deduced. Yet it must not generate as a well-formed pair the above sentence and the presupposition 'Hoisin sauce is used to kill fleas which collect in ducks' feathers' (unless of course there are additional presuppositions such as 'Ducks become edible when fleas are removed from their feathers'). As it stands, this sentence-presupposition pair is not grammatical: speakers know that killing fleas on ducks has nothing to do with cooking. But the semantic specification of both the sentence and the presupposition contains the word *duck* and therefore there seems no way of preventing the deductive mechanism from predicting that this sentence-presupposition pair is grammatical. The problem is not restricted to this particular sentence-presupposition complex. Consider (9) and (10).

(9) S: Pope John is dying and the cat's in the bath.
     Pr: I have a brother who is a schizophrenic Catholic and whenever he hears a Catholic is sick he puts the cat in the bath.
(10) S: Pope John is dying and the cat's in the bath.
     Pr: I have a schizophrenic brother who puts the cat in the bath when he has a turn.

Of these pairs, I take it that the conjunction in (9) is meaningful relative to its presupposition; but in (10) the same conjunction is not, since there is not sufficient relation between the sentence and the postulated presupposition in this latter case. In the case of (9), a relatively simple deduction process allows us to predict a common topic between the conjuncts of the sentence since from both conjuncts one can deduce, via the presupposition, that a Catholic is sick. But it is equally possible for the formal mechanism to deduce a common topic in (10) via its presupposition where the predicted existence of a common topic does not match our intuitions; for the first conjunct entails that someone is sick and from the second conjunct, via the presupposition, we can deduce that since my brother is sick, someone is sick. Thus the mechanism is forced to predict a common topic and hence the grammaticality of (10). The point is this: if the mechanism has sufficient power to predict the required sentence-presupposition pairs, it will have absolute and unconstrainable power. It is thus not a valid means of avoiding the charge of unpredictability. The problem thus remains: speaker relative presuppositions cannot be incorporated into the linguistic model without giving up all of the four essential prerequisites on one's formal model (cf. p. 60 fn. 2 above). This being so, I shall assume that presupposition defined in terms of speaker assumptions must not be part of a formal semantic theory.[1]

4.2 Lexical presuppositions: Fillmore

Though the Lakoff account of presupposition has been influential among their followers, it has not evoked the widespread cross-theoretical interest that is enjoyed by the concept of lexical presupposition put forward independently by Fillmore (1969, 1971) and the Kiparskys (1970). Both sets of authors define presupposition in terms of what a speaker presupposes as opposed to what he asserts, so it would appear *prima facie* that their use of presupposition does not correspond to the logical use either. However this is misleading. The criterion that both the Kiparskys and Fillmore apply to determine what elements of a sentence are presuppositional is a negation test. This test divides the semantic components of a sentence into two sets – those which may fall within the scope of negation (i.e. which may be interpreted as false when the corresponding positive sentence is asserted to be false), and those which can never fall within the scope of negation (i.e. which must

[1] The more recent work of the Lakoffs (e.g. G. N. Lakoff 1972a, R. Lakoff 1972) does not swerve from the main assumptions adopted in the articles discussed here and is therefore open to the same objections.

be interpreted as true when the corresponding positive is asserted to be false). Now this is equivalent to the defining criterion of logical presupposition that the truth and falsity of S_1, the presupposing sentence, be a sufficient condition for the truth of S_2, the presupposed sentence. In the case of a lexical item its presuppositions are said to be those elements of its meaning which are unaffected by negation: i.e. they cannot be denied. In terms of the semantic representation of negative sentences, which we have already seen involves a disjunction, the semantic components of a sentence or word which are presuppositional must therefore be those which cannot enter into the disjunction. Unfortunately this disjunction is not always taken into account. For example, the item *bachelor*, in the relevant sense of the word, is claimed to have 'unmarried' as its meaning and the components 'adult' and 'male' as its presuppositions (Fillmore 1969, p. 123; Kiparsky and Kiparsky 1970, p. 156), on the grounds that *That person is not a bachelor* is not used to deny that the person is a male adult, but only to deny that he is unmarried. But this assumes that negative sentences have a single fully specified interpretation, which, as we have seen (1.3.3), is false. In fact, each of the components of *bachelor* can be interpreted as falling within the scope of negation:

(11) That person is not a bachelor – he's married.

(12) That person is not a bachelor – he's only five years old.

(13) That person is not a bachelor – it's a woman.

(14) That person is not a bachelor – it's a woman, who is married.

(15) That person is not a bachelor – it's a spinster.

(16) It was not a bachelor that frightened Mary-Ann – it was a scarecrow.

If we take the negation test strictly, this set of sentences provides five contradictory results:

  I *bachelor* Meaning: unmarried
             Presupposition: male, adult, human   (11)
 II *bachelor* Meaning: adult and unmarried
             Presupposition: male and human   (12)
III *bachelor* Meaning: male and unmarried
             Presupposition: adult and human   (13), (14)
 IV *bachelor* Meaning: male
             Presupposition: unmarried, adult, human   (15)
  V *bachelor* Meaning: male, human, unmarried, adult   (16)

Clearly this is wrong. What has been ignored is the inherent vagueness of negative sentences and the variability in the interpretation of their scope. Furthermore, since the examples demonstrate that any part of the meaning of *bachelor* can be interpreted as not matching the state of affairs described then in no case is a component presupposed. On the contrary, the variability in scope of negation is a defining criterion of an entailment relation (cf. chapter 3, p. 49, table 1, line 3) since the denial of the entailing sentence has no consequence for the entailed sentence, which can be either true or false when the entailing sentence is false. It therefore appears that *That person is a bachelor* entails the maleness, adultness, etc., of the object described and does not presuppose them. Thus none of the components of *bachelor* constitutes presuppositional components.

This confusion of entailment and presupposition lies at the heart of Fillmore's analysis of verbs of judging (1971), his fullest discussion of presupposition. Thus, to take one pair of examples, consider the verbs *criticise* and *accuse*, which Fillmore specified as

> *accuse* (Judge, Defendant, Situation)   (Performative)
> Meaning: SAY (Judge, 'X', Addressee)
> Presupposition: BAD (Situation)
>
> *criticise* (Judge, Defendant, Situation)
> Meaning: SAY (Judge, 'X', Addressee)
> Presupposition$_1$: RESPONSIBLE (Defendant, Situation)
> Presupposition$_2$: ACTUAL (Situation)

These in effect claim that for X (the judge) to be described as accusing Y (the defendant) of Z (the situation), X must say to someone, not necessarily the defendant Y, that Y is responsible for Z, and it must in addition be presupposed that the situation is bad. Conversely for *criticise*, with the additional presupposition that Z actually happened.[1] But this analysis predicts incorrectly that, of the following sentences, only (18)–(22) are not contradictions.

(17) John didn't accuse Mary of taking his books: he merely suggested that she had.

[1] It is not easy to test this analysis because of an equivocation over who does the presupposing. Fillmore allows the following formulae (where x is what is presupposed): 'Suppose there's no question in anybody's mind that x' (p. 285), 'There is no question about x' (p. 282), and 'If I say (36), I presuppose that x' (p. 282). Thus it is not clear whether the presupposed element has to be true, to be generally assumed to be true (whether it is or not), or to be assumed to be true by the hearer.

(18) John didn't accuse Mary of taking his books because he knew she hadn't done so.

(19) John didn't accuse Mary of taking his books: he didn't say anything.

(20) John didn't accuse Mary of taking his books because he assumed he'd lost them.

(21) John didn't criticise Mary for taking his books because he knew there was nothing wrong in doing so.

(22) John didn't criticise Mary for taking his books: he didn't say anything.

(23) John didn't criticise Mary for taking his books because he knew she hadn't done so.

(24) John didn't criticise Mary for taking his books, because he assumed he'd lost them.

Yet none of these sentences is contradictory. Sentences (18)–(22), where the lexical meaning components (reflexes of entailment) are interpreted as falling within the scope of negation, are no different in status from sentences (17), (23) and (24) where the presuppositional components are denied. Yet no presuppositional account can predict this: it follows naturally only from an entailment analysis. Thus the test of negation provides evidence against Fillmore's analysis and in favour of an analysis which does not differentiate among the set of truth conditions contributed to sentence meaning by either *accuse* or *criticise*. Furthermore I think this procedure of testing a purported presupposition by seeking interpretations of negative sentences which deny it (an impossibility for a true presupposition) shows that there is no such thing as lexical presupposition in the sense Fillmore has used it. Every case of lexical presupposition that he proposes can be interpreted as falling within the scope of negation, and these lexical properties seem to be no more than reflexes of entailment[1] in just the way that the semantic components of Leech (1969), Katz and Fodor (1963), Bierwisch (1969, 1970, 1971), etc., are set up on lexical items by virtue of entailment relations between sentences in which the items occur.

It might be said in defence of Fillmore that a reduction of Fillmore's presupposition to entailment is irrelevant since he himself is not concerned with a truth-based definition of presupposition at all but with a speech-act account. And indeed his examples of presupposition are set in the framework of a use theory of language. However such a

[1] For a more detailed criticism, cf. Kempson 1973, D. Cohen 1973.

defence cannot be sustained, since the speech-act theory of semantics Fillmore purports to adopt is terminologically equivalent to a componential truth-based semantics: it gives no account of illocutionary force, nor of the speech acts carried out in uttering sentences, except in so far as these are made explicit. More specifically, though he claims that the meaning of sentences should be analysed in terms of two levels, the illocutionary and the presuppositional, the latter constituting 'those conditions which must be satisfied in order for a particular illocutionary act to be effectively performed in saying particular sentences' (p. 276), he adds to this account two *ad hoc* caveats which render it non-distinct from a truth-based componential semantics. First the illocutionary level is called the 'explicit' level of communication, ruling out in an *ad hoc* manner the fact that a statement may be used to boast, warn, etc. – i.e. ruling out that aspect of communication which is a central part of a use theory of meaning; and second, at the presuppositional level he claims to be concerned 'only with those [conditions] that can be related to facts about the linguistic structure of sentences' (p. 277), ruling out some of the conditions which are normally seen as an indisputed part of a speech-act theory of meaning (cf. the preparatory and sincerity conditions on promising etc given in Searle 1969). Such a theory of meaning is a speech-act theory in name only. Since moreover the definition of presupposition as a necessary implication of both the positive and the corresponding negative sentence is equivalent to a logical definition, the conflation of presupposition and entailment is a charge Fillmore cannot I think avoid.

4.3 Factive verbs: Kiparsky and Kiparsky, and Karttunen

Similar problems arise with the Kiparskys' account of factive verbs. Like Fillmore, they claim to be concerned with the distinction between assertion and presupposition, but like Fillmore also, they adopt the negation test, so their characterisation of presupposition is none other than the logical one. That they are restricting themselves to the semantic account of presupposition (contrasting with entailment) is confirmed by their own account of the negation test. For, as they say of the test, 'it must be emphasized that it is the SET of assertions that is operated on by...negation' where the assertions of a sentence are 'all those propositions which follow from it by virtue of its meaning' (p. 148). In this sense assertion corresponds by definition to entailment. However they maintain, in agreement with Fillmore, that certain elements of meaning are presuppositional and cannot enter into the scope of negation. So for example they give the following set of examples (p. 152) as possible interpretations of *Mary didn't clean the house*:

(25) Someone may have cleaned the house, but not Mary.

(26) Mary may have done something, but not clean the house.

(27) Mary may have cleaned something, but not the house.

(28) Mary may have done something to the house, but not clean it.

(29) Mary may have been cleaning the house, but it didn't get clean.

However they exclude as a possible interpretation

(30) It wasn't dirty – so she can't have cleaned it.

Thus *Mary didn't clean the house* is said to presuppose that the house was or has been dirty.

Now their reason for excluding (30) as a possible interpretation of *Mary didn't clean the house* provides the core of the presupposition problem. Their use of the negation test has one important caveat: the presuppositions of a sentence may be denied, but this does not constitute 'the straightforward denial of an event or situation, but rather the denial of the appropriateness of the word in question' (p. 151). Thus certain interpretations of negative sentence are excluded by fiat as not constituting 'straightforward denial'. With their particular example, *clean* is said to presuppose that the object of which it is predicated was or has been dirty, and it follows that (31) would be described as an example of straightforward denial, but (32) by contrast apparently would deny the appropriateness of the word *clean*.

(31) The boy didn't clean the room – the woman did.

(32) The boy didn't clean the room – he made it dirty.

The assumption of different types of negation I shall assess in detail later (5.2). But this distinction as characterised by the Kiparskys is in any case dubious. We have seen earlier (pp. 34–5) that to deny some proposition P is to claim that the conditions specified by P do not correspond to the state of affairs in question. Pragmatically, one might say that it is not appropriate to use P unless there is an exact correspondence between P and the state of affairs.[1] Thus in the examples cited, it is just as inappropriate to the situation to say *John cleaned the room* if in fact Mary did as it is to say *John cleaned the room* if in fact

---

[1] Cf. the Gricean maxim to be discussed in chapter 7 'Do not say what you believe to be false'.

he made it dirty. To deny some proposition, for example *John cleaned the room*, is to say it is inappropriate to relate the predicate in question to the particular subject, whatever the cause of the non-correspondence.[1]

The Kiparskys characterise this 'special' type of negation as characteristically having contrastive stress. But if one legislates against the type of negation in (32) as being merely a denial of the appropriacy of the word *clean*, one is bound to legislate against all contrastive stress negations, and such an exclusion would have also to exclude (31). In this example, the scope of negation was interpreted as being restricted to the set of conditions represented by *boy*. Since it is precisely these conditions which fail, one might say – parallel to (32) – that the word *boy* is inappropriate in this context. Yet the Kiparskys clearly would not wish to exclude (31) along with (32). And if negative assertions which deny the presupposition are thought to be characterised by some special feature such as contrastive stress not shared by straightforward negation, it is not clear how this can include the presupposition-denying example (32), which seems to be of exactly the same status as (31). On balance therefore, there seems to be at least no *a priori* reason for considering negative sentences to be ambiguous in the way the Kiparskys suggest (cf. 4.5 and 5.2 below for further problems meeting an ambiguity account of negation).

The Kiparskys' discussion of presupposition is by way of introduction to the semantic and syntactic properties of the predicates they call factive, e.g. *regret, realise, be angry*, which – as is well known – they claim to presuppose the truth of their complements. Here again, however, I think it can be shown that sentences negating these verbs can be interpreted as negating their complements as well. While the implication in a positive sentence of the truth of the complement cannot be cancelled – the resulting sentences are contradictory – in a negative sentence, it can be. Witness the distinction between each pair of the following set:

(33a) ?Edward regretted that Margaret had failed even though he knew she hadn't.

(33b) Edward didn't regret that Margaret had failed because he knew it wasn't true.

(34a) ?Sue realised that Edward had been unfaithful to Margaret though he hadn't been.

---

[1] Cf. 5.2 for arguments against postulating the more special kind of denial as a separate sentence-operator.

(34b) Sue did not realise that Edward had been unfaithful to Margaret: you must have been mistaken – I know Edward has never been unfaithful.

(35a) ?Bill regretted that his sister caused a lot of trouble even though she didn't cause any trouble.

(35b) Bill didn't regret that his sister caused a lot of trouble – how can he have done – she didn't.

The status of each sentence of these pairs is not the same. While the (b) sentences are undeniably not the natural interpretation of the negative sentences in question, they are equally undeniably not contradictory. Yet on a presupposition account of factives the status of the sentences in each pair is predicted to be identical. It is only an entailment analysis which predicts that the truth value of the complement sentence is independently specifiable when the positive sentence is negated. This is not of course to deny that there is some difference between what the Kiparskys hoped to characterise as the normal interpretations of negation and the unnormal: it is merely that the difference cannot be captured by the concept of presupposition since the criterion of presupposition is that under no circumstances at all can the presupposed sentence be false if the presupposing sentence is false. It is logically necessary that if the presupposing sentence is false, the presupposed sentence be true. And as the pairs (33)–(35) demonstrate, the factive verbs do not fulfil this requirement.

If the status of presupposition rested solely on this problem of negative sentences, the issue might never be resolved: each protagonist would remain entrenched in his own academic fortress, merely adding to the fortifications argument by argument. However it has been pointed out increasingly in the literature (Morgan 1969; Langendoen and Savin 1971; Karttunen 1973) that the initial account of the Kiparskys is in any event too simple, and several additional complications have had to be added to the original account. Now each such complication presents – as we shall see – serious anomalies to the application of three-valued logic to the semantics of natural language. On the contrary however, each such problem is naturally explained within a two-valued framework.

The difficulty which linguists have seen as arising in the Kiparskys' account constitutes the so-called 'projection problem'. The Kiparskys' account of presupposition predicts that if a sentence which presupposes some sentence X is embedded in some other sentence Y, then Y will presuppose X. Yet there are several specifiable environments where presuppositions on embedded sentences are not part of the interpretation of the whole. Thus, for example, none of the following sentences themselves presupposes the presupposition of the embedded sentence.

(36) John pretended to regret that the captain was in prison so that no-one would know that he had escaped.

(37) John is married and regrets that he is.

(38) Either John regretted going to the party or he didn't go.

(39) If John went to the party, then he regrets it.

These sentences all contain predicates which are 'plugs' or 'filters' in the sense of Karttunen 1973. In an attempt to solve the projection problem, Karttunen distinguished between three types of predicate: plugs – predicates which block off all the presuppositions of the complement sentence; holes – predicates which allow all presuppositions to be presuppositions of the matrix sentence; and filters – predicates which, under certain conditions, cancel some of the presuppositions of the complement. The central examples of the group of plugs, are the verbs of saying, which have the inherent semantic property that the subject is merely reporting and is not committed himself to the truth of what he is reporting: more formally their complements have a truth value independent of the truth value of the sentence containing the verb. This property can be stated in either a two-valued or a three-valued system and these verbs of saying do not therefore provide evidence either for or against a presupposition analysis. Holes are verbs such as the factives which either entail or presuppose the truth of the complement. If these are in the matrix sentence (with no logical operator) then there can be no test between presupposition and entailment analyses since in both cases the truth of the implied sentence is a necessary consequence of the truth of the implying sentence. It is the filters which pose one of the two main problems: these allow the presupposition to be maintained or dropped. Yet by definition a presupposition should be carried over to the matrix sentence. The second main problem is posed by verbs such as *pretend*, which do not fit easily into this categorisation at all; because a three-valued analysis predicts that they should be holes but in fact they are not – they are plugs. Since these bring out the awkwardness of the system in a particularly direct way, I shall consider them first.

4.3.1 The problem of pretence. *Pretend* is a verb which very generally implies the falsity of its complement.[1] If then sentences containing a
factive verb are embedded as a complement of *pretend*, that complement
will be implied to be false. But on the hypothesis that sentences containing factive verbs presuppose the truth of their complement it
should follow that the complement of the factive verb must still be
implied to be true, even though the sentence containing the factive
verb is itself implied to be false. In other words, *pretend* should be a hole.
But on the hypothesis that positive sentences containing factive verbs
entail the truth of their complement, this prediction will not of course
follow since if the entailing sentence is implied to be false (as it will
be when embedded as the complement of *pretend*) the entailed sentence
(the complement of the factive verb) may be either true or false. The
prediction made by the presupposition analysis is not borne out. Each
of the examples (40)–(44) can be interpreted in one of two ways – either
the complement of the factive predicate taken to be true or taken to be
false:[2]

(40a) Sue pretended that her boss realised she had an IQ of 180 in
order to get a better job.

(40b) Sue pretended that her boss realised she had an IQ of 180
though in fact he didn't know how clever she was.

(41a) I pretended to realise I was dying of cancer though I knew it
was only sciatica.

(41b) I pretended to realise I was dying of cancer though in fact I
couldn't make myself believe it.

(42a) I pretended to regret that John was leaving when I knew he had
no intention of doing so.

(42b) I pretended to regret that John was leaving because I didn't
want anyone to see how relieved I was.

---

[1] It is arguable that this property is based on an entailment relation between any
assertion containing *pretend* and the complement of the verb; but examples such as
*John pretended that he was ill and he found out later that in fact he had been ill for a
very long time* suggest that the relation is not that strong. (I am grateful to John
Lyons for pointing out to me examples of this type.) Cf. pp. 210–11 for a further
discussion of the nature of this relation.

[2] In fact this variability extends to the entire range of purported presuppositions as we
shall see. Cf. G. N. Lakoff 1972a and Karttunen 1973 who notice that judgements
seem to differ in such cases. Both Karttunen and Lakoff fail to point out that this
variability is an unambiguous indication that the relation in question is not one of
presupposition, but of entailment.

(43a) The teacher pretended that he was angry that Pete was late though he knew that Pete was there on time.

(43b) The teacher pretended that he was angry that Pete was late so that Pete would be frightened.

(44a) Gerald pretended that it was most unfortunate that Ann was pregnant though he knew in fact it wasn't true.

(44b) Gerald pretended that it was most unfortunate that Ann was pregnant though secretly he was very pleased.

This evidence suggests fairly unambiguously that the relation between positive sentences containing factive verbs and the complements of those verbs is not one of presupposition at all, but is a relation of entailment.[1] So posing a plugging mechanism on *pretend* to account for these cases would merely be an *ad hoc* device with no intrinsic explanatory power whatever. Similar problems arise with *believe* and *dream*, as Karttunen himself pointed out.

4.3.2 Filtering: the problem of the connectives. The main body of filters are the logical connectives (said by Karttunen to be predicates). Before considering each connective in detail, it is worth pausing to anticipate the predictions the entailment and presupposition analyses make about embedding in logically compound sentences. In the case of S_1 *and* S_2, an entailment-based analysis predicts that any entailments of either sentence will be entailments of the whole, and a presuppositional account should be similar. If some sentence S_3 is a pre-condition of S_1 being true or false, it should also be a pre-condition of S_1 *and* S_2 being true or false. With S_1 *or* S_2 the predictions are not parallel. Since in uttering S_1 *or* S_2 the speaker is not committing himself to the truth of either conjunct, and since on an entailment account, the implications only follow if the entailing sentence is true or implied to be true, it follows that the entailments of S_1 and S_2 are not a necessary implication of the compound S_1 *or* S_2 (unless some sentence is entailed by both S_1 and S_2). In contrast to this, if S_1 presupposes S_3, then S_3 is a necessary condition for S_1 to be assessed either as true or as false. Since in claiming S_1 *or* S_2 one is presumably committing oneself to the view that both could have been true, one might anticipate that pre-

[1] I do not mean to imply by criticising the Kiparskys' use of the term presupposition that their entire analysis is thereby falsified. On the contrary, as we shall see in 6.4 below, the evidence they provide suggests fairly conclusively that a syntactic class of factive predicates needs to be distinguished, but these are a subset of predicates which entail the truth of their complement propositions.

suppositions of S_1 or of S_2, unlike entailments, should be a presupposition of the whole. Finally *If S_1 then S_2*, where a similar point
holds. Since on an entailment account a speaker does not commit
himself to either conjunct, the entailments of S_1 and S_2 are not entailments of the entire sentence. Presuppositions though, as pre-conditions
for either of the values true or false, might be expected to be maintained
of the whole. It is no coincidence that these predictions about presuppositional properties in logically compound sentences are uncertain,
even vague: for the definition of the corresponding connectives in
presuppositional logic is disputed. What we shall see immediately is
that no single definition of any one of the connectives enables the
insights captured by a presuppositional analysis of simple sentences to
carry over to compound sentences.

First consider *and*. The problem as Karttunen presents it is that
sometimes presuppositions are maintained in compound sentences
conjoined by *and*, but sometimes not.

(45a) Susie was sick and James regretted going to the circus.

(45b) James went to the circus and he regretted going to the circus.

(45a) appears to presuppose that James went to the circus but (45b)
does not – it asserts it. In formal terms, if it were false to say that
James had been to the circus (45b) would be false, not truth-valueless;
but it seems that (45a) should be characterised as neither true nor false
under these circumstances – it is presumably just as odd to say (45a) if
James did not go to the circus as to say simply *James regretted going to
the circus*. But this is not a point where we can say that *P and Q* presupposes *R* (*a*) if *P* presupposes *R*, (*b*) if *Q* presupposes *R* unless *R*
equals *P* (in which case *P and Q* entails *R*), though this is effectively
what Karttunen does. One cannot make this move, because implicit in
such a step is a double definition of *and*. That is, if we say that *P and Q*
presupposes some sentence *R* which *Q* presupposes, then when *R* is
false *Q* will be neither true nor false and *P and Q* will also be neither
true nor false (since it too presupposes *R*). But if *P and Q* is said to
entail *R* which *Q* presupposes just in case *R* happens to be identical with
P then when *R* (*P*) is false, *Q* will be neither true nor false, but this
time *P and Q* will be false. And, though there is no ambiguity in *and*,
this gives us two conflicting truth-table definitions of *and*:

P	Q	P and Q		P	Q	P and Q
T	T	T		T	T	T
T	F	F		T	F	F
F	T	F		F	T	F
.	.	.		.	.	.
.	.	.		.	.	.
F	−(T v F)	−(T v F)		F	−(T v F)	F

The only way out of this impasse is to give up the relation between the truth-tables and the implications of ordinary language; either assigning the value false when one conjunct is neither true nor false despite the assumption which may be inherent in the conjoined sentence (as in (45a)), or to assign *P and Q* the value neither true nor false under these circumstances ignoring the fact that the purported presupposition is in fact asserted, rather than assumed (as in (45b)). An entailment analysis however has no such problems. Both (45a) and (45b) will be false if either of their conjuncts is false. More particularly, since on this account *James regretted going to the circus* entails that James went to the circus, if the latter is false, the factive sentence will also (necessarily) be false and so the whole conjunction will under those circumstances be false.

Anomalies of this kind arise for a presuppositional account with each logical connective. Consider a three-valued truth-table for *P or Q*. What happens when one conjunct is true and the other conjunct neither true nor false: is the entire proposition true or neither true nor false? Some cases suggest one assignment, some the other. If we maintain the intuition that a third value is used to enable us to capture what a speaker assumes in uttering sentences, then presumably of (46) we would wish to say that *Johnny gave his favourite teddy to Oxfam* is presupposed – it would certainly be assumed to be true by anyone who spoke it under all normal conditions:

(46) Either Johnny regrets that he gave his favourite teddy to Oxfam or he is moping about something else.

Along these lines then, we would want to say that if Johnny did not give his favourite teddy to Oxfam then the entire proposition made by (46) is neither true nor false, regardless of the truth of the second conjunct. In contrast to (46) consider (47).

(47) Either Max regrets twisting his sister's arm or he didn't twist it. If in this case the second conjunct is true, then it seems clear that the

whole claim is true, despite the fact that the first conjunct is necessarily neither true nor false. Again we are facing a contradiction. Either we have to depart from the intuition for which presuppositions were set up in the first place by defining *or* in such a way that *P or Q* will be true just in case either conjunct is true (ignoring the assumptions speakers make in uttering sentences),[1] or we have to allow more than one definition of *or* (quite apart from the problem of exclusive *or*). Yet again there is no problem with an entailment analysis. Since neither *P* nor *Q* are themselves asserted, it may be the case that an entailment of either holds but it need not. Thus there is predicted to be nothing contradictory about (47). On the contrary an entailment-based analysis predicts that it be true if the second conjunct is true.

Finally let us consider *If P then Q*. Here speaker's intuitions are notoriously hazy. But consider a three-valued truth-table of *If P then Q*. Again the third value causes problems. If *Q* is neither true nor false but *P* is true, is the entire claim false, or is it neither true nor false? If *Q* is neither true nor false but *P* is false, is the entire claim true or is it, like *Q*, neither true nor false? As with all the other connectives, the intuition that presupposition corresponds to what speakers assume in saying sentences cannot be maintained without multiplying definitions of *If P then Q*. Consider the following.

(48) If Julian went home at one o'clock, then Jason will regret having had a big breakfast.

(49) If Joe married Sue, then Ed will regret being a civil servant.

(50) If Jim saw the peep show, then he regrets it.

(51) If you are unwell, you will soon realise it.

(48) and (49) take for granted that Jason had a big breakfast and that Ed is a civil servant respectively, in a way which a presupposition analysis might be expected to capture. This being so, one would presumably want to say that *If P then Q* is neither true nor false whenever *Q* has the value neither true nor false, irrespective of the value of *P*. But (50) and (51) suggest the opposite – in these cases if *P* is false then *Q* is neither true nor false, yet the whole is surely true. Whatever presuppositional approach is adopted, some part of the speakers' intuitions about language will be ignored. But, pace Karttunen, both assignments cannot be adopted. Thus the original motive for incorporating presupposition into semantics – that it captures what speakers assume in

[1] This is the option taken by Keenan 1972.

saying sentences – cannot be maintained here. Yet in striking contrast to the clumsiness of the three-valued system, in every case where a presupposition analysis meets anomalies, an entailment analysis makes predictions entirely consonant with the data. In examples (48) and (49), if it should turn out that the antecedent is false and the complement of *regret* false then since the consequent itself will (necessarily) be false, the whole would be true. And in (50) and (51) the same conclusion holds for a different reason: that if the antecedent is false the consequent must also be, but this is sufficient for the truth of the whole.

One final piece of evidence provides further confirmation of the entailment nature of the relation between factives and their complements. Both G. N. Lakoff (1972a) and Horn (1972), anticipating Karttunen (1973), discussed the suspension of presuppositions under certain conditions. Predictably, one of these was that the presupposing sentence be negated. Thus in the pairs (52)–(53) and (54)–(55) only the latter sentence is contradictory.

(52)   John doesn't realise Sue loves him, if indeed she does.
(53)   ?John realises Sue loves him, if indeed she does.
(54)   John doesn't regret having his money stolen, if in fact it was.
(55)   ?John regrets having his money stolen, if in fact it was.

And again, this is prohibited by definition for presupposition, and constitutes the hallmark of entailment.[1] Hence we have still not seen evidence for the necessity of changing the original framework of chapters 1 and 2 to accommodate a different logical relation of presupposition.

4.4 Some remaining examples of logically defined presupposition: Keenan

Keenan (1971) provides a large range of examples which are said to demonstrate the reality of the relation of logical presupposition in natural language, but all his examples can I think be handled as entailments, in a way similar to the examples of Fillmore and the Kiparskys. Keenan himself would not consider this counter-evidence since, unlike Strawson, he explicitly claims that presupposition is a type of entailment. However, so far we have had reason to suggest that presupposition as linguists use it is non-distinct from entailment. The defining criterion of presupposition is that the truth of S_2 follows from

[1] Cf. Karttunen 1971d for a different analysis of sentences such as these.

the falsity (negation) of S_1 as well as from the truth of S_1. His examples include '"factive" predicates, "definite" names, "cleft" sentences, selectional restrictions, temporal subordinate clauses, non-restrictive relatives, certain aspectuals, iteratives and presuppositional quantifiers' (pp. 46–7).[1] Factives I have already dealt with; definite noun phrases I shall consider in some detail in chapter 5, when I shall turn to some problems in the Strawsonian and Van Fraassen analyses; selectional restrictions I argued in chapter 1 must be formulated as mere components of the lexical items in question and not as a separate entity (cf. pp. 4–7) – thus anticipating the discussion here. The remaining constructions are exemplified in (56)–(61).

(56) It was John who was sick. (presupposition: Someone was sick)

(57) John left before Margaret came. (presupposition: Margaret came)

(58) Fred ate another helping. (presupposition: Fred ate at least one helping)

(59) John stopped working. (presupposition: John was working)[2]

(60) Only Fred shot himself. (presupposition: Fred shot himself)

(61) John, who saw Bill, burst out laughing. (presupposition: John saw Bill)

These involve various problems. Some of them do not have straightforward negations for syntactic or semantic reasons, and are thus not amenable to the negation test (e.g. non-restrictive relatives, adverbial constructions and *only* constructions). But it is not clear that even in these cases the falsity of the presupposing sentence necessarily implies the truth of the presupposed one. Consider the following examples, contextualising denials of the truth of the above examples:

(62) ??It is false to say that the King, who opened the exhibition in January, was assassinated in February, since the exhibition wasn't opened until March.

(63) It is false to say that it was John who caught the thief since the thief got away.

(64) It is false to say that John left before Margaret came, because Margaret never came.[3]

---

[1] I shall not discuss quantifiers such as *any*, *every*, *many*, *some*, either here or in chapter 5, since the interpretations of quantified, plural and generic noun phrases provide too many additional problems to be able to incorporate them in this book. For some indication of the general treatment of noun phrases, cf. p. 119.

[2] These are among the examples which Karttunen (1973) shows to be problematical.

[3] In some dialects of English this relation is not entailment either. An announcement

(65) John has not stopped working. How can he have – he hasn't even started.

(66) Fred didn't eat another helping – he even refused the first one.

(67) It is false to say that only Fred shot himself because he was the only one that did not.

Furthermore, these cases allow an interpretation when embedded below a verb such as *pretend* in which the presupposition fails to hold:

(68) Bill pretended that it was John who was sick though he realised that none of them were.

(69) Bill pretended that he had eaten one flower. Then he pretended that he had eaten another flower. Then he pretended to stop eating.

(70) Bill pretended that only Fred shot himself when in fact it was Bob and not Fred that did.

As we saw in the case of the factive verbs, this interpretation is predicted by an entailment analysis but not by a presuppositional one. This predicts, against the evidence, that the purported presupposition of the constructions in question must be implied to be true when, as here, the presupposing statement is implied to be false.

Moreover these purported cases of presupposition meet anomalies similar to those demonstrated by the factive predicates in conjoined sentences (either by *and*, *or*, or *if-then*). In none of the following cases conjoined by *and* is the purported presupposition of the second conjunct presupposed by the example as a whole: if the apparently presupposed sentence is false then the entire sentence is presumably false, not truth-valueless and 'odd' as presupposition failure is supposed to guarantee.

(71) Somebody killed John and it was Bill that did.

(72) Someone was sick and it was Gavin that was.

(73) James ate one helping and then he ate another helping.

(74) Sue was working and then she stopped working.

(75) John came and Sue left before John came.

(76) Fred and only Fred shot himself.

All these examples of Keenan, therefore seem, like the factives, more naturally explicable as relations of entailment, an analysis which makes exactly correct predictions.

on the news, 1 August 1972, contained the sentence *They defused the bomb before it exploded.*

The case for which this seems perhaps the least plausible is non-restrictive relatives (cf. my prefixed question marks to example (62)). But there is independent evidence for not analysing these clauses as presupposed. Consider examples (77)–(79).

(77) The King, who opened Parliament on January 10th, was assassinated in February.

(78) The King, who was assassinated in February, opened Parliament on January 10th.

(79) The King opened Parliament on January 10th, and he was assassinated in February.

If non-restrictive relative clauses are analysed as presuppositional, these three sentences will not be synonymous since they will have different truth conditions. Yet in terms of propositional content, these seem identical. It would surely be counter-intuitive to say that in a state of affairs in which the King was assassinated in February but Parliament was not opened until March, one would be bound to analyse utterances of (77) and (78) differently, assigning the value neither true nor false to (77) and the value false to (78). The relation between the statements (77)–(79) and the state of affairs in question is surely the same – viz. a mis-match of exactly the same order. Thus if one is false, as indeed both (78) and (79) are, then (77) must be false too. I therefore see no reason for analysing (77) and (78) as non-synonymous.[1]

In general then, though Keenan's examples are somewhat more intractible and border-line than the Kiparskys' or Fillmore's, we have not yet come across any strong evidence that semantics of natural language should be based on a three-valued logic incorporating presupposition. In chapter 5, I shall consider further reasons why such a logic should not be taken as the corner stone of semantics.

4.5 Summary

What sort of conclusion can be drawn from this medley of negative criticisms? First, I argued that speaker relative concepts cannot be included in a predictive semantic theory because if they are, then the semantics automatically loses its predictive power. I therefore concluded that speaker relative concepts must be excluded by fiat. Secondly, I have argued that none of Fillmore's, the Kiparskys' or Keenan's

[1] To analyse non-restrictive relative clauses in terms of presupposition is in any case counter to the Frege analysis (cf. Geach and Black (eds.) 1966, p. 73).

examples provide counter-examples to an entailment analysis of the data in question, since – among other reasons – in each case the purported presupposition can be interpreted as denied when the presupposing sentence is denied, a possibility excluded by a presupposition analysis. Furthermore a presupposition analysis, though it may capture some intuitions about the nature of negation in simple sentences, meets serious anomalies in compound sentences where it cannot maintain the insights it was set up to explain. On the one hand then, I have legislated against speaker presuppositions: on the other hand, I have rejected every linguistic account of logical presupposition as confusing presupposition and entailment. The concepts of presupposition thus seem to be being squeezed out of theoretical existence. So, on present evidence, the framework outlined in chapters 1 and 2 does not appear to require revision.

Four main forms of rejoinder could however be made. First, I have still not touched on the problem of reference, for which presupposition was first introduced. Thus a semantic theory has still to predict a presuppositional relation in order to explain the nature of the relation between a definite noun phrase and its referent. Secondly, in analysing the Fillmore–Keenan–Kiparsky examples as entailment, I have excluded the possibility of capturing what constitutes a natural interpretation, a concept which is captured by their use of presupposition. Each of the cases I constructed as a falsifier to a presupposition-based analysis constituted a less likely interpretation as opposed to the most likely interpretation. Thus, for example, *I didn't regret going to the party because I didn't go* is clearly not the natural interpretation of *I didn't regret going to the party*.

These two complaints can however be met – the first trivially: I shall consider the Strawsonian and Van Fraassen accounts of presupposition in the following chapter. Less trivially, I think arguments along the lines of earlier sections of this chapter can be extended to the whole concept of presupposition. The second complaint claims in effect that an analysis in terms of entailment could not be correct since it does not distinguish between more and less likely interpretations. Presupposition on the other hand can be used to distinguish between these two.[1] However, even if this could be consistently carried out, the use of presupposition to distinguish more and less likely interpretations

---

[1] Notice how Keenan (1972) in discussing presupposition is careful to refer to 'natural denial' (p. 49).

constitutes a misuse of the term presupposition. The definition of presupposition is in terms of necessary implication, and it is clear I think that the falsity of the apparently presupposing sentence does not of necessity guarantee the truth of the presupposed sentences, in the cases we have considered. Furthermore, one of the aims of a semantic theory outlined initially was to predict all possible interpretations of every well-formed sentence of the language. Thus a semantic theory is not only committed to predicting the obvious interpretations of sentences but all possible interpretations. Analogously, it is now standard to reject a syntax which only describes the obvious sentences of any language on the grounds that it would not only be a very uninteresting one but it would also not capture the necessary generalisations. It is however arguable that a complete account of natural languages should contain some form of prediction as to what constitutes a natural interpretation; but I shall argue in chapters 7–9 that this is naturally explained within the domain of a theory of communication (pragmatics) as part of an over-all theory of performance. The explanation of why a sentence such as *I didn't regret going to the party because I didn't go* is extremely unlikely ever to occur will thus be comparable in status to the explanation of the impossibility of *I met the man the girl the boy bit seduced*.

This relegation of speaker-assumptions in the use of factives to pragmatics, even where they seem as in negative sentences to be *prima facie* a linguistic convention, receives indirect support from Karttunen's account of presupposition within semantics (Karttunen 1973). For one of his main points is that his filtering conditions (which I have here rejected for independent reasons) must be made sensitive to assumptions in the sense accorded to presupposition by the Lakoffs. That is, for example, his filtering mechanism should be able to predict that the following sentences do not have the same presuppositions:

(80) Either the governors of the Opera House are worrying about the financial prospects of the House or they regret having included a famous singer in the administration.

(81) Either the governors of the Opera House have not appointed Tito Gobbi as its Secretary, or they regret having included a famous singer in the administration.

The first assumes that the governors of the Opera House have included a famous singer in the administration, the second does not. But this lack of presupposition in (81) is not due to the inherent semantic relation between the conjuncts since there is none, but to other contextual assumptions which guarantee the (non-semantic) equivalence of *The governors of the Opera House have appointed Tito Gobbi as its Secretary* and *The governors of the Opera House have included a famous singer in the administration*. But if my criticisms of the Lakoff concept of presupposition are even correct in principle, it follows that any device for ruling out interpretations which depends on situation-specific assumptions cannot be part of any type of semantics. Thus the relation between *Either Mary regretted inviting a maniac to the party or John was sick* and *Mary invited a maniac to the party* – or more generally the relation between any sentence containing a factive predicate embedded inside any one of the operators *not*, *or*, and *if-then*, and the truth of the factive complement sentence – cannot be a semantic dependency but must rather be a relation which can only be explained at a pragmatic level.

The third rejoinder might be that the entire discussion of more or less likely interpretations of a single sentence completely misses the point. For in considering a sentence such as *Bill didn't regret seducing Gertrude* one is not considering a single sentence but two – that is, the sentence is ambiguous. On this view, distinguishing between internal and external negation, *Bill didn't regret seducing Gertrude* has one reading in which *Bill seduced Gertrude* is presupposed and one in which it is not. While I shall consider the problem of ambiguity in detail in chapter 5 in connection with definite noun phrases, notice in any case that this argument is undermined by the disjunctive nature of the interpretation of any negative sentence. More importantly, what this view can give no account of is the interpretation of factive complements when the factive predicate itself is embedded inside any of the other operators – *and*, *or*, and *if-then*. But the problem is fundamentally the same for each of the four operators: viz. under what conditions can sentences be false? This problem is not specific to negation. Thus to analyse negative sentences as ambiguous is to miss a general account. For there is no way in which *If P then Q*, *P or Q*, or *P and Q* can be said to be analogously ambiguous. Moreover, if sentences such as *Edward didn't regret leaving Rachel* are said to be ambiguous, then it follows as an automatic consequence that *Edward regretted leaving Rachel* will simultaneously presuppose and entail the truth of its complement. Yet on the one hand, the sentence is not ambiguous in the required way, and on the other hand it is impossible for a non-ambiguous sentence both to presuppose and to entail another.[1] This is so because for any two sentences S_1 and S_2, the falsity of S_1 cannot both be a necessary condition for the truth of S_2 and not a necessary condition for the truth of S_2. So the analysis of negative sentences as ambiguous cannot be correct.

There is one final over-all criticism which should be made. My analysis dismissed somewhat off-handedly contrastiveness of *but*, temporal sequence and *and*, and the concept of common topic, yet each of these clearly contributes to the interpretation of sentences in some sense. Moreover, I have offered no explanation whatever of G. N. Lakoff's examples of reciprocal contrastive stress, such as *John told Mary that she was ugly and then SHE insulted HIM*. What all these examples have in common is that none of them falls naturally within the domain of a truth-based semantics. Furthermore, there is the more general problem of contrastive stress,[2] which I argued explicitly in chapter 3 could not be accounted for by a logical definition of presupposition because it could not be explained in terms of truth conditions. This group of examples together might seem to constitute the falsifying counter-examples to my claim that meaning for natural languages can be explained in terms of truth conditions. However, the exclusion of most of these examples from semantic theory can be justified (cf. the reasons given in analysing *but* (pp. 56–7) and *and* (pp. 55–6). There is one yet more serious putative counter-example. At least one lexical item has a meaning which appears not to be explicable at all in terms of truth conditions: *even*.

Even, like many other items, has been analysed in terms of presupposition.[3] It has been said for example that in saying *Even Max tried on the pants* a speaker asserts that Max tried on the pants and presupposes (*a*) that other people tried on the pants and (*b*) that it is surprising that Max tried on the pants. However Fraser (1971) points out that presupposition is not the right relation to describe the properties of *even*. In particular the implication that 'other people tried on the pants', though a semantic property of the sentence in question, is not a presupposition and nor is it an entailment. For as Fraser points out 'there is certainly something very strange about (2) [*Even Max tried on the pants*] if Max turned out to be the only one to try on the pants, but I

---

[1] Cf. Wilson (forthcoming) for a proof of this.

[2] The phenomenon of contrastive stress is a well-known one, and has been discussed in some detail recently by Chomsky 1971. Cf. 1.3.5 above and 8.6.1 below for a discussion and re-analysis of Chomsky's data.

[3] Cf. Horn 1969 and Fraser 1971.

think we can still assert that (2) is either true or false depending on the empirical evidence' (p. 153). He suggests that the implication that 'other people tried on the pants' is rather an implication as defined by Austin (cf. Austin 1962, p. 48). Similarly for the implication of surprise (cf. p. 154). But this is the relation which holds between my saying *Max tried on the pants* and my believing that Max tried on the pants, which is generally agreed to be pragmatic and not a semantic relation. *Even* therefore seems to constitute a clear counter-example to the claim that the contribution lexical items make to the meaning of sentences can be defined in terms of truth conditions.

It is no coincidence that the exceptions I have listed here have at some stage been labelled as involving presupposition, since they are all naturally explicable in terms of what a speaker presupposes (or assumes) as opposed to what he asserts. I do not however believe, despite the evidence which these counter-examples present, that the theory of truth conditions has thereby been shown to be false and should be replaced by a non-predictive speaker-oriented semantics. On the contrary, I hope to show in chapter 8 that these apparent counter-examples are not falsifying examples, and that the generalisations captured within the framework put forward here can – and must – be maintained. As with the concept of 'natural interpretation' I shall in general explain these apparent counter-examples within the framework of a theory of pragmatics – viz. a theory which seeks to characterise how speakers use the sentences of a language to effect successful communication.

5 The problem of reference and the semantic interpretation of noun phrases

In chapter 4 we considered a wide range of evidence which suggested not only that the notion of presupposition has been misunderstood by linguists but also that if the two quite separate uses of the term are distinguished, then it is no longer obvious that either of them plays any part in an explanation of the semantics of natural language. It is now time to turn to the source from whence the trouble came – definite noun phrases.

5.1. The referring properties of definite noun phrases: entailment or presupposition?

First let me briefly recapitulate the main differences between Russell's analysis and that of Strawson. Russell (1905) claimed that sentences such as *The King of France is wise* should not be analysed in a simple subject-predicate form but as the conjunction of

There is a King of France
There is not more than one King of France
There is nothing which is the King of France and not wise,

any such statement therefore entailing each of these conjuncts. On Strawson's account however it is only false to say that the King of France is wise if he is not wise. If there is no such man, then it is neither true nor false to say that he is wise. Conversely *The King of France is not wise* is only true if there is such a man. If there is not, then – like its positive congener – it is neither true nor false.

Thus these examples constitute the *prima facie* cases for the negation test discussed in chapter 4. Yet though it should be contradictory to negate a sentence containing a definite noun phrase and simultaneously to imply that the existential sentence corresponding to the implication of reference on the noun phrase is false, even Strawson draws attention to examples where this is not the case:

(1) The moon wasn't hidden by the clouds because there weren't any.

(2) A: Did the neighbours break the window?

    B: No, it wasn't the fault of the neighbours – we haven't got any neighbours.

(3) The exhibition was not visited by the King of France – France hasn't got a King.

(4) Jones has not spent the morning at the local swimming pool – there isn't a swimming pool in this town.

(5) Neither Aristotelian nor Russellian rules give the exact logic of any expression of ordinary language; for ordinary language has no exact logic.[1]

In commenting on such sentences, he points out (1964a, p. 112) that 'it may seem natural enough to say that it is quite untrue, or is false that Jones spent the morning at the local swimming pool, since there isn't one; that, however Jones spent the morning, he did *not* spend it at the local swimming pool, since there's no such place'. The linguistic corollary to this statement is that these examples demonstrate how, among the possible interpretations of negative sentences, there is one in which the reference properties of a noun phrase fall within the scope of negation.

What examples (1)–(5) have in common is that the definite noun phrase in question is not in subject position; and Strawson points out (1954, p. 226) that it is much less natural to interpret the implication of existence on a noun phrase as falling within the scope of the denial if that noun phrase is in subject position. However, I think it is fairly clear that counterparts to examples (1)–(4) in which the relevant noun phrase is in subject position can be interpreted as having their existence denied. Such an interpretation will normally demand contrastive stress, unless the sentences are a conjunct of some other sentence (cf. pp. 90–5).

(6) The clouds weren't hiding the moon – there weren't any clouds.

(7) No, the neighbours didn't break it – we haven't got any neighbours.

(8) The King of France didn't visit the exhibition – France hasn't got a king.

---

[1] Examples (1)–(4) are modified examples from Strawson 1964a; but (5) is the concluding sentence of 'On Referring'! Its existence as a counter-example to the analysis presented in that article is pointed out by Bar-Hillel 1954.

(9) The swimming pool at Ely wasn't closed – there isn't a swimming pool there.

Compare also

(10) My husband didn't come to meet me – I'm not married.

Now, as before, there is no doubt but that these examples provide
unnatural interpretations of negative sentences. However I would argue
again (cf. pp. 80–1) that negative sentences have a semantic representation
which allows a disjunct set of interpretations and that the initial aim
of the semantic model must be to predict what the logical limits to the
possible number of interpretations are before it can characterise which
is more or less likely. These examples therefore suggest that the implication of reference of definite noun phrases may fall within the scope
of negation though clearly it need not. This being so, even the relation
of reference would seem to be an entailment relation and not one of
presupposition.

Anyone wishing to maintain an analysis in terms of presupposition
must explain away such examples as these. One such way might be to
argue for an ambiguity between external and internal negation as is
implicit in Van Fraassen's account (cf. Van Fraassen 1968, 1969, 1970),
though – as we have already partly seen in connection with factives –
there are serious anomalies in adopting such a line of attack. But Strawson chooses a different way out. He attempts to defend his position by
analysing the concept of truth and truth-value assignment in terms of
'topic', where the topic of a statement is what the statement is about.
What he claims is that 'assessments of statements as true or untrue are
commonly, though not only, topic-centred in the same way as the
statements assessed; and when, as commonly, this is so, we may say
that the statement is assessed *as* putative information *about its topic*'
(p. 116). Thus he claims that since in the case of an example such as (3)
the exhibition is the established topic then it can be the case that it is
false to say of the exhibition that it was visited by a non-existent person.
But if *the King of France* is claimed to be the topic, as in *The King of
France visited the exhibition*, and this noun phrase does not have a
referent, there is no topic about which to assess the truth-value of the
predicate. In this case, it has no truth value. It follows that a passive
form of a sentence may be false while, under the same circumstances,
the active form has no truth value at all. Furthermore, the same active
sentence may be false in one speech-act situation and truth-valueless in

another while the state of affairs to which the sentence refers remains constant. What has been varied is the speaker's choice of topic. Thus *The King of France visited the exhibition* will lack a truth value if the King of France is the topic and there is no such man, or if the exhibition is the topic and there was no exhibition. If however the King of France is the topic and there is such a man, but there was no exhibition, then the statement will merely be false. Similarly if the exhibition is the topic and the speaker is correct in thinking there was an exhibition but mistaken in thinking there was a King of France.

But such an analysis is untenable. This constitutes a radical change in the conception of truth: it is no longer defined as a relation between an abstract statement (or sentence) and a particular state of affairs but rather in relation to a speaker, a hearer, and a state of affairs. That is, the assignment of truth value is dependent on what information the speaker is intending to convey to the hearer. Notice first that a large body of contradictions will no longer be labelled as such since the conjunction of any sentence containing a definite noun phrase with its negative counterpart will not be necessarily false. It may be neither true nor false.[1] Notice secondly that if this definition of truth were correct, the statement of meaning of a sentence as a set of truth conditions would have to be abandoned, since the truth of a sentence under this characterisation would not depend solely on the relation between the constituent parts of the sentence and the objects and relations to which they refer, but also on what information the speaker was intending to convey. It follows from this that sentences, on a truth-condition account of meaning, could not be said to have a particular meaning independent of the context in which they are spoken. The meaning would be dependent on what information was already known beforehand by the speaker and his audience. This consequence follows because, since truth is dependent on the information a speaker is intending to convey, the meaning of an utterance must also be dependent on the speaker's intentions. But if this holds, sentences become indefinitely ambiguous, the limits on a semantic theory are not definable, and semantics thereby becomes an inoperable discipline. Exactly the same consequences follow as follow from the incorporation of speaker presupposition into semantics.

Moreover the argument seems unavoidably circular. The definition of truth is dependent on a concept of topic. Topic itself is more or less

[1] Cf. Hochberg 1970.

undefined. However, informally, a characterisation of topic will depend on what a speaker assumes to be true, and is thus in some real sense dependent on the notion of presupposition. But presupposition is defined in terms of truth: hence the circle.

A definition of truth which avoids this circularity is given by Dummett (1958/59). According to his definition,

A statement, so long as it is not ambiguous or vague, divides all possible states of affairs into just *two* classes. For a given state of affairs, either the statement is used in such a way that a man who asserted it but envisaged that state of affairs as a possibility would be held to have spoken misleadingly, or the assertion of the statement would not be taken as expressing the speaker's exclusion of that possibility. If a statement of the first kind obtains, the statement is false; if all actual states of affairs are of the second kind, it is true. It is thus *prima facie* senseless to say of any statement that in such-and-such a state of affairs it would be neither true nor false.

This analysis casts doubt on the premises of a presuppositional logic, the possibility of a truth-valueless statement. If the definition provided by Dummett is in the main correct, as I believe it is, the counter-examples (1)–(10) raised earlier remain unexplained.

The philosophical literature on this problem is of course extensive,[1] and I shall not consider it all. Some independent evidence provided by Nerlich (1965) might however be briefly mentioned. It is well known that entailment is a transitive relation such that for any sentences S_1, S_2 and S_3, if S_1 entails S_2 and S_2 entails S_3, then it follows that S_1 entails S_3. A straightforward example is *This rose is crimson* entails *This rose is red*. The latter in its turn entails *This rose is coloured*, and hence *This rose is crimson* entails *This rose is coloured*. Nerlich points out that by the rule of transitivity *The King of France in 1965 is bald* must entail *There is a king of France in 1965*, since the former entails *There is a bald king of France in 1965* which itself entails *There is a king of France in 1965*. To postulate a separate logical relation of presupposition to account for this is therefore a matter of legislation, and the law of transitivity will have to be relinquished. Moreover both he and Linsky (1967) noticed that if a statement S_1 is a necessary condition of the truth and falsity of a statement S_2, then it must by definition be a necessary condition of the truth of S_2. This in its turn entails that S_2 is a sufficient condition for the truth of S_1. But this defines entailment.

[1] Cf. Geach 1958–9, Caton 1959, Odegard 1963, Roberts 1969, Cassin 1970a, 1970b, Jacobson 1970, Hochberg 1970, Schnitzer 1971, to name but a few.

In drawing a conclusion against Strawson, we cannot afford to ignore the important and influential work on three-valued logic by Van Fraassen, who, as a means of solving the traditional problem of self-referential sentences such as *What I now say is false*, uses two negation operators corresponding to internal (choice) and external (exclusion) negation (cf. Van Fraassen 1969, p. 69). However we saw in chapter 4 that the problems which face the application of three-valued logic to natural languages are not restricted to negation. So before turning in detail to the ambiguity problem of negation, let us first check whether the other problems posed for a presuppositional account of factive complements carry over to definite noun phrases. On the basis of sentences such as (1)–(10) which provide (marked) interpretations of negative sentences in which the existence of the referent implied by the definite noun phrase is denied, we might anticipate that, like factive complements, the occurrence of a definite noun phrase in the complement of a verb which implies the falsity of that complement does not – despite the prediction of a presuppositional analysis – guarantee an implication of reference. This anticipation is borne out: *John pretended that the King of France seduced his sister* can clearly be true even if there is no king of France. Thus it does not necessarily imply the existence of the King of France, despite the fact that an assertion of pretence implies the falsity of the complement of *pretend*. A similar phenomenon occurs in sentences with *believe* and *dream* as the superordinate verbs.

(11) Bill dreamt the Queen of Germany was dying.

(12) Amahl believes that Franklin Roosevelt is the King of America.

The problem of the connectives *and*, *or* and *if-then* also carries over in exactly the same way. And this problem presents perhaps the most damaging evidence against a presupposition-based framework since (*a*) there is no possible escape route *via* ambiguity as there is with negation and (*b*) it is in compound sentences that a presuppositional analysis cannot, despite its claims, capture consistently the assumptions which speakers make in saying sentences. Thus though the concept of neither true nor false matches the native speaker's intuition about the oddity of saying either *The King of France is bald* or *The King of France is not bald* when there is no such man, it cannot do so for all cases of compound sentences containing definite noun phrases, any more than it could for factive complements. For example, since it is just as odd to make the complex claim

(13) The King of France is coming to the exhibition and Mary has
got a headache.

if there is no such man as it is merely to assert the first conjunct, we
might be prepared in principle to agree with Keenan (1972) that if
either conjunct of *P and Q* is neither true nor false, then the whole
claim will be neither true nor false. Yet this truth-value assignment
sometimes conflicts with our intuitions. Compare (14) and (15).

(14) John beats his wife and his children.
(15) John is married and he beats his wife.

(14) is like (13) in matching neatly our intuitions that if a presupposition
of one conjunct is false, the entire sentence will be odd. However in
(15), this is not so: if John is not married, then the claim is simply false.
Furthermore it is not odd at all to say *It is false that John is married and
he beats his wife* if he is not married: on the contrary it is true. But we
cannot allow the truth-functional definition of *and* to depend on the
semantic properties of its parts. Thus we are faced with the same contradiction as before. When one of the conjuncts of *P and Q* is neither
true nor false, we appear to need to assign the entire statement sometimes the value neither true nor false, but sometimes the value false.

There is a further problem associated with the definition of *and*.
Suppose I bet example (16).

(16) In 1976, the Pope will not give the annual address but it will
be the Prefect of the Sacred College of Rites who gives it.

What in fact happens is that the Pope dies in 1975 and they do not
replace him. So in 1976, the Prefect of the Sacred College of Rites gives
the address. Do I win my bet? It seems clear that I do. Yet this intuition
cannot be captured in a presuppositional three-valued logic.[1] A presuppositional logic claims that both the positive and negative claims
containing a definite noun phrase are vitiated and are neither true nor
false if there is no referent corresponding to the definite noun phrase.
Thus the claim that the Pope will not give the annual address must turn
out to be neither true nor false if there is no Pope. But since *P but Q*
can only be true (like *P and Q*) if both conjuncts are true, a presuppositional logic must predict that under the circumstances described, I do

---

[1] The only possible solution within a three-valued semantics is to invoke the ambiguity
of negation at this point claiming that the bet is won on one reading (that of external,
denial, negation) and is invalid on the other (that of internal, descriptive, negation).
But this solution is itself fraught with difficulties (cf. 5.2).

not win my bet. None of these problems arises if we assume the validity of a two-valued logic. In particular the fact that I win the bet stated in (16) if it turns out that there is no Pope and that the Prefect of the Sacred College of Rites delivers the address is naturally predicted. If there is no Pope, then the prediction that the Pope will not give the annual address will turn out to be true.

The anomaly repeats itself with *P or Q* and the problem of its truth value when one conjunct is true and the other conjunct neither true nor false. Again some cases suggest one assignment, some the other. Compare (17) and (18).

> (17) Either the Mayor of London visited the exhibition or the organiser was very upset.

> (18) Either there wasn't a mayor of London or the Mayor of London visited the exhibition.[1]

(17) suggests, on the basis of the over-all implication that there is a Mayor of London, that the whole be neither true nor false if the first conjunct be neither true nor false. But (18) is surely true if the first conjunct is true, despite the fact that the second conjunct is necessarily neither true nor false. Again either we have to depart from the intuition for which presuppositions were set up in the first place, or we have to allow more than one definition of *or*.

And, as with *and*, we face problems with bets. Suppose John bets (19),

> (19) Either the Mayor of Inglesham won't go to the meeting or the motion will be defeated.

and what in fact happens is that the Mayor dies shortly before the meeting and so does not go. There is therefore no argument against the motion and it is passed. Does John win his bet? Or if he bets (20),

> (20) On January 1st 1976, either the Pope will not give the annual address, or America will drop 100 bombs on Moscow.

what is the outcome when it turns out that America does not drop any bombs on Moscow but since the Pope is dead somebody else gives the

---

[1] It has been suggested to me by John Lyons that a three-valued account makes the correct predictions if in making a prediction one is in fact predicting of a particular man (who is President, Pope or whatever) at the time of the prediction that he will not open exhibitions, give annual addresses, etc. But this is I think to miss the point that definite noun phrases are not logical proper names: they do not refer uniquely to some one individual. Hence the truth of the bet in (16) under the circumstances specified is not affected by the fact that the definite noun phrase does not refer to any such individual. For a further discussion of the uniqueness requirement on definite noun phrases, cf. 5.5 below.

annual address? Are the bets successful? Though these cases are less clear than the case of conjunction by *and*, it seems to me that there is little doubt that strictly speaking in both cases John has won his bet.[1] But a three-valued logic cannot account for this intuition. Since in both cases one conjunct is false, and one conjunct is truth-valueless, whatever the value the entire proposition may have it cannot be true. But if John wins his bets, then the propositions are true. And just as before with *and/but*, what provides an anomaly for a three-valued logic is automatically accounted for by a two-valued logic. A two-valued logic predicts that if there is no object for a definite noun phrase to refer to then a negative statement containing it must be true. Thus the first conjuncts of (19) and (20) are true under such conditions and the whole proposition will therefore be true even if the second conjunct is false.

Finally *If P then Q*. Suppose I say (21).

(21) If the Regent of Lithuania visited Enid's art gallery, then I'm a Dutchman.[2]

Now since the expression *If X, then I'm a Dutchman* is commonly used to suggest the absurdity of X, it seems reasonable to suggest that (21) is true if there is no Regent of Lithuania and I'm not a Dutchman. But what if the negative statement *The Regent of Lithuania did not visit Enid's art gallery* replaces the positive statement in (21)? According to a three-valued logic this will have the same truth value as its positive counterpart if there is no such man as the Regent of Lithuania – neither true nor false. So a three-valued logic predicts that the substitution of the negative statement for its positive counterpart in (21) should not alter the truth value of the whole. But it seems clear that it does. If there is no Regent of Lithuania and I am not a Dutchman then the claim made in (22) is surely false.

(22) If the Regent of Lithuania did not visit Enid's art gallery, then I'm a Dutchman.

To put it another way, if you promise that if the Regent of Lithuania does not visit Enid's art gallery, then you will eat your hat, when it

[1] Whether these bets could be upheld in a court of law is not relevant since the legal doctrine of frustration which is relevant here is not defined in terms of the semantics of the statement (contract) in question but refers to extra-linguistic knowledge concerning the particular circumstances involved (e.g. a tanker contracted to carry oil from A to B will not be in breach of contract if, when B is at war, it refuses so to do, unless of course this is specifically provided for in the contract).

[2] This type of example was pointed out to me by Deirdre Wilson.

transpires that he did not because there is no such man then you should feel forced to eat your hat. That is to say, the antecedent of both conditionals is true if there is no Regent of Lithuania, and thus the entire proposition is true only if the consequent is true. Otherwise it is false. Thus the claim in (22) is false if there is no Regent but I am not a Dutchman. This is precisely the result predicted by a two-valued logic – but not by a three-valued logic, which predicts that in both the cases (21) and (22) the entire proposition will be true if I am not a Dutchman. Like the examples with *or* and *and*, this prediction does not match the native speaker's intuition.

There is one further example involving *If P then Q* which concerns a counter-argument given by Strawson (1964a) in an attempt to disprove the validity of a three-valued logic. The argument Strawson cites runs as follows. Let *P* be a statement which is neither true nor false. Then the statement *P is true* is false. If it is false that *P* is true, then *P* must be false. But the statement *P is false* is also false. If it is false that *P* is false, then *P* is true. Therefore *P* is both true and false. Since this is self-contradictory, the three-value theory is false. Strawson's counter-argument (*ibid*, p. 109) is that if *P* lacks a truth value, then any statement assessing it as true, or any statement assessing it as false similarly lack a truth value. But this counter-argument will not I think do. Consider (23),

(23) If John has won his bet, then it is false that the Mayor opened the exhibition.

in conjunction with a state of affairs in which (*a*) John bet that there was no mayor and (*b*) John won his bet. A three-valued logic has three alternatives: (i) to say that (23) is neither true nor false since the antecedent is true and the consequent neither true nor false, (ii) to say that *If P then Q* can be true when the antecedent is true and the consequent neither true nor false, (iii) to admit that if it is true that there was no mayor then the statement *It is false that the Mayor opened the exhibition* is true. I take it that no-one would be prepared to support the second alternative. But the first does not match one's intuitions. (23) seems true, given the state of affairs in question. Thus we seem bound to accept alternative (iii). But this is an admission that the relation between the two statements *The Mayor opened the exhibition* and *There was a mayor* is one of entailment and not presupposition.

Thus we find that despite its initial apparent ability to capture certain properties of definite noun phrases, an analysis based on a three-valued logic not only makes a considerable number of wrong predictions with respect to negation and opaque environments such as *pretend*, but also faces a number of embarrassing anomalies. Yet for each of the cases raised against a presuppositional analysis, an analysis of the referential properties of definite noun phrases in terms of entailment makes predictions consonant with the native speaker's intuitions. Thus the sum conclusion of the evidence I have presented is that definite noun phrases, as delimited by Russell (cf. Russell 1905), do not presuppose the existence of their referents but rather entail it.

5.2 The problem of ambiguity

It must be pointed out that in arguing that the relation between definite noun phrases and their implied referent is reducible to a relation of entailment, I have not only flown in the face of the Strawsonian and the Van Fraassen account of presupposition, but I have also departed from Russell's account. For even Russell claims (1905, pp. 489–90) that the negation of a sentence containing a definite description is ambiguous. In the light of such a strong philosophical tradition, it would be foolhardy to dismiss the case for considering negative sentences to be ambiguous (at least with reference to scope and definite noun phrases) without considerable hesitation. However I think the evidence leads unerringly to that conclusion.

Informally, ambiguity of negation between external and internal (choice) negation has traditionally been said to correspond to the distinction in natural language between denial and descriptive negation. Descriptive negation is defined as the falsity operator of logic – true if the positive assertion is false, false if it is true:

P	$-P$
T	F
F	T
$-(\text{T } v \text{ F})$	$-(\text{T } v \text{ F})$

But external negation (which I shall characterise by the symbol '¬') is not so easily defined. Two definitions might be suggested:

(a)	P	$\neg P$	(b)	P	$\neg P$
	T	F		T	F
	F	F		F	T
	$-(T\,v\,F)$	T		$-(T\,v\,F)$	T

Definition (a) characterises $\neg P$ as mutually exclusive with standard negation and this is the definition which, *prima facie*, linguists might turn to since it corresponds to the claim that a sentence such as *John doesn't regret that Sue was sick* is true under two quite disjoint conditions – either if she was not ($\neg P$) or if she was but John did not regret it ($-P$). This is presumably the characterisation of 'special' negation used by the Kiparskys since their so-called 'denial of the appropriateness of the word in question' is said to be quite a 'different level' from the 'straightforward denial of an event or situation' (p. 151). However it is quite counter-intuitive that a definition of 'not true P' should be false when P is false, and it is not widely accepted by logicians. Moreover it does not capture the concept of denial since under this definition $\neg P$ would only be true for those cases which are counter-examples to a presuppositional analysis and would be false of a sentence such as *Bill didn't kneel at the feet of the Sultan of Mongolia because he missed the reception* if the circumstances are as described, irrespective of whether it is used as a denial or as a negative assertion. Since in any case, the problems that arise with definition (b) arise also with definition (a), I shall only consider in detail here the definition (b) (though cf. pp. 99–100).

Definition (b), given by Van Fraassen (1969, p. 69) and discussed by Herzberger (1970, p. 27), is more interesting in that it is equivalent to a characterisation of natural-language negation within a bivalent system except that what would be different types of falsity in the latter are given separate truth-value assignments (false and neither true nor false). Thus anyone holding that natural-language negation is ambiguous need not deny any of my arguments concerning negation but could say in rejoinder that only the one type of negation had such a free distribution. In particular, on this view there is an overlap between denial and descriptive negation, so a sentence such as

(24) John didn't set eyes on the Queen of Sheba because he wasn't at the reception.

is predicted to be ambiguous according as the negation is '¬' or '−', whereas

(25) John didn't set eyes on the Queen of Sheba because there is no such person.

is predicted to have one well-formed reading only.[1] Since this corresponds to the intuition that whereas (24) may be either a descriptive account of John or a denial of a previous statement (25) can only be a denial, the '¬' operator so defined appears to capture exactly the concept of denial and thus have an explanatory value quite independent of the descriptive negation operator.

Unfortunately for the presupposition account, the incorporation into natural-language semantics of an additional denial operator has some awkward consequences. First of all, notice that it is hard to avoid the consequence that all sentences are two- or three-, if not many-ways ambiguous, for positive sentence sentences can also be used as denials.

(26) A: John has passed his exams.
     B: He hasn't passed his exams.
(27) A: John hasn't passed his exams.
     B: He has passed his exams.

The status of B's utterance in conversations (26) and (27) is the same – he is denying the truth of A's statement. On the argument that $\neg P$ corresponds to natural-language denial, the second sentence of (27) would therefore have to be given a semantic characterisation corresponding to

$$\neg \, (-(\text{John has passed his exams}))$$

But the problem does not stop here. The conversation could have repeated itself, A saying "He hasn't", B replying obstreperously "He has". Yet the principle involved is now getting out of hand. It involves yet another semantic representation of the positive and negative sentences respectively as

$$\neg \, (\neg \, (-(\text{John has passed his exams})))$$

for A's response and

$$\neg \, (\neg \, (\neg \, (-(\text{John has passed his exams}))))$$

for B's response. And even if such multiple ambiguity can be explained

---

[1] Actually it would be analysed as being ambiguous between one contingently true reading and one contradictory reading.

away as logical equivalences, this is not a viable way out for the three formulae

> ¬ (−(John has passed his exams))
> ¬ (¬ (John has passed his exams))
> John has passed his exams

if the denial operator is to retain any substance, since a denial of a negative statement is surely different from a denial of a denial of a positive statement, and both of these are different from an assertion of a positive statement, in a way that setting up a denial operator might be expected to capture.

And this is only the first of the problems. Recall also that any analysis of negative sentences as ambiguous is committed to the contradictory view that a positive sentence both presupposes and entails the implied sentence in question (cf. p. 83).[1] Furthermore while the concept of denial may, in general, correspond to the marked (contrastive stress) interpretations of negative sentences in simple sentences (cf. pp. 86–7), this correspondence – as we have already partly seen (4.3.2) – does not carry over to compound sentences. Thus in examples (5), (16), (19), (20) and (22) (repeated here for convenience) there is no question of the sentences being exclusively denials, if indeed they have that potential at all.

> (5) Neither Aristotelian nor Russellian rules give the exact logic of any expression of ordinary language; for ordinary language has no exact logic.
>
> (16) In 1976, the Pope will not give the annual address but it will be the Prefect of the Sacred College of Rites who gives it.
>
> (19) Either the Mayor of Inglesham won't go to the meeting or the motion will be defeated.
>
> (20) On January 1st 1976, either the Pope will not give the annual address, or America will drop 100 bombs on Moscow.
>
> (22) If the Regent of Lithuania did not visit Enid's art gallery, then I'm a Dutchman.

Yet it is only if the ambiguity of negative sentences can be invoked that these sentences can be explained at all within a presuppositional framework. Thus in (16) one might seek to say that on an internal

---

[1] This was, to my knowledge, first pointed out by Schnitzer 1971, who draws attention to other anomalies in the Russellian ambiguity account. In particular he argues that on this account, *The King of France is bald* will neither entail nor presuppose *Whoever is the King of France is bald*.

(choice negation) reading of negation the bet is off since one conjunct is neither true nor false, and on an external reading of negation (given that the other conjunct is true), the bet is won. But this is to give up the characterisation of external negation as denial which justified its application to natural-language semantics. There is one alternative to this position: to retain '¬' as a denial operator and to agree that the truth conditions of '−' must be extended to cover all these cases (and of course the parallel factive ones). But this is to relinquish the very claim on which the entire presuppositional analysis is based − that the truth of any implied existential is a necessary condition for the truth of $-P$ as well as P. Moreover such a step has the consequence that both negation operators apply to the same range of cases, despite the fact that the second denial operator was set up to explain cases which were not originally thought to fall within the scope of the falsity operator. (Notice incidentally that the fact that descriptive negation covers the same range of cases as denial is what one might expect if denial was considered to be not a semantic operator but merely one of the uses to which negative (and positive) sentences could be put.) Since I take it that no supporters of a three-valued account of natural language would agree to this particular retraction of their claims, they cannot I think escape the conclusion that not only does the denial operator which proved necessary to save the account from counter-examples not capture the concept of denial in positive sentences, but it has to be used to characterise some negative sentences which cannot under any circumstances be used as denials.[1] At this stage of the game, it goes without saying that these anomalies simply evaporate if the ambiguity account of negation is given up.

Finally let us look at the standard tests for ambiguity in connection with both possible definitions of the denial operator. Recall that ambiguity is preserved across verb-phrase pronominalisation and so is vagueness (cf. 1.3.3). So in the case of ambiguity, any interpretation of the first sentence must be preserved in the pronominalised conjunct. Along these lines, definition (*a*) of the denial operator should predict that verb-phrase pronominalisation cannot take place across distinctions in negation scope differing as to whether a definite noun phrase falls in its scope. Definition (*b*) of the denial operator should predict that verb-phrase pronominalisation cannot take place across a distinction between a denial and a descriptive statement. Contrary to these, the analysis of

[1] Cf. Gale 1970 for further arguments against equating negation and denial.

scope in negative sentences as being entirely unspecified predicts that scope specification can differ across conjuncts in the structure in question. Furthermore since the distinction between denial and desscriptive negation is not captured by this analysis (being only a pragmatic distinction) the analysis predicts that the use of either conjunct of the test structure is separately specifiable. The evidence matches the latter pair of predictions, not the former.

> (28) Germany didn't invite the Mayor of London to their centenary dinner in 1973 and nor incidentally did France to theirs in 1974. Germany didn't because there wasn't a mayor at that time, and France didn't because the President so disliked the current mayor.
>
> (29) The King of France didn't visit the Duke's world-famous exhibition and Prince Ivan didn't either. The King of France didn't because France doesn't have a king, and I heard the news about Prince Ivan from someone who had shared the same room with him in a prison hospital.

Both (28) and (29) have the scope of negation including the relevant definite noun phrase in one of the conjuncts only (in defiance of definition (*a*)) and both can be said in denial of someone else's previous assertion of the first conjunct to the contrary, adding the second conjunct merely as additional information (in defiance of definition (*b*)). Exactly parallel cases could be provided for factive complements. The evidence therefore suggests fairly conclusively that negative sentences are not ambiguous, even in the case of definite noun phrases. In any case the attempt to analyse negative sentences as ambiguous in order to save the case for presupposition is to miss the point. The same type of phenomenon arises in all logically compound sentences, not merely negation, and there is no possible second operator analogous to denial to resort to for *and*, *or* and *if-then*.

5.3 Assertion: Strawson *v.* Russell

All my arguments have led in the same direction, that presupposition, as a new logical relation, is in natural language not distinct from entailment. Natural language therefore appears to be analysable in terms of a two-valued logic and not some other logic. Since many of my arguments have centred on the problem of negation, one might expect that this was the source of Strawson's disagreement with Russell.

But this is not so. Their disagreement can I think be traced to a confusion over the term *assertion*. Assertion is not used by Strawson in the same sense as Russell, though Strawson appears to assume that there is no radical difference. The distinction is analogous to the distinction I made earlier (3.3) between *statement* defined logically and *statement* defined as an illocutionary act. Assertion is used by Russell in the sense of a commitment to the truth of certain conditions. Thus Searle (1969) defines assertion as 'a (very special kind of) commitment to the truth of a proposition' (Searle 1969, p. 29). This definition has as an automatic consequence that if a speaker asserts (is committed to the truth of) some sentence then he is automatically asserting (committed to the truth of) all the entailments of that sentence. To infer that 'anyone who asserted S [*The King of France is wise*] would be asserting that (1) There is a king of France (2) There is not more than one king of France (3) There is nothing which is king of France and is not wise' (Strawson 1950, p. 324) is therefore not an incorrect inference, given the above characterisation of assertion. But this concept of assertion is clearly not equivalent to *assert* in the sense of 'to give information of some kind to an audience'. Only the latter stands in contrast to what a speaker assumes. This latter sense is used by Strawson. He claims that 'To use the sentence [*The table is covered with books*] is not to assert, but it is (in the special sense discussed) to imply, that there is only one thing which is *both* of the kind specified (i.e. a table) *and is being referred to*[1] by the speaker' and '...referring to or mentioning a particular thing cannot be dissolved into any kind of assertion. To refer is not to assert, though you refer in order to go on to assert' (Strawson 1950, p. 333). Yet Strawson appears to assume that there is no difference between his sense of assertion, and that of Russell. He argues that one of the false things that Russell claims is that in asserting *The King of France is wise* a speaker would also be asserting that there at present existed one and only one king of France. Further he argues that since all a speaker would be asserting is the wiseness of such a man, then it is only on the grounds of his putative wiseness that that assertion can be assessed as true or false. It is this claim which conflates the two uses of the term *assert* and it leads directly to the incorporation of some undefined notion of topic into the definition of truth, a procedure which I have already argued leads to circularity.

The argument in favour of presupposition seems therefore to be

[1] Strawson's italics.

founded on a misconception. Clearly Russell would not accept the characterisation (and the consequences) of assertion that Strawson assumes. Such a characterisation is indistinguishable from a non-truth-functional use of assertion, in which *JOHN hit Mary* asserts that it was John that hit Mary but assumes (presupposes) that someone hit Mary (cf. pp. 50–1). The conflation of an illocutionary definition and a logical definition also emerges in Strawson's use of the word *state*. He claims that 'to use the word *the* is...to imply that the existential conditions...are fulfilled. But to use *the* in this way is not to "state" that these conditions are fulfilled' (1950, p. 332). Here he appears to use *state* in an illocutionary sense. But this sense of *state* is not of the same class as a logically defined statement, to which Russell was seeking an explanation. This type of confusion is best (i.e. most crudely) displayed not by Strawson, but by Searle, who claims that Russell's analysis is incorrect on the grounds that 'it is absurd to suppose that someone who asks "Does the queen of England know the king of France?" makes two assertions, one of them true and one false' (Searle 1969, p. 162). The absurdity lies rather in Searle's refusal to recognise that assertion is being used in two quite separate ways. Moreover it is *not* so obvious that the supposition he outlines is incorrect, given the Russellian use of assertion. Indeed Geach (1965) – along the lines of Russell – claims exactly this. He suggests not only that the assertion *John is aware of the fact that his wife is unfaithful* is equivalent to the pair of assertions *John is convinced that his wife is unfaithful* and *John's wife is unfaithful* but that in asking the question *Is John aware of the fact that his wife is deceiving him?* 'I am not just asking a question; I am asserting that John's wife is deceiving him' (p. 454). Since I have argued earlier that meaning is quite separate from aspects of the speech act (cf. 2.4.2) and moreover that meaning on a truth-conditional basis therefore relates directly not to the speech act of stating, to which it is logically prior, but to the logical statement, I shall therefore assume that an analysis of reference for definite noun phrases cannot be in terms of what a speaker assumes in uttering sentences. This assumption, together with the earlier arguments given against an analysis of reference in terms of a three-valued logic, commit me to asserting that presupposition, as Strawson defines it, is not part of a semantic explanation of natural language, since it appears to have been conceived on the basis of a conflation of the logical structure of statements and their illocutionary function.

5.4 Anaphora: the problem of coreference

I have assumed so far that the property of reference of the definite noun phrase is a unitary phenomenon. This is clearly an oversimplification. There are two main functions of the definite article as an indicator of definite reference:

(1) anaphoric:
   I saw a man hanging around this morning and when I came back the man had moved.
   Jack dismissed an employee and the next day he deliberately antagonised the man he had dismissed.
(2) non-linguistically anaphoric:
   Did you wind the clock?
   The King of France is bald.
   The planets that have more than one sun are larger than the earth.

In all that precedes, I have only discussed type (2) and I have argued that this implication of reference can be interpreted as falling within the scope of negation. But anaphoric definite noun phrases never can be: *A dog and a cat ran across the road and the dog wasn't chasing the cat* implies the existence of a specific dog and a specific cat. So one might argue that these at least constitute a clear case of presupposition (as Keenan (1971) does). However this would not I think be justified. Let us look at the evidence more closely.

A descriptive account of *the* in this type of example is relatively straightforward. The function of *the* is as a linguistic coreference indicator to some noun phrase previously occurring. The linearity involved in the distribution of *a* and *the* is essential to the interpretation of the definite article. Consider examples (30)–(33).

(30) Someone came into the room and told a boy that the police were outside, while the boy was talking to a pretty girl.
(31) While a boy was talking to a pretty girl, someone came into the room and told the boy that the police were outside.
(32) Someone came into the room and told the boy that the police were outside, while a boy was talking to a pretty girl.
(33) While the boy was talking to a pretty girl, someone came into the room and told a boy that the police were outside.

In both (30) and (31) the indefinite noun phrase is to the left of the lexically identical definite noun phrase[1] and this allows a reading of coreference. When this condition is not fulfilled as in (32) and (33) the readings are that these two instances of *boy* do not refer to the same object. Thus (30) and (31) are synonymous but (31), (32) and (33) are not. But it is sentence-pairs (30) and (33), and (31) and (32), which are identical morpheme for morpheme and which would – other things being equal – have identical representations (both semantic and syntactic). Thus, however the distribution of *a* and *the* is to be predicted, it is clearly dependent not on deep-structure order but on surface structure. Moreover, if an interpretation of coreference is required, *the* is obligatory. If *a* is substituted for *the* in (30) and (31), there is a necessary implication that two boys are involved, not one. The evidence therefore suggests that we explain these occurrences of *the* as indicating a second-mention instance of the noun phrase it modifies, and analyse definite and indefinite noun phrases as differing only in that a definite noun phrase is a second instance of the indefinite noun phrase, since this would provide an automatic means of explaining the synonymy of (30) and (31) despite their non-identity morpheme for morpheme.

Definite noun phrases with relative clauses are exactly comparable to non-modified definite noun phrases: the function of the definite article is to establish anaphoric coreferentiality:

(34) A man with a moustache was talking to a man who was bald on the pavement at the side of the road when suddenly the man who was bald took out a gun.

Here, as with the simple definite noun phrase, the occurrence of *the* must be analysed as differing from the indefinite noun phrase only in that it constitutes a second occurrence of the noun phrase, since again *the* is obligatory if an interpretation of coreference is required.

If this analysis is correct, and the anaphoric use of the definite article is a reflex of a second mention of the object to which the noun phrase is referring, then there is an automatic explanation of why this use of the definite noun phrase cannot be interpreted as falling within the scope of negation. The law of contradiction predicts that a sentence cannot be simultaneously both true and false. So for example, the semantic interpretation of a sentence such as *John met a girl at the party* predicts that the sentence will be true if, among other things, there was a girl at the

---

[1] There are numerous problems about this statement of identity. For some discussion, cf. G. N. Lakoff 1968, pp. 63–74, and Karttunen 1971c.

party.[1] But the sentence *John didn't dance with the girl because there weren't any girls there* is true under contrary conditions. Thus general principles of contradiction predict the oddity of *John met a girl at the party but he didn't dance with the girl because there weren't any girls there.* Similarly *A man with a moustache was talking to a man who was bald at the far end of the room but the man who was bald was not replying* must imply that there was such a bald man, since to interpret *The man who was bald was not replying* as true because there was no such man provides a contradiction with the preceding conjunct. On these grounds, a noun phrase with linguistically anaphoric *the* can never be interpreted as falling within the scope of negation, since to do so will always set up a contradiction with the preceding instance of that noun phrase. Non-linguistically anaphoric *the* differs from anaphoric *the* in just this respect. There is no prior explicit commitment to the existence of some object in the former case, and so a necessary contradiction does not arise – this use of *the* is interpreted as falling within the scope of negation. Hence the nondeviance of

(35) I didn't wind the clock because we haven't got one.

(36) The moon wasn't hidden by the clouds, because there weren't any.

It therefore seems that the natural explanation for anaphoric definite noun phrases, with or without relative clauses, is that they constitute second mention of the object the noun phrase describes, thus automatically providing an account of why they are not interpretable as falling within the scope of negation. If this is a correct explanation, then there are no grounds for setting up a new logical relation of presupposition just to account for these cases.

Evidence that this general analysis is correct is provided by the contrastive interpretations of indefinite, anaphoric-definite and non-anaphoric-definite noun phrases when embedded in a complement sentence below *pretend*, the verb whose use commonly implies the falsity of its complement. We saw earlier that the implication of existence of non-anaphoric *the* could be interpreted as false within a *pretend* complement. Thus *John pretended that the King of France seduced his*

---

[1] Examples such as *John saw a ghost* which do not entail that there was a ghost do not affect the validity of this relation, since the properties of *see* guarantee that there need be no referent to the object seen. Contrast this with *John met/touched/kissed/ beat up a ghost* which do have as a necessary condition of their truth that there be a ghost.

sister does not depend for its truth on there being a king of France. This may, or may not be, true. Thus (37) is not a contradiction.

(37) John pretended that the King of France seduced his sister though there is no such man.

Compare also

(38) John pretended that the clouds were hiding the moon though there weren't any.

(39) John pretended that he was winding the clock, though there wasn't one there.

By contrast the anaphoric uses of *the* cannot normally enter sentences in a similar way without contradiction:

(40a) ??John pretended that he was stroking the woman beside him though there was no-one there.

(40b) John pretended that he was stroking the woman beside him though he never touched her.

(41a) John pretended that he was stroking a woman beside him though there was no-one there.

(41b) John pretended that he was stroking a woman beside him though he never touched her.

(42a) ??John pretended that he was stroking the woman who was standing beside him though there was no-one there.

(42b) John pretended that he was stroking the woman who was standing beside him though he never touched her.

(43a) John pretended that he was stroking a woman who was standing beside him though there was no-one there.

(43b) John pretended that he was stroking a woman who was standing beside him though he never touched her.

In each of these cases, an account of the contrast between interpretations with indefinite and definite noun phrases in terms of first and second mention of some object predicts this distribution in the following way. The indefinite noun phrase can be interpreted as false since there is no prior commitment to the truth of the existence of the object to which the noun phrase refers. The definite noun phrase if anaphoric cannot, as there is such a prior commitment – it constitutes a second mention of some object previously referred to and, because the previous mention of this object is not explicitly included within the scope of *pretend* in these examples, it is understood to be outside the scope of the verb. Hence, as in the other cases (cf. pp. 104–5) general rules of contradiction predict the deviance of such an interpretation.

A presupposition supporter might well retort at this point that to eliminate presupposition only to bring in a notion of 'prior commitment' is in effect to bring presupposition in again by the back door. But this would be quite unjustified. This notion of prior commitment is not in these cases relative to the world which guarantees the truth of the sentence in which the definite noun phrase occurs (as a presuppositional analysis would predict): rather it is relative to the world in which the first mention of the noun phrase in question was asserted.[1] Consider the following sentences.

(44) John pretended there was a woman beside him and that he was striking the woman.

(45) John dreamt that he seduced a woman, and the woman fought him.

(46) John wants to buy a car which is convertible and the car must be green.

(47) John wants to catch a fish this afternoon when the tide is out and then eat the fish he has caught for supper.

(48) My great-grandfather seduced a woman and the woman therefore became a nun.

(49) John will catch a fish this afternoon and we shall make sure that the fish is shared amongst us all.

Each of the above sentences contains an indefinite noun phrase and a definite noun phrase which are coreferential. However, none of them unambiguously implies a specific referent to whose existence the speaker must be committed in asserting the sentence. On the contrary, all of them constitute opaque contexts: that is to say, they describe worlds or states of affairs which may be compatible with the actual world but which need not (in some cases, must not) be co-extensive with the real world. Thus for example John may want something which exists, but he may want something which only exists in the hypothetical state of affairs that he envisages and desires.[2] So it is that in each of the above examples, the referent that the two noun phrases refer to may be a real-world referent, but it may not be. Thus for example (49) is true under two possible interpretations – either if John is going to catch a

<hr>

[1] Cf. Hintikka 1969, pp. 157–62 and 1972 for a lucid account of reference in modal contexts, using the concept of possible world.

[2] This is the concept of possible world which I introduced in chapter 2.

specific fish, which – say – he has seen, or if there is going to be a state of affairs such that there is a fish which he catches. Analogously, (48) can be true whether or not there is a specific woman who my great-grandfather seduced alive at the time of utterance. It does not affect the truth conditions of the sentence if in fact there is no such woman to refer to in the world relative to the speaker.[1] But these opaque contexts are not restricted to a particular set of verbs. They include future and past tense, as we have seen. Moreover, like negation, each of these opaque operators is vague with respect to its scope and not ambiguous.[2] Each passes the vagueness test (cf. p. 15) in allowing verb-phrase pronominalisation without demanding agreement in the specification of whether or not the noun phrase in question has a specific referent.

(50) My great grandfather seduced a woman, and so did my grand-father. Only my grandfather's woman is alive today.

(51) John wants to buy a car and so does Bill, but only Bill knows exactly the car he wants.

(52) John dreamt a woman was sleeping in bed beside him, and so did Bill. Bill woke up to find there was.

Now in the cases I considered previously – in which I claimed there was a 'prior commitment' – the definite noun phrase has no precursor within the opaque context, but is understood to be anaphoric. This being the case, its precursor is generally understood to be outside the opaque context,[3] preventing the definite noun phrase from being inter-

---

[1] This appears to be the basis of Chomsky's suggestion (1971) that *Einstein taught John physics* would be used if Einstein were dead, as opposed to *Einstein has taught John physics* which assumes that he is alive. An account more in line with the analysis here would be that past tense is an opaque context describing a world which is necessarily not co-extensive with the present, whereas perfect aspect does not provide an opaque environment but is interpreted as co-extensive with the present.

[2] Despite numerous claims to the contrary. Cf. C. L. Baker 1966, Jackendoff 1971, Hall-Partee 1972.

[3] Actually the relation between worlds is more complex than this. Coreference may either cross into an opaque world as in (i) or from an opaque world to the real world as in (ii) or remain within the opaque world as in (iii):

(i) John met a girl and he dreamt he seduced her.
(ii) Yesterday John dreamt that he hurt a girl and today she came round.
(iii) John dreamt that he hurt a girl and she cried.

In the two cases where coreference is across worlds, the two worlds must agree in the interpretation given to that referent. In terms of referential indices, the constraints are as follows: if within one world an object can be referred to by more than one name, each of these references must bear the same index. This is true for both real world coreference and coreference in an opaque world. Where coreference occurs across worlds, these worlds must agree in assigning the same index to a particular object. Cf. Hintikka 1969, 1972.

preted as within the opaque state of affairs. The exceptions to this general position are cases where the predicate responsible for the opaque environment is repeated in a discourse. Thus examples in (40a) and (42a) do not imply the actual existence of a referent if they occur in the following environment:[1]

(53) John pretended that there was a woman beside him. Then he pretended that he was stroking the woman beside him though in fact there was no-one there.

(54) ??John pretended there was a woman standing beside him. Then he stood up and pretended to stroke the woman who was standing beside him, though in fact there was no-one there.

These examples, particularly (53), provide us with further evidence that the implication of reference on an anaphoric definite noun phrase is not based on a relation of presupposition, but on entailment since only the latter predicts the variability of reference implications within opaque environments. The evidence thus suggests that all definite noun phrases entail the existence of their referent, despite the fact that in negative sentences they divide into two classes, only one of which allows an interpretation that denies the existence of the referent. The other class – those whose existence has already been implied by a preceding indefinite (or definite) noun phrase – cannot do so on account of the contradiction that would be set up. The nature of this relation between two noun phrases which are lexically identical save that where one has an indefinite article and the other a definite article can be formally captured simply by means of the linear representation of sentences. It would therefore be redundant to add any additional inherent specification to definite noun phrases to distinguish them from their corresponding indefinite noun phrases. It follows that definite anaphoric noun phrases and indefinite noun phrases have an identical semantic representation.[2]

5.5 Definite noun phrases and the implication of uniqueness

One final question remains: are all definite noun phrases semantically

---

[1] For some reason that I cannot explain, the occurrence of an explicit tense marker within the definite noun phrase in (49) makes it worse than (48). Since I have not given any detailed consideration of the enormous problems involved in the semantics of tense, this remains an anomaly.

[2] I am not alone in analysing indefinite noun phrases in terms of reference. Cf. Hall-Partee 1972, who talks about the referring properties of indefinite noun phrases.

identical to indefinite noun phrases in merely entailing (in non-opaque contexts) that there be some specific object having the properties assigned to it or do definite noun phrases imply some further condition? Russell assumes that they are not identical, and claims that definite noun phrases contain an implication of uniqueness. That is *The King of France visited the exhibition* entails, in his analysis, that there is one and only one king of France, whereas *A king of France visited the exhibition* does not. It is doubtful however whether this relationship is one of entailment. If it were, and the semantic representation of *The King of France visited the exhibition* had to include a conjunction of the statements *There is one and only one King of France* and *The King of France visited the exhibition* (I ignore the noun phrase in the predicate), then it should follow that the statement will be false if either one of its conjuncts is false (an argument which is by now familiar). However the statement *It is not true that the King of France visited the exhibition because there is more than one king of France* seems quite as incoherent as the same sentence with an indefinite noun phrase, where uniqueness is clearly not entailed:

(55) It is not true that a king of France visited the exhibition because there is more than one king of France.

The truth of the statement in question in both cases is quite unaffected by whether or not there is more than one king of France. Compare:

(56) It is not true that the head of school came to see me because we have two heads of school.

(57) It is not true that a head of school came to see me because we have two heads of school.

It is simply irrelevant to the truth of the statement *The head of school came to see me* that there may be more than one head of school. Similarly with (58):

(58) The glass has fallen on the floor.

This does not entail that only one glass has fallen on the floor since if in fact seven other glasses fell on the floor as well (58) would not thereby be false. Rather the conditions under which (58) be true are exactly those which guarantee the truth of *A glass has fallen on the floor*. What is additionally implied in the use of the definite noun phrase is however that the object referred to by the definite noun phrase is uniquely identifiable by the hearer; but this implication is not an entailment either. The truth of any of the statements *The King of France visited the exhibition, The head of school came to see me, The glass has fallen on the floor* is clearly not affected by whether or not the hearer is in fact able to identify the particular objects referred to in any speaker's utterance of the sentences. Thus, as we would predict of a relation involving speaker-hearer interaction, the implication of uniqueness on non-anaphoric definite noun phrases is not a truth-conditional implication and hence is not merely not an entailment relation but is arguably not even a semantic relation. Since, as we have seen, this is the only putative distinction between (non-anaphoric) definite noun phrases and indefinite noun phrases, I shall therefore assume that, like the anaphoric *the*, the non-anaphoric *the* is non-distinct in its semantic representation from the indefinite article.

One important exception to this conclusion is the predicative use of the indefinite noun phrase, which does not enter into a relation of reference at all. It is also an exception to the generalisation adopted in the formalism described in 1.3.2 that all noun phrases bear a referring index. It is not at all obvious how to deal with these examples except possibly by setting up two mutually exclusive indefinite articles, one referring and one not. This solution is not entirely *ad hoc* since their behaviour is importantly different. (It does not however explain the anomaly in the formalism of referring indices.) Notice for example that a referring use of the indefinite article cannot occur after the definite article and maintain an implication of coreference. Thus *The man came into the room and a man immediately did up his coat* cannot imply that the same man both came into the room and did up his coat. This is not so with the non-referring use:

(59) The man is a big lout.
(60) John hit the man, a big lout of a fellow.

The indefinite noun phrase clearly does indicate properties of the object referred to by the definite noun phrase, and not some other object. For reasons such as these I shall assume that the predicative use of the indefinite article has to be represented as quite distinct from its referring use. And in all that follows, I shall only be concerned with this referring use of the indefinite noun phrase.[1]

---

[1] I shall also not take into account here the generic use of either the indefinite or the definite article. While the concept of reference as I have used it here might reasonably be expected to include reference to a whole class, generics provide additional problems of their own which are not relevant to the main arguments of this book. I have also omitted the use of the definite article in superlative constructions on the ground that this is an extended and not a central use.

5.6 Summary

The central argument of this chapter has been – like that of the previous chapter – a negative one: I have suggested that the logical relation necessary to describe the implication of reference in definite noun phrases is entailment, and not presupposition. Thus the conflation by linguists of presupposition and entailment is not merely a foolish and philosophically insensitive misuse of relations defined within logic but stems from the fact that in natural language presupposition is not logically distinct from entailment, despite Strawson's claim to the contrary. What I am in effect suggesting is that the discussion of presupposition within a formal linguistic framework has been a red herring, since the arguments originally establishing the need for such a new logical relation are not valid. A consequence of my argument is that both definite and indefinite noun phrases entail the existence of the object to which they refer and should therefore be given the same semantic representation. We shall see in the following chapter how the conclusions of this chapter can be characterised in our formal framework.

The list of counter-examples or anomalies to a truth-based semantics has grown longer with each chapter. This chapter has added to the list not only the extremely 'marked' nature of the interpretations of negative sentences which include the implication of reference in the scope of negation, but also (more seriously perhaps) the implication in definite noun phrases of the hearer's ability uniquely to identify the object described, an implication which is the basis of the distinction between definite and indefinite noun phrases. However on the basis that a semantic theory must not only be predictive but must also make the correct predictions (cf. 1.1), I suggest that the restriction is a legitimate one and the apparent anomalies which arise can be naturally explained by a theory of pragmatics. Two large problems thus remain: (1) the further specification of our linguistic framework to predict the data we have discussed in this and the preceding chapter; (2) the specification of a theory of pragmatics. These form the burden of the four remaining chapters.

6 The formalisation of the solution

The conclusions reached in chapters 4 and 5 provide two main problems of formal description:

1. How should the theoretical account reflect the demonstrated relations of entailment – (*a*) between a non-opaque sentence containing a factive verb and its complement (*b*) between a non-opaque sentence containing a specific noun phrase (definite or indefinite) and the consequent claim of existence of the referent of that noun phrase?

2. How can the distribution of the definite article be predicted (*a*) where the two coreferring noun phrases (of which the second contains the definite article) are within the same sentence, (*b*) when the coreferring noun phrases are not within the same sentence, (*c*) when there is no explicit prior noun phrase for the definite noun phrase to corefer to?

As we shall see, there is reason to suppose that cases such as factive verbs which entail the truth of their complements should be analysed as containing a definite noun head. This being so, the formal representation of factives depends on the analysis given to definite noun phrases. I shall therefore discuss first the means of capturing the distribution of the definite noun phrase – i.e. problem (2).

6.1 The syntactic relation between definite and indefinite noun phrases

I have already argued that definite and indefinite noun phrases should have an identical semantic representation. On this basis, some linguists have argued that they should be given the same underlying syntactic representation, deriving the definite article by a rule of definitisation from an underlying indefinite article.[1]

What syntactic justification is there for this analysis? According to the principles suggested in chapter 1, the evidence would have to show that

[1] Cf. Annear 1965, Robbins 1968, Kuroda 1968.

113

indefinite and definite noun phrases did not differ in their syntactic constraints. Two putative counter-examples to this claim are the hypotheses that only definite noun phrases can take non-restrictive relative clauses, and that indefinite noun phrases cannot occur in negative sentences.[1] Thus one might argue that of the following examples, (1), (3), (5), (6), (8) and (10) are acceptable, but (2), (4), (7), (9) and (11) are not:

(1)   The book, which is about linguistics, would be very helpful.

(2)   ?*A book, which is about linguistics, would be very helpful.

(3)   A book which is about linguistics would be very helpful.

(4)   ?*Any book, which is about linguistics, would be useful.

(5)   Any book which is about linguistics would be useful.

(6)   He is an anthropologist who studies Indian tribes.

(7)   ?*He is an anthropologist, who studies Indian tribes.

(8)   The halfback didn't run with the ball.

(9)   ?*A halfback didn't run with the ball.

(10)   John didn't see the salesman.

(11)   ?*John didn't see a salesman.[2]

The evidence given is insufficient. There are circumstances in which an indefinite noun phrase can take a non-restrictive relative clause and does enter negative sentences:

.(12)   John didn't see a lorry which was coming round the corner.

(13)   John didn't see a lorry, which was coming round the corner.

(14)   John didn't buy a car which was convertible.

(15)   ??John didn't buy a car, which was convertible.

(16)   *A picture, which has a gold frame, may soon be painted by John.

(17)   A book, which was written by Paisley, was publicly burned by Catholics today.

(18)   A man didn't see me and stepped off the pavement in front of the car.

The negation constraint is shown by these examples to be simply wrong.[3] So too is the constraint on non-restrictive relative clause formation. (13), (15) and (17) all contain non-restrictive relatives modifying indefinite noun phrases. What then is the nature of the relation between

[1] Cf. Smith 1964, who distinguishes between two uses of the indefinite noun phrase, only one of which can take non-restrictive relatives, and C. L. Baker 1966.

[2] Examples (9) and (11) are from C. L. Baker 1966.

[3] Stockwell *et al.* 1973 wisely disagree with Baker's data (cf. p. 72).

indefiniteness and negation on the one hand, and non-restrictive relative clauses on the other? (13) appears to contain a referring instance of an indefinite noun phrase in a negative sentence, with a non-restrictive clause modifying it. So does (15). (12) and (14) are of the same negative contruction (containing an indefinite noun phrase with a restrictive relative clause) but their interpretations do not seem parallel. (12) seems to suggest that there was a specific lorry, but (14) does not suggest the existence of a specific convertible. These four examples indicate that an indefinite noun phrase in a negative sentence can either be interpreted as referring to a specific object or as not doing so.[1] If this evidence is correct, it should enable one to predict that *John didn't see a lorry* has (at least) two possible interpretations:

(19) John didn't see a lorry $\left\{\begin{array}{l}\text{– in fact he didn't see any traffic.}\\\text{and it nearly ran him down.}\end{array}\right.$

Similarly with examples (9) and (11):

(20) A halfback did not run with the ball $\left\{\begin{array}{l}\text{– he didn't even touch it.}\\\text{– you don't have half-backs in rugby.}\end{array}\right.$

The hallmarks of entailment are in evidence, and the postulated negation constraint thus seems non-existent.

What of constraints on non-restrictive relative clause formation? Notice that in each of (13), (15) and (17) the interpretation of the indefinite noun phrase must imply the existence of some referent, even (as in (13) and (15)) when the indefinite noun phrase is contained in a negative sentence. Moreover examples (4), (7) and (16), which all seem clearly deviant, contain indefinite noun phrases which do not imply the existence of a specific referent. A first explanation for this distribution is that there is a constraint on non-restrictive relative clauses such that they can only modify noun phrases which imply a specific referent. Restrictive relative clauses have no prohibition of this kind since (6) and (14) are grammatical though only the latter is even able to carry a referential interpretation. Since I have argued that negative sentences

---

[1] (13) also demonstrates the incorrectness of a constraint suggested by Smith 1964 that non-restrictive relatives cannot occur with either *the* or *a* in the predicate of negative sentences. The deviance of her example, *He didn't write a novel, which was published by McGraw-Hill*, is particular to verbs such as *write* which take objects of result. Cf. example (16). For some discussion of these, cf. Fillmore 1968, pp. 4–5, and also Vendler 1967a, pp. 97–121, who calls them 'accomplishment' verbs.

with an indefinite noun phrase allow this noun phrase to fall within the scope of negation, it follows that examples (2) and (15) will only be deviant if they are not given an interpretation in which the noun phrase in question has a referent. Though this interpretation may be difficult to evoke in some cases,[1] for example (15), the sentence (and others like it), must be allowed a referential interpretation on the ground of its interpretation when embedded in a sentence such as (21):[2]

(21) In the end John decided not to buy a car, which then stayed in the showrooms for six months.

Moreover, the constraint on non-restrictive relative clauses as reformulated should predict that whenever a noun phrase is open to either a referring or a non-referring interpretation, a modifying non-restrictive clause will disambiguate the sentence, though a restrictive clause will not. There are two types of environment in which indefinite noun phrases have varying interpretations: negative sentences and opaque environments.

(22) John is looking for a car.

(23) John is looking for a car which is convertible.

(24) John is looking for a car, which is convertible.

(22) and (23) are indeterminate as to whether John has a specific car he wishes to buy, but (24) must mean that there is a particular object. These examples of relative clause modification demonstrate that the constraints involved in non-restrictive relative clause formation are dependent not on the form of the article but on the referring properties of both definite and indefinite noun phrases.[3]

However, the analysis given above is simplistic for exactly the same reasons as a description of definite noun phrases as necessarily implying a specific real-world referent is simplistic. Though a non-restrictive relative clause may force an implication of a specific referent, as in examples (13), (15) and (17) above, it need not.

(25) John dreamt he seduced a woman, who fought him.

In (25), as in the examples with a definite noun phrase on p. 107, and

---

[1] This is particularly difficult in (2) which contains the modal *would*, an opaque operator like *will*. Cf. pp. 107–9.

[2] The referential interpretation is the natural one in this type of example if *a* is replaced by *one*. Cf. Perlmutter 1970 for an argument that *a* is the unstressed variant of *one*.

[3] The existence of this constraint (though yet to be modified: cf. pp. 117–18) provides added support for this rather wider use of the term *reference* than is common among philosophers.

unlike the earlier examples in this section, the non-restrictive relative clause allows an interpretation in which the action described takes place within the dream. The noun phrase it modifies is therefore not necessarily interpreted as implying a specific real-world referent. The reason for this is straightforward. The syntactic evidence for deriving non-restrictive relative clauses from an underlying conjoint structure is reasonably convincing (cf. G. N. Lakoff, pp. 41–60). This being so, sentences of the form *John bought a car, which is green* will be derived from the structure underlying *John bought a car and the car is green*. But non-restrictive relative clauses therefore correspond to the second-mention anaphoric definite article. It follows that non-restrictive relatives should have the same constraints as the definite article.[1] This prediction is borne out by examples (26)–(29).

(26) *Any book, which is about linguistics, would be useful.

(27) *Any book would be useful and the book is about linguistics.

(28) *John is an anthropologist, who hit me.

(29) *John is an anthropologist, and the anthropologist hit me.

Neither anaphoric definite noun phrases nor non-restrictive relative clauses can occur where the preceding noun phrase has no implication

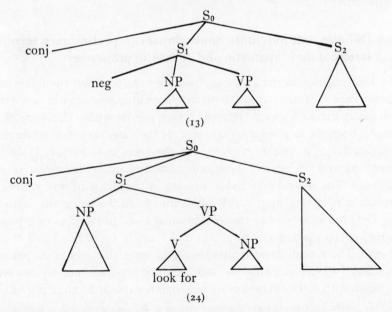

(13)

(24)

---

[1] Cf. also pronominalisation which occurs in a similar range of environments. Though cf. Hall-Partee 1972 for a discussion of the many problems involved.

of a referent. Their shared constraint is therefore that the noun phrase in question must imply the existence of a referent in some world, and that where coreference is across worlds, the worlds must agree in their interpretation at this point (cf. p. 108 fn. 3 above). It follows from this (by virtue of their underlying conjunct structure) that the non-restrictive relative clauses lie outside the scope of negation in examples (13) and (15) above, and outside the scope of *look for* in (24). (13) and (24) will have deep structures as shown (p. 117). The interpretation of S_2 in both cases is therefore relative to the speaker (by virtue of the deictic property of the tense). To avoid contradiction, the interpretation of the indefinite noun phrase in S_1 of (13) as having a referent must therefore not be included in the scope of negation. Thus not only do non-restrictive relative clauses occur with definite and indefinite noun phrases under the same conditions, but these conditions are exactly those which allow the occurrence of anaphoric definite noun phrase.

And so both the two counter-arguments to the proposed identity of definite and indefinite noun phrases fall to the ground. We can therefore conclude in the absence of further putative counter-examples that syntactic constraints on definite and indefinite noun phrases are identical.[1]

6.2 Definite and indefinite noun phrases: a preliminary formulation of their syntactic and semantic properties

In a formulation of the above analysis, we have to reflect the following facts: Fact 1: Noun phrases, both definite and indefinite, will be interpreted as having a specific referent if they are not within the scope of a modal operator or a negation operator. If they are, they may retain the implication of a specific referent, but they may not. Fact 2: Definite noun phrases in general constitute second mention indefinite noun phrases. The second fact I shall capture in the standard way within a sentence by postulating a rule of definitisation assigning the feature [+Def] to the second of two coreferential noun phrases, to take place after adverb movement (cf. p. 124 and Kuroda 1968, Stockwell *et al.* 1973). The morphological rules then guarantee that any noun phrase marked [+Def] acquires *the* and any noun phrase not so marked remains with *a*. The exceptions – non-anaphoric definite noun phrases –

---

[1] This conclusion has of course the same caveats as did the corresponding conclusion in chapter 5 about the semantic representation of definite and indefinite noun phrases. Cf. p. 111.

will arbitrarily have *the* in underlying structure, with a syntactic feature [+Def]. For further details of this formulation, see the next section, where more difficult counter-examples are also considered.

The formalisation of the semantic properties of noun phrases is not so straightforward. The form of the interpretation will depend to a large extent on how the interpretation of quantified, plural and generic noun phrases is formalised. Yet each of these constitutes a study of its own and I cannot go into these problems here. Bierwisch (1971) has argued that the quantification theory of modern logic is not suited to an analysis of quantification in natural language on the ground that unlike the existential and universal quantifiers, which characterise sets by enumerating the individuals in those sets, the quantifiers (and plural noun phrases) of natural language appear to operate with sets as primitive terms. Evidence for this is given by (*a*) sentences such as

(30) The boys saw the girls.
(31) The boys hit the girls.

since only the former necessitates that each boy stands in the specified relation to each girl, and an interpretation in terms of logical quantifiers would therefore have to distinguish between the two sentences; and (*b*) sentences such as *The Romans destroyed Carthage* where the act of destroying Carthage is not even understood as applying to each or indeed any one Roman individually but rather to the group as a whole. On the basis of evidence such as this Bierwisch sets up a different type of semantic element from that considered in chapter 1 – namely, a semantic element which delimits the set substitutable for the variable X_i in the semantic reading of a noun phrase, and I shall adopt his formulation here. Unlike the predicating features already discussed which specify the conditions to be met by the objects of the set referred to, the delimiting features apply to the set as a whole. Bierwisch suggests two ways in which these features might be formulated: an operator (QX_i) is formed by combining the delimiting feature Q with the variable X_i and this operator is either prefixed to the reading of the whole sentence (or the next higher constituent) or it is prefixed to the reading of the noun phrase itself. As in logic, brackets indicate the scope of the operator. The two alternative formulations are then as follows for some sentence containing a two-place predicate:

(i) $(QX_1)([B]X_1 . (QX_2)([C]X_2 . [S]X_1X_2))$
(ii) $[S] (QX_1)([B]X_1) (QX_2)([C]X_2)$

Though Bierwisch does not choose between these two formulations, we shall see that alternative (i) allows for a correct prediction of the interpretation of negative sentences (with one additional rule for interpreting negation in combination with such an operator) whereas alternative (ii) does not.

Let us assume then that each noun phrase is assigned a reference index in its underlying structure (needed for syntactic purposes such as relativisation) and that whether a noun phrase has the feature [+Def] or not,[1] the semantic representation of the noun phrase will include the operator $(SpecX_i)$ to characterise the fact that a single fixed object is referred to by that noun phrase. The interpretation of a sentence such as *A/The King bought a/the chandelier* will then (ignoring tense) be along the lines of one of the following schema:[2]

(a) $(SpecX_1)([K]X_1 . (SpecX_2)([C]X_2 . [B]X_1X_2))$

(b) $[B] (SpecX_1)([K]X_1) (SpecX_2)([C]X_2)$

The interpretation of the negation of such a sentence must then be able to predict that the positive statement could be false for at least any one of the following reasons: that the King sold the chandelier, that he sold a candlestick, that he bought a candlestick, that the Duke bought or sold the chandelier, that there was no chandelier, or that there was no king. To what extent are either of the above formulations successful in predicting such a disjunction of possibilities? Before answering this question we need some formulation of the interaction of negation and $(SpecX_i)$ and I tentatively suggest the following addition to the negation rule given in chapter 1:[3]

$Neg(SpecX_i)([S]X_i) \equiv A/ (SpecX_i)([S]X_i)$

$A/ (SpecX_i)([S]X_i) \equiv (A/SpecX_i)([S]X_i) \text{ v } (SpecX_i)A/([S]X_i)$

In the limiting case where [S] is a single predicate:

$A/ (SpecX_i)([S]X_i) \equiv (A/SpecX_i)([S]X_i) \text{ v } (SpecX_i)([A/S]X_i)$

Informally what this rule states is that if it is not true that some fixed object has the attribute (or complex of attributes) [S], the neither there is no such fixed object (with the attribute [S]) or there is some fixed

---

[1] It is only non-anaphoric definite noun phrases which have [+Def] present in deep structure: cf. p. 124.

[2] [K] represents the complex of features characterising *king*, [B] the complex of features characterising the two-place relation *buy*, and [C] the complex of features characterising *chandelier*.

[3] [S] represents any complex of features whose arguments contain the variable X_i bound by the operator $(SpecX_i)$. 'A/' is the antonymy operator: cf. 1.3.3 above.

object but it does not have the attribute [S]. The negation rule then applies to the sentence reading (*a*) (alternative (i)) as follows:

$$A/ (SpecX_1)([K]X_1 . (SpecX_2)([C]X_2 . [B]X_1X_2))$$
$$\equiv (A/SpecX_1)([K]X_1 . (SpecX_2)([C]X_2 . [B]X_1X_2)) \text{ v}$$
$$(SpecX_1)A/([K]X_1 . (SpecX_2)([C]X_2 . [B]X_1X_2))$$
$$\equiv (A/SpecX_1)([K]X_1 . (SpecX_2)([C]X_2 . [B]X_1X_2)) \text{ v}$$
$$(SpecX_1)([A/K]X_1 \text{ v } A/(SpecX_2)([C]X_2 . [B]X_1X_2))$$
$$\equiv (A/SpecX_1)([K]X_1 . (SpecX_2)([C]X_2 . [B]X_1X_2)) \text{ v}$$
$$(SpecX_1)([A/K]X_1 \text{ v } (A/SpecX_2)([C]X_2 . [B]X_1X_2) \text{ v}$$
$$(SpecX_2)A/([C]X_2 . [B]X_1X_2))$$
$$\equiv (A/SpecX_1)([K]X_1 . (SpecX_2)([C]X_2 . [B]X_1X_2)) \text{ v}$$
$$(SpecX_1)([A/K]X_1 \text{ v } (A/SpecX_2)([C]X_2 . [B]X_1X_2) \text{ v}$$
$$(SpecX_2)([A/C]X_2 \text{ v } [A/B]X_1X_2))$$

This gives exactly the result we need – namely that a given statement will be false if one or any combination of the semantic properties is not met in the state of affairs it describes.[1] In particular it allows the combination of $[A/K]X_1$ and/or $[A/C]X_2$ and/or $[A/B]X_1X_2$. Bierwisch's alternative (ii) cannot predict this range of possibilities. It would predict the following reading:

$$A/ [B] (SpecX_1)([K]X_1) (SpecX_2)([C]X_2)$$
$$\equiv [A/B] (SpecX_1)([K]X_1) (SpecX_2)([C]X_2) \text{ v}$$
$$[B] A/(SpecX_1)([K]X_1) \text{ v } A/(SpecX_2)([C]X_2)^2$$
$$\equiv [A/B] (SpecX_1)([K]X_1) (SpecX_2)([C]X_2) \text{ v}$$
$$[B] (A/SpecX_1)([K]X_1) \text{ v } (SpecX_1)([A/K]X_1) \text{ v}$$
$$(A/SpecX_2)([C]X_2) \text{ v } (SpecX_2)([A/C]X_2)$$

But this formulation does not allow the combination of [A/B] and either [A/C] or [A/K] a combination clearly demanded by sentences such as *The King didn't buy the chandelier: what happened was that the Duke sold the candlestick.* I shall therefore assume that the first alternative is the correct one.

---

[1] In fact the situation is more complicated since $(A/SpecX_i)([S]X_i)$, when [S] is a complex of predicates [P] and [Q], appears to be equivalent to:

$$(A/SpecX_i)([P]X_i) \text{ v } (A/SpecX_i)([Q]X_i)$$

For example, if there is no object such that it is the Queen of France and proud, then either there is no Queen of France or there is no-one who is proud. To obtain a more complete account in the negative sentences considered here, this further equivalence has to be included in their specification. However, since nothing hangs on its validity, I have omitted it for the sake of exegesis.

[2] The negation rule I have applied here is the equivalent to that given above, viz:

$$A/ [S] (SpecX_i) \text{ v } [S] (A/SpecX_i)$$

In addition to such a negation rule, analogous rules will be needed for the interpretation of opaque contexts, since these provide exactly the same indeterminacy in the interpretation of the reference of noun phrases within their scope as negation (cf. pp. 90, 105–9).[1] These rules will differ according as for example the operator demands that the 'world' it describes not be co-extensive with the real world (of which a possible example is *pretend*, though cf. p. 71 fn. 1 above), or whether the operator allows the case where the 'world' it describes is co-extensive with the real world (e.g. *look for, believe*). I shall not provide a formalisation of these since the details are not central to the argument of this thesis. However I think the existence of these rules in principle cannot be doubted. Furthermore these rules will only affect the interpretation of the noun phrases and their indices: they will not constitute deletion rules. The syntactic function of the index for relativisation, etc., will therefore be unaltered despite the fact that the interpretation of the index may be that there is no real-world referent (as in for example: *John did not buy a car which is convertible – he bought a lorry*).[2]

6.3 Inter-sentence relations – which solution?

I have so far argued about and formalised the relation between definite and indefinite noun phrases within the framework of a sentence-based grammar, and I have more or less ignored the problem of relations between indefinite and definite noun phrases across sentence boundaries. Yet it is well known that anaphora is not restricted to the confines of

---

[1] For a different proposal, cf. Jackendoff 1971, who argues that any formalism which uses quantifiers whose scope is as large as an entire proposition (e.g. traditional quantificational logic) is in principle incapable of capturing the appropriate interpretation of sentences containing opaque contexts, on the ground that for example *John is trying to find a pretty girl* does not mean 'John is trying to cause there to be a pretty girl such that he finds her' since he is not trying to make someone exist. His translation of the predicate calculus formula is not however the only possible one. It could read 'John is trying to cause it that there be a pretty girl such that he finds her' which does not entail that John is trying to cause the girl's existence. (For a related discussion of operators like *cause* which do not 'penetrate' to the entailments of their propositional argument, cf. Dretske 1970). In any case, when his own analysis of the referential properties of noun phrases is extended to entire sentences, Jackendoff's system falls prey to all the problems of quantificational logic, and is thus no more than a terminological equivalent.

[2] This avoids the problem pointed out by Baker 1966 that a noun, though it have no referent, may still allow restrictive relative clause modification which apparently demands coreference between the superordinate noun phrase and the noun phrase in the embedded sentence.

the single sentence, and the critical reader may have doubted my conclusions on the strength of these examples. This problem must now be faced. There are three possible solutions:

(A) to treat definite noun phrases as always constituting a second mention of some indefinite noun phrase and as therefore containing – either in the underlying structure or in the semantic interpretation – the information that there was a prior mention of that noun phrase; (B) to treat sentences with only a definite noun phrase as different in principle from sentences containing coreferring pairs of indefinite and definite noun phrases; (C) to treat indefinite and definite noun phrases identically, and to treat sentences with only a definite noun phrase in an *ad hoc* manner on the basis that inter-sentence relations are excluded by fiat, since they constitute part of a theory of discourse, not a theory of semantics. Alternative (A) has occasionally been put forward (Baker 1966; Jackson 1971). However it is in my view untenable. The syntax of a simple sentence cannot be allowed to have a conjoint sentence as part of its underlying structure for two reasons: (i) there is no syntactic evidence to justify such an underlying structure – I can conceive of no relevant syntactic constraints which a simple sentence such as *A man hit the girl* would share with a conjoint structure such as *There is a girl and a man hit the girl* (cf. 1.2); (ii) general conditions on recoverability prohibit such an analysis, since the details of the sentence preceding the occurrence of any given definite noun phrase are quite undecidable. It is not even possible to predict that the preceding sentence contain an indefinite noun phrase since it may not. The preceding noun phrase might itself be definite, or a pronoun (as in (32)):

(32) A man came. He sat down and eventually a girl came. At that point the man left.

Similar reasons militate against a semantic rule stating as part of the interpretation of a simple sentence that the preceding sentence has contained in it an indefinite noun phrase. To incorporate either type of rule into the grammar would be to transform the grammar from a grammar predicting the sentences of some language into a grammar predicting the discourse of some language. But, as the example above shows, the structure of a discourse is not predictable in the way that the structure of a sentence is. One cannot predict what sentence will precede or follow any given sentence. Thus any attempt to incorporate such a prediction into the grammar is in principle doomed to failure.

The second alternative, (B), treats definite noun phrases with no preceding coreferential noun phrase as different in kind from definite noun phrases which form such a pair. This is in effect a weaker form of a presupposition-based theory. Definite noun phrases with no preceding indefinite noun phrase (whether with a relative clause or not) would be said to presuppose the existence of the referent, whereas in co-ordinate structures where the constraints are naturally explicable in terms of entailment, an analysis of the definite noun phrases in question as entailing the existence of their referent would seem more appropriate.[1] Such an analysis is not however satisfactory, since the very general claim that inter-sentence relations are in principle different from intra-sentence relations would follow as a consequence. But it is not the case that all inter-sentence relations are different in kind from relations within a sentence. Indeed, coreference causes this theoretical difficulty just because it is the same phenomenon which is operating both between and within sentences. A framework which treats one and the same phenomenon in the form of two quite different statements, referring to two different logics, is not one to be accepted lightly.

The third alternative, (C), is to admit the limits of one's model openly, to provide a mechanism which deals with the counter-examples albeit in an *ad hoc* manner and which provides a general theory within which the *ad hoc* distinction can be explained away. It is this final alternative which – in the face of no adequate alternative solution – I wish to put forward. Definite noun phrases which have no preceding noun phrase with which they explicitly corefer, must be entered in the underlying structure of the sentence as definite noun phrases. To effect this, we shall say that all noun phrases have a referring index in underlying structure and they may optionally have an additional syntactic feature [+Def]. This feature does not take part in any transformation and is not interpreted by the semantic rules operating at the base. The definitisation rule then operates on coreferential noun phrases, without taking these [+Def] features already in the phrase marker into account. That is, it applies irrespective of whether the first noun phrase of the coreferring pair is marked [+Def] and it applies redundantly where a [+Def] feature was assigned in the base on a coreferential noun phrase. The morphological rules then guarantee the spelling out of *the* and *a*. The feature [+Def],

---

[1] This solution is not in fact adopted by anyone, but unless some such solution is adopted the examples given here in preceding sections provide an embarrassing wealth of counter-examples.

like the feature [+Pro], will not be given any interpretation by the grammar, which will predict synonymy between *The man hit me* and *A man hit me*. This is arguably not counter-intuitive. The distinction between *The man hit me* and *A man hit me* is, as we have already seen (cf. pp. 110–11), explicable in terms of the speaker's assumption of what the hearer knows. *The man hit me* implies that the hearer knows who is being referred to, while *A man hit me* does not. But as I have already argued in chapter 4 (pp. 59–60) this type of relation cannot and should not be handled within a formal model and so must be excluded by fiat.

6.4 The formulation of factive complements

In the light of the formulation given to definite noun phrases in the last two sections, we are now in a position to discuss a possible formulation of the interpretation of the factive verbs. We saw in chapter 1 that some predicates take propositions as arguments (e.g. [CAUSE]; and from the discussion of factives in chapter 4, it becomes clear that propositions which operate as arguments must be divided into at least two types – those whose truth is entailed by the superordinate predicate and those whose truth-value assignment is independent of the superordinate predicate. The factive predicates delimited by the Kiparskys (1970) constitute a subset of those predicates which entail the truth of their (propositional) argument, and the Kiparskys argued on syntactic and semantic grounds that sentences containing factive predicates plus *that* complements or gerunds should be derived from an underlying structure identical to sentences containing an explicit definite noun phrase complement – i.e. that *John regretted that Susie was sick* and *John regretted the fact that Susie was sick* should have the same underlying structure. The syntactic evidence that has been put forward as evidence of the distinction between factive and non-factive verbs is:

(i) Only factives can take the full range of gerundives (without tense or adverbial constraints) as object complements – hence the distribution

(33) John regretted Bill's having whipped the dog so hard.
(34) John resented Edward's seeing his sister every day.
(35) *John thought Bill's whipping Mary.
(36) *Edward assumed Alice's creating a fuss in each lecture.
(37) *Sue proved Mary's being neurotic.

(ii) Only non-factives allow the transformation of raising to object position:

(38) *John regretted Mary to be right.

(39) *Edward resented Bill to be the winner.

(40) Jane believed Deirdre to be wrong.

(41) Edward expected Bill to be the winner.

(42) Sam proved Einstein to be a fraud.

(43) John was discovered to be a genius.

(iii) Only non-factives allow the rule of negative transportation: (cf. R. Lakoff 1969) – thus

(44) John thought that Bill wasn't there.

is equivalent to

(45) John didn't think that Bill was there.

but this is not true of the pair (46)–(47):

(46) John regretted that Bill wasn't there.

(47) John didn't regret that Bill was there.

(iv) Only factives can be freely followed by *the fact that S* construction, which is synonymous with a simple *that* complement:

(48) John regrets the fact that Mary came early.

(49) John resents the fact that Mary came early.

(50) *Jo thinks the fact that Bill is right.

(51) *Jo imagined the fact that Peter was there.

(v) Only non-factive verbs require that the tense of the embedded complement clause must agree with the superordinate verb:

(52) At first my parents deeply regretted that $\left\{ \begin{array}{c} \text{I've} \\ \text{I'd} \end{array} \right\}$ decided not to have any more children.

(53) My parents eventually realised that $\left\{ \begin{array}{c} \text{I'm} \\ \text{I was} \end{array} \right\}$ determined not to have any children.

(54) At first my parents thought/believed/imagined that $\left\{ \begin{array}{c} \text{*I've} \\ \text{I'd} \end{array} \right\}$ decided not to have any children.

(55) Last year I discovered that my daughter $\left\{ \begin{array}{c} \text{*has been} \\ \text{had been} \end{array} \right\}$ a heroin addict.

(vi) Only non-factives allow adverb preposing from the embedded complement clause to the front of the superordinate clause. Thus we get

(56) I think he'll be in York tomorrow.

(57) Tomorrow I think he'll be in York.

(58) I imagine that Tom will give the game away tomorrow.

(59) Tomorrow I imagine that Tom will give the game away.

(60) I suggest we go to Windsor tomorrow.

(61) Tomorrow I suggest we go to Windsor.

(62) I've just discovered we'll be on holiday next week.

(63) Next week I've just discovered we'll be on holiday.

(64) It happens to be Nixon's birthday tomorrow.

(65) Tomorrow it happens to be Nixon's birthday.

(66) I regret that Mary is leaving tomorrow.

(67) *Tomorrow I regret that Mary is leaving.

(68) I resent it that Mary is leaving tomorrow.

(69) *Tomorrow I resent it that Mary is leaving.

(70) I'm surprised that Mary is leaving tomorrow.

(71) *Tomorrow I'm surprised that Mary is leaving.

Of this list, two criteria do not in fact distinguish factives from other verbs which entail the truth of their complement. Thus the equivalence which is said to provide evidence for negative transportation does not hold for any verb whose assertion entails the truth of the verb's complement. Thus *John didn't discover that Mary was sick* is not equivalent to *John discovered that Mary wasn't sick*. Similarly any such verb can be followed by *the fact that S* construction, though it is not obvious that for non-factive verbs these constructions are synonymous with the simple *that* construction:

(72) John discovered the fact that some soaps are inflammable.

(73) John discovered that some soaps are inflammable.

But it is arguable in any case that these properties are semantic and not syntactic. In general though, the remaining evidence suggests that there is a syntactic distinction between the Kiparskys' factive verbs and other verbs, even though they do not possess the semantic distinctiveness attributed to them.

This conclusion has been attacked by R. Lakoff (1972) who claims that while the semantic account is in the main correct, the syntactic account is not. But this attack depends on accepting a claim of Karttunen's (1971a, 1971b) that there are three classes of verbs which imply the truth of their complement: factives, semi-factives, and implicatives. It is not the implicatives which cause the problem since these are consistent with either the Kiparskys' account (re-analysed in terms of entailment) or Karttunen's. For the so-called implicatives do indeed constitute a separate semantic subclass of verbs which, while their assertion entails the truth of their complement, their negation entails the falsity of their complement. Moreover they have quite different properties from factives. But the third class, semi-factives, containing *prove*, *discover*, and *happen*, are said to have some of the semantic properties of factives but not their syntactic properties. And this R. Lakoff claims constitutes a cross-classification which is hard to account for under the Kiparskys' syntactic analysis of factives.

But there is reason to believe that the purported semantic distinction between factives and semi-factives is incorrect. The difference between factives and the so-called semi-factives is said (by R. Lakoff) to be shown by the following pair of sentences, the latter only implying the possibility of the truth of the complement:

(74) If I regret later that I have not told the truth, I will confess it to everyone.

(75) If I discover later that I have not told the truth, I will confess it to everyone.

But the data considered are insufficient. Compare:

(76) If I regret later that I have had a child, I will get a professional nanny.

(77) If I regret after the party that I have been seduced, I shall stop going to parties.

Neither of these imply that the complement of *regret* is true. Thus what appeared to be a means of subclassifying verbs which entail the truth of their complement is in fact merely a property of all such verbs. And the distinction between the two types of verbs is now reduced to the set of syntactic distinctions which the Kiparskys used to delimit the factive verbs. But this being so, the apparent partial overlap between syntactic and semantic properties of factives and the so-called semi-factives disappears. Semantically they form a homogeneous group of verbs (entailing the truth of their complement) but syntactically the Kiparskys' group of factive verbs is distinct from all other verbs which take complement sentences,[1] irrespective of any semantic dependence.

---

[1] There are several verbs which do not fulfil all the criteria of the semantic class to which they belong, but in each case the verb will fulfil a majority of the conditions: e.g. *imagine*. This verb takes the full range of gerundives but it allows raising (*I imagined Edward to be at my side*) and adverb preposing (cf. (58)–(59)); and it

Since moreover the Kiparskys' account provides a principled explanation of this syntactic distinction, I shall assume, together with the Kiparskys, that factive and non-factive complements differ in that the former is assigned an underlying structure of the form:

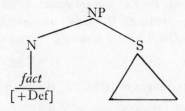

The problem we now meet of formalising the semantic interpretation of factive complements thus becomes one of formalising the interpretation of those definite noun phrases where the head noun and the entire modifying proposition are coreferential.

Bierwisch (1971) has argued (p. 425) that these 'fact' noun phrases should be interpreted – along lines indicated by Reichenbach (1947) – as involving the specification of a given fact where the proposition expressed is the name of that fact.[1] Formally, this is expressed as $(\mathrm{SpecX_i})$ $([\mathrm{P}]\mathrm{X_i})$[2] for some proposition P whose truth is entailed by the statement in which it is embedded as a complement.[3] For example, if we represent the semantic components of *regret* schematically as [REGRET], those of *king* as [K] and those of *The Queen is sick* as [P], then the semantic representation of *The King regrets that the Queen is sick* will be:

$$(\mathrm{SpecX_1})([\mathrm{K}]\mathrm{X_1} . (\mathrm{SpecX_2})([\mathrm{P}]\mathrm{X_2} . [\mathrm{REGRET}]\mathrm{X_1X_2}))$$

Now, in the case of the Kiparskys' factive verbs, there is a close correspondence between the deep-structure syntactic representation and the semantic representation, the syntactic representation reflecting the syntactic behaviour of this class of items. Yet this form of semantic

---

requires sequence of tense agreement (**They imagined that you are sick*). In addition, it allows negative transportation (*I don't imagine he'll come to our party*) and cannot take *the fact that S* constructions.

[1] Cf. Keenan 1972, pp. 419–20, for a similar formal characterisation of factive predicates.

[2] This formulation assumes the position argued earlier (5.3) that definite and indefinite noun phrases are semantically non-distinct.

[3] Definite noun phrases containing relative clauses are distinct from this since there is no variable ranging over the proposition itself. Thus the ambiguity of *the fact that Mary forgot* is reflected schematically in two different semantic representations:

(*a*) for the relative: $(\mathrm{SpecX_1})([\mathrm{F}]\mathrm{X_1} . (\mathrm{SpecX_2})([\mathrm{M}]\mathrm{X_2} . [\mathrm{Fo}]\mathrm{X_2X_1}))$
(*b*) for the non-relative: $(\mathrm{SpecX_1})([[(\mathrm{SpecX_2})([\mathrm{M}]\mathrm{X_2} . [\mathrm{Fo}]\mathrm{X_2})]\mathrm{X_1})$

representation is not restricted to the factive predicates: it is general to all semantic predicates which take a proposition as argument whose truth is entailed. Thus [CAUSE] for example, which in positive statements entails the truth of its complement proposition, will be of the form represented here. So *The King of France killed the Queen of Persia*, which contains the predicate [CAUSE] and entails the truth of *The Queen of Persia died*, will have a semantic representation which is not

$$(\mathrm{SpecX_1})([\mathrm{K}]\mathrm{X_1} \;.\; (\mathrm{SpecX_2})([\mathrm{Q}]\mathrm{X_2} \;.\; [\mathrm{CAUSE}]\mathrm{X_1}([\mathrm{DIE}]\mathrm{X_2})))^1$$

where the second argument of [CAUSE] is a proposition, but rather

$$(\mathrm{SpecX_1})([\mathrm{K}]\mathrm{X_1} \;.\; (\mathrm{SpecX_2})([[(\mathrm{SpecX_3})([\mathrm{Q}]\mathrm{X_3} \;.\; [\mathrm{DIE}]\mathrm{X_3})]\mathrm{X_2} \;.\; [\mathrm{CAUSE}]\mathrm{X_1}\mathrm{X_2}))^2$$

Implicit in this formulation is the claim that the relation between a true proposition and the state of affairs which it expresses can be explained by means of the same formal mechanism as the relation between a symbol and the specific object to which it refers. There are many philosophical problems attendant on this claim: and suggestions which have been put forward along these lines have proved controversial – cf. particularly Reichenbach's 'fact functions' (Reichenbach 1947, pp. 269–74) and Frege's concept of truth value being the referent of a proposition (Frege 1892, translated 1966, p. 63). I cannot enter here into all the issues which such a formulation implies. However, should the claim that objects and facts can legitimately be treated as the same type of formal object prove too strong, it would be a straightforward matter to allow another form of quantifier which ranged only over propositions. Since this would be a weakening of the theory, I shall maintain the more restrictive form in the absence of further evidence.[3] Some confirmation of the correctness of this analysis can however be gained by seeing how this formal mechanism interacts with the rule of negation. Given the schematic semantic representation of *The King of France*

---

[1] I assume here and elsewhere in this section for simplicity that [DIE] is primitive, since its internal structure is not germane to the arguments here.

[2] It might seem that the semantic representation should have the quantifier scope of $\mathrm{X_2}$ and $\mathrm{X_3}$ reversed so that the existence of the Queen of Persia in the above example is outside the range of the [CAUSE] predicate. Arguments to this effect have been given by Jackendoff 1971. For arguments against this alternative, cf. p. 122 fn. 1 above.

[3] For some discussion of this question cf. Martin 1971a, who first argues against Reichenbach's use of the same operators over facts and objects, but who later (pp. 129–30) admits that a perfectly satisfactory formal system would also hold if the distinction between the two were not taken as primitive. For support of the weaker view that propositions should legitimately be quantified over, cf. Vendler 1967b.

killed the Queen of Persia suggested on the previous page, and given the rule of negation:

$$A/[P \cdot Q] \equiv [A/P \text{ v } A/Q] \qquad \text{(cf. p. 12)}$$

and its subparts

$$[A/P] \equiv [-P] \text{ where P is the sole member of a set} \qquad \text{(cf. p. 12)}$$

$$A/(SpecX_i)([S]X_i) \equiv (A/SpecX_i)([S]X_i \text{ v } (SpecX_i)([A/S]X_i))$$

$$\text{(cf. p. 120)}$$

the negation rule would predict that *The King of France did not kill the Queen of Persia* be assigned a semantic interpretation as follows:

A/ $(SpecX_1)([K]X_1 \cdot (SpecX_2)([[(SpecX_3)([Q]X_3 \cdot [DIE]X_3)]X_2 \cdot [CAUSE]X_1X_2))$

$\equiv (A/SpecX_1)([K]X_1 \cdot (SpecX_2)([[(SpecX_3)([Q]X_3 \cdot [DIE]X_3)]X_2 \cdot [CAUSE]X_1X_2)) \text{ v } (SpecX_1)A/([K]X_1 \cdot (SpecX_2)([[(SpecX_3)([Q]X_3 \cdot [DIE]X_3)]X_2 \cdot [CAUSE]X_1X_2))$

$\equiv (A/SpecX_1)([K]X_1 \cdot (SpecX_2)([[(SpecX_3)([Q]X_3 \cdot [DIE]X_3)]X_2 \cdot [CAUSE]X_1X_2)) \text{ v } (SpecX_1)([A/K]X_1 \text{ v } A/(SpecX_2)([[(SpecX_3)([Q]X_3 \cdot [DIE]X_3)]X_2 \cdot [CAUSE]X_1X_2))$

$\equiv (A/SpecX_1)([K]X_1 \cdot (SpecX_2)([[(SpecX_3)([Q]X_3 \cdot [DIE]X_3)]X_2 \cdot [CAUSE]X_1X_2)) \text{ v } (SpecX_1)([A/K]X_1 \text{ v } (A/SpecX_2)([[(SpecX_3)([Q]X_3 \cdot [DIE]X_3)]X_2 \cdot [CAUSE]X_1X_2)) \text{ v } (SpecX_2)A/([[(SpecX_3)([Q]X_3 \cdot [DIE]X_3)]X_2 \cdot [CAUSE]X_1X_2))$

$\equiv (A/SpecX_1)([K]X_1 \cdot (SpecX_2)([[(SpecX_3)([Q]X_3 \cdot [DIE]X_3)]X_2 \cdot [CAUSE]X_1X_2)) \text{ v } (SpecX_1)([A/K]X_1 \text{ v } (A/SpecX_2) ([[(SpecX_3)([Q]X_3 \cdot [DIE]X_3)]X_2 \cdot [CAUSE]X_1X_2) \text{ v } (SpecX_2)(A/[(SpecX_3)([Q]X_3 \cdot [DIE]X_3)]X_2 \text{ v } [A/CAUSE]X_1X_2))$

$\equiv (A/SpecX_1)([K]X_1 \cdot (SpecX_2)([[(SpecX_3)([Q]X_3 \cdot [DIE]X_3)]X_2 \cdot [CAUSE]X_1X_2)) \text{ v } (SpecX_1) ([A/K]X_1 \text{ v } (A/SpecX_2)([[(SpecX_3)([Q]X_3 \cdot [DIE]X_3)]X_2 \cdot [CAUSE]X_1X_2) \text{ v } (SpecX_2)([[(A/SpecX_3)([Q]X_3 \cdot [DIE]X_3) \text{ v } (SpecX_3)A/([Q]X_3 \cdot [DIE]X_3)]X_2 \text{ v } [A/CAUSE]X_1X_2))$

$\equiv (A/SpecX_1)([K]X_1 \cdot (SpecX_2)([[(SpecX_3)([Q]X_3 \cdot [DIE]X_3)]X_2 \cdot [CAUSE]X_1X_2)) \text{ v } (SpecX_1)([A/K]X_1 \text{ v } (A/SpecX_2)([[(SpecX_3)([Q]X_3 \cdot [DIE]X_3)]X_2 \cdot$

$$[CAUSE]X_1X_2) \text{ v } (SpecX_2)([[(A/SpecX_3)([Q]X_3 .$$
$$[DIE]X_3) \text{ v } (SpecX_3)([A/Q]X_3 \text{ v } [A/DIE]X_3)]X_2 \text{ v }$$
$$[A/CAUSE]X_1X_2))$$

This is just the result we want. We have (at least) seven possible interpretations,[1] each of which is exemplified in the following contextualisations (corresponding in order to the order of the disjuncts):

(78) The King of France didn't kill the Queen of Persia – there's no such person as the King of France.

(79) The King of France didn't kill the Queen of Persia – it was the Shah who did.

(80) The King of France didn't kill the Queen of Persia – she's here.

(81) The King of France didn't kill the Queen of Persia – there's no such person as the Queen of Persia.

(82) The King of France didn't kill the Queen of Persia – he killed the Queen of Ethiopia.

(83) The King of France didn't kill the Queen of Persia – he merely made her very ill.

(84) The King of France didn't kill the Queen of Persia – nobody did, she just died.

Informally, the rule states that *The King of France did not kill the Queen of Persia* is true just in case any one or more of the predicate terms falls within the scope of negation and hence the property to which it corresponds fails to hold in the state of affairs being described. Furthermore, it states that if any of the delimiting argument features is interpreted as falling within the scope of negation, then all the components which depend on the argument in question must of necessity fail. Thus if there is no referent corresponding to X_1, not only is there no King of France but there cannot have been a killing of the type described; if there was no fact corresponding to X_2 (i.e. the Queen of Persia did not die), then the King of France cannot have killed her; and if there was either no Queen of Persia or she did not die or someone else was killed, then there cannot have been a fact corresponding to the conditions specified of X_2. Thus our independently justified negation rule predicts correctly that (*a*) if the statement *There is a King of France* is false, then of necessity *The King of France did not kill the Queen of Persia* is true;

---

[1] There are more than seven possible interpretations, since the 'v' of the negation rule is inclusive. Cf. also p. 121 fn. 1 above.

(*b*) if the entailed fact is false then either it is false because she did not die, or because *There is a Queen of Persia* is false; and (*c*) if *There is a Queen of Persia* is false independently of whatever the action the King of France may or may not have taken[1] then not only is it of necessity false that the Queen of Persia died in the manner specified, but also it is of necessity true that the King of France did not kill the Queen of Persia.

As a further example, take *The King regrets that the Queen is sick*, which we represented schematically before as:

$$(SpecX_1)([K]X_1 . (SpecX_2)([P]X_2 . [REGRET]X_1X_2))$$

If we now break down the semantic structure of 'P' giving the components of *queen* as [Q] and those of *sick* as [S] we get:

$$(SpecX_1)([K]X_1 . (SpecX_2)([(SpecX_3)([Q]X_3 . [S]X_3)]X_2 . [REGRET]X_1X_2))$$

The semantic representation of *The King does not regret that the Queen is sick* is then predicted to be

$$A/ (SpecX_1)([K]X_1 . (SpecX_2)([(SpecX_3)([Q]X_3 . [S]X_3)]X_2 . [REGRET]X_1X_2))$$

$$\equiv (A/SpecX_1)([K]X_1 . (SpecX_2)([(SpecX_3)([Q]X_3 . [S]X_3)]X_2 . [REGRET]X_1X_2)) v (SpecX_1)A/([K]X_1 . (SpecX_2)([(SpecX_3)([Q]X_3 . [S]X_3)]X_2 . [REGRET]X_1X_2))$$

$$\equiv (A/SpecX_1)([K]X_1 . (SpecX_2)([(SpecX_3)([Q]X_3 . [S]X_3)]X_2 . [REGRET]X_1X_2)) v (SpecX_1)([A/K]X_1 v A/(SpecX_2)([(SpecX_3)([Q]X_3 . [S]X_3)]X_2 . [REGRET]X_1X_2))$$

$$\equiv (A/SpecX_1)([K]X_1 . (SpecX_2)([(SpecX_3)([Q]X_3 . [S]X_3)]X_2 . [REGRET]X_1X_2)) v (SpecX_1)([A/K]X_1 v (A/SpecX_2)([(SpecX_3)([Q]X_3 . [S]X_3)]X_2 . [REGRET]X_1X_2) v (SpecX_2)A/([(SpecX_3)([Q]X_3 . [S]X_3)]X_2 . [REGRET]X_1X_2))$$

$$\equiv (A/SpecX_1)([K]X_1 . (SpecX_2)([(SpecX_3)([Q]X_3 . [S]X_3)]X'_2 . [REGRET]X_1X_2)) v (SpecX_1)([A/K]X_1 v (A/SpecX_2)([(SpecX_3)([Q]X_3 . [S]X_3)]X_2 . [REGRET]X_1X_2) v (SpecX_2)(A/[(SpecX_3)([Q]X_3 . [S]X_3)]X_2 v [A/REGRET]X_1X_2))$$

---

[1] The complication caused here by the use of the verb *kill* in this example is irrelevant to the general point.

$$\equiv (A/SpecX_1)([K]X_1 \cdot (SpecX_2)([(SpecX_3)([Q]X_3 \cdot$$
$$[S]X_3)]X_2 \cdot [REGRET]X_1X_2)) \text{ v } (SpecX_1)([A/K]X_1 \text{ v}$$
$$(A/SpecX_2)([(SpecX_3)([Q]X_3 \cdot [S]X_3)]X_2 \cdot$$
$$[REGRET]X_1X_2) \text{ v } (SpecX_2)([(A/SpecX_3)([Q]X_3 \cdot$$
$$[S]X_3) \text{ v } (SpecX_3)A/([Q]X_3 \cdot [S]X_3)]X_2 \text{ v}$$
$$[A/REGRET]X_1X_2))$$

$$\equiv (A/SpecX_1)([K]X_1 \cdot (SpecX_2)([(SpecX_3)([Q]X_3 \cdot$$
$$[S]X_3)]X_2 \cdot [REGRET]X_1X_2)) \text{ v } (SpecX_1)([A/K]X_1 \text{ v}$$
$$(A/SpecX_2)([(SpecX_3)([Q]X_3 \cdot [S]X_3)]X_2 \cdot$$
$$[REGRET]X_1X_2) \text{ v } (SpecX_2)([(A/SpecX_3)([Q]X_3 \cdot$$
$$[S]X_3) \text{ v } (SpecX_3)([A/Q]X_3 \text{ v } [A/S]X_3)]X_2 \text{ v}$$
$$[A/REGRET]X_1X_2))$$

As before, the output of the rule predicts that if any of the quantifiers is negated, and hence there is no specific argument to which to attribute the respective predicates, then all the predicate features which depend on that argument must also fail to correspond to properties in the state of affairs being described. Thus for example, if there is no king, then *The King does not regret that the Queen is sick* must be true since the *regret* predicate must also fail to hold (though it may still be true that the Queen is sick, since the specification of X_2 itself does not depend on X_1); if there is no fact X_2, then either there is no queen or she is not sick and of necessity the King cannot have regretted it; and if there is no queen corresponding to X_3, then *The Queen is sick* (X_2) must be false and hence again the King cannot have regretted it. This is exactly the result we need – specifically that if there is no fact corresponding to X_2 and *The Queen is sick* is false, then (of necessity) *The King does not regret that the Queen is sick* is thereby true; and if there is no queen, then (*a*) *The Queen is sick* is false and (*b*), as before, *The King does not regret that the Queen is sick* is therefore true. It thus seems that our independently motivated formal mechanism gives the correct result in a non-vacuous way.

Some details of the formulation must now be made more explicit. All propositional arguments in the semantic interpretation of a sentence whose truth is entailed are represented as falling within the scope of the 'Spec' quantifier, which also binds object-variables, according to the schema $(SpecX_i)([P]X_i)$. Their semantic representation is thus closely analogous to specific noun phrases. In the case of factive verbs and adjectives, this semantic parallel is explicitly reflected in the syntactic representation, which contains an underlying definite noun phrase. The feature of definiteness is specified at the level of deep structure since the definite article in phrases such as *the fact that Mary came* are never anaphoric (cf. p. 124). Indeed this type of construction demands the definite article: *a fact that Mary came* is ungrammatical as a noun-phrase construction.[1] A syntactic subcategorisational restriction on the lexical entry *fact*[2] will therefore guarantee that a rule assigning [+Def] to noun phrases optionally will in this case be obligatory. The semantic interpretation of the entailed complements of factives in both positive and negative sentences is then predicted by rules of interpretation which are independently justified.

6.5 Summary

We have seen in this chapter how if we assume (*a*) that definite and indefinite noun phrases are in general non-distinct both in their underlying syntactic representation and in their semantic representation and (*b*) that factives are non-distinct from definite noun phrases of the type *the fact that S* in their underlying syntactic and semantic representation, then the already existing framework proposed by Bierwisch, with only minor extensions (cf. p. 120), makes all and only the predictions the data demand. While the prediction of correct interpretations only provides functional justification for the analysis in hand, I take it that such predictive success provides at least strong partial confirmation of the philosophical assumptions on which it is based. Thus concepts such as Reichenbach's 'fact functions' receive some confirmation.

More generally, in this central section, I have considered what evidence there is for the incorporation into natural language semantics of either a logical or a speaker-oriented concept of presupposition. The conclusions were however negative: the evidence suggests on the contrary that the semantic component of the grammar should not be revised to allow for the concept of presupposition, whichever way it is defined.

One of the most important assumptions I have made throughout has been the need to predict all the possible interpretations of negative sentences (given the agreement that 'interpretation' be understood in a truth-conditional sense). So there has been no attempt to predict in the specification of negative sentences what constitute likely interpretations

---

[1] It is not of course in sentences such as *It's a fact that Mary came* but these constitute cases where extraposition has taken place.

[2] Of the form $+[+\text{Def}\underline{\quad}S]$.

and what much less likely ones – either in the case of sentences containing factive verbs or in the case of sentences containing definite noun phrases. In both, the rule of negation merely predicts all the logical possible ways in which negative sentences can be true. It might be argued (as I suggested on p. 81) that likely interpretations (as the more 'natural') should be distinguished from unlikely ones, and that this becomes a problem only if a relation of presupposition, however it is defined, is not recognised. But we shall see in the following section that an explanation of this problem is not a semantic matter.

7 Towards a pragmatic theory

Throughout chapters 4–6 I have had constant recourse to a theory of pragmatics. Whenever I faced counter-examples, both more and less serious, my excuse has been that this is a phenomenon which it is the function of a pragmatic theory to explain, and not that of a semantic theory. This excuse is little more than a lame fudge if there is no pragmatic theory to carry out the task assigned to it. We must now therefore ask what form such a pragmatic theory could take. Unfortunately there are almost as many divergent delimitations of pragmatics as there are of semantics.[1] When Morris first introduced the trichotomy of syntax, semantics and pragmatics (1938, 1946), pragmatics was characterised as the study of the relation between an utterance and its interpreters (speaker and hearer). But since Bar-Hillel suggested in 1954 that pragmatics concern itself with the interpretation of indexical expressions, there have arisen two quite separate applications of the term *pragmatics*. It can be applied to the study of speech acts (cf. Stalnaker 1972, pp. 383–4) or to an interpretation of indexical sentences (cf. Stalnaker *ibid.*; Montague 1972). However in arguing that the semantics of a natural language involves a statement of the necessary and sufficient condition for the truth of the sentences of that language, I have already assumed (cf. p. 38) that such a statement in the case of indexical sentences is part of semantics (as argued by Davidson 1967; Lewis 1972; Wiggins 1971). In any case I have referred to the need for a pragmatic theory at the points where the interpretation of sentences in natural language appears to involve phenomena which do not play any part in a truth definition for that language. And a pragmatics such as Montague's (Montague 1968, 1970) which assigns a truth value to indexical (and other) sentences (relative to some arbitrary world) is no nearer to explaining these phenomena than a semantics stating necessary and sufficient conditions for truth. I am not therefore using pragmatics

[1] Cf. Hintikka 1968, Martin 1971b, Stalnaker 1972, Thomason 1973.

here in the sense of Bar-Hillel, Montague and others. In the sense to be adopted here, pragmatics refers to the study of sentences in use, and I shall be assuming that a pragmatic theory is a theory which has to explain how a language is used to enable any speaker to communicate with any hearer (cf. Thomason 1973 and Wiggins 1971, who make an equivalent use of the term). Such a theory is put forward by Grice (1957, 1961, 1968a, 1968b, 1969), and in the remainder of this study, I shall attempt to show how the problems and implications pertaining to non-truth-conditional properties of utterances (or sentences) can be explained within the theory of conversation set out by Grice. Since the concept and status of a pragmatic theory within an over-all theory of language is still quite unclear, the greater part of what follows must be assumed to be in the nature of a tentative initial suggestion. Despite this caveat however, what I hope minimally to show is that Grice's framework can provide a natural explanation of the phenomena to which both linguists and logicians have given the label *presupposition*. If this explanation is at least in part correct, I shall take it that the restriction of semantics to a framework which is both truth-conditional and based on a two-valued logic receives double confirmation – (*a*) from internal arguments such as the prediction for any given sentence of its entailments and contradictions arising from those entailments, and (*b*) from the demonstration that those phenomena which are not accounted for by this form of semantics appear to be naturally explicable within a more general theory of communication (pragmatics).

7.1 Grice's theory of meaning

7.1.1 A definition of speaker's meaning: 'meaning$_{nn}$'.
Grice's theory has two parts: (i) a definition of speaker's meaning, (ii) the setting up of maxims of behaviour to explain the co-operative nature of communication.[1] With respect to speaker's meaning ('meaning$_{nn}$'), Grice argues that (roughly speaking) in uttering 'x', a speaker (S) is intending for indicative utterances[2] (*a*) that the hearer (H) should believe that S believes some proposition *p*, and (*b*) that by virtue of his

---

[1] In all that follows, I shall give references wherever possible to the published accounts of Grice's work. Where the only account is the mimeo version of Grice's William James 1967/8 lectures, I have had no option but to give references to this unpublished but widely circulated account. I have not given detailed page references in this case.

[2] Cf. 7.2.1 for a generalisation of Grice's definition of meaning to include imperatives and questions.

belief that S believes *p*, H should also believe *p*. In more formal terms, Grice gives the following definition:[1]

For some specific occasion, a speaker S makes an utterance 'x' to a hearer H indicating that p if he intends that:

(1) H should think x has f (where f is a feature)

(2) H should think that he S intends H to think x has f

(3) H should think f is correlated in way c with the state of believing that p (where p is the propositional content)

(4) H should think that S intends that he (H) thinks f is correlated in way c with the state of believing that p

(5) H should think he S intends H (*via* 1 and 3) to think that S believes that p

(6) on the basis of (5), H should think that in fact S does believe that p

(7) H should think that S intends (6)

(8) on the basis of (6) H should believe that p.[2]

That is to say, there is a general convention which all speakers (and necessarily therefore all hearers) know (and moreover know that they all know)[3] that in communicating some proposition *p*, a speaker is communicating his belief that p with the intention that the hearer, knowing that the speaker only says *x* if he believes that p, will also believe that p.[4]

The obscure part of Grice's definition of so-called 'meaning$_{nn}$' is the relation between 'x', 'f', 'c' and 'p'. There are two possible interpretations. The weaker one is that the relation between 'x', 'f', 'c' and 'p' is that conventionally provided by the rules of the language.[5] This

---

[1] This definition (given in the William James lectures) combines the revisions to the 1957 account outlined in Grice 1969, with one omission which is not essential here (cf. Grice 1969, p. 165), with the change made in the 1968a account that H believe *p* only from his belief that S believes *p*, rather than directly from S's intentions (cf. Grice 1968a, p. 230).

[2] I have not adopted Schiffer's revision of Grice's definition here (cf. Schiffer 1972), since this revision depends on the assumption that the regress involved in this definition is not harmless. Cf. 7.2.2 below for an argument that this is not the case.

[3] Hence the constant inclusion of a defining criterion 'S intends that H should think X' with a following criterion 'S intends that H should think that S intends H to think X'.

[4] This definition of utterance meaning depends on the assumption that we all speak the truth, a problem to which I shall shortly return.

[5] Cf. Apostel's (1971) paraphrase of Grice's conditions which includes the condition that the perception of the event E' (caused by the speaker A) by the hearer B 'causes the epistemic state in B about A because B believes that E' belongs to a set of events {E'} whose structural description is such that only systems behaving in accordance

weaker thesis is straightforwardly compatible with the framework suggested in this book. The interpretation which Grice intends is however a stronger thesis: 'x', 'f', 'c' and 'p', as part of a definition of utterance meaning, are intended to cover what on any occasion an utterer may mean by using a sentence. And – as Grice points out – what a sentence means ('timeless meaning') is not necessarily the same as what an utterer might mean (speaker's meaning) in saying that sentence on a particular occasion. In saying, for example, *He's a fine friend* of somebody who has just left you in the lurch, you do not mean to indicate the proposition p which is correlated by the rules of the language to the sentence you have uttered.

In its strongest form, Grice's explanation of meaning is not compatible with a truth-based definition of semantics, but is rather in direct conflict with it. What Grice has aimed to show (with Strawson as his articulate second – cf. Strawson 1964a, 1964b, 1971b; and also Schiffer 1972) is that (*a*) occasional (utterance) meaning can be defined as above in terms which do not presuppose the concept of linguistic meaning, and (*b*) linguistic meaning can then be defined in terms of occasional meaning. It follows from this that – if Grice, Strawson and Schiffer are correct – linguistic meaning can and should be defined in terms of the speaker's belief and intention in saying sentences.[1] The clarification of 'x', 'f', 'c' and 'p' in Grice's definition are therefore essential to an assessment of his claim.

While I am by no means certain that my interpretation of Grice is the correct one, I should like to consider some problems which appear to arise under the strong version of Grice's definition. We have already seen that to incorporate into a linguistic theory what a speaker might mean in saying a sentence on some particular occasion is to face the consequence that the meaning of sentences is unpredictable (cf. 4.1). Now, if sentence meaning is claimed to be derived from a definition of utterer's meaning, and this definition allows 'f', 'c' and 'p' to range over features, modes of correlation and propositions respectively which are not conventionally indicated by the utterance 'x', then it is by no means clear how the consequence of non-predictability can be avoided. One possible way to avoid it would be to restrict 'f', 'c' and 'p' precisely

with certain rules R (speaking a certain language) will produce elements of {E′}. Moreover B believes that these rules are such that only believing p and wishes others to know f(p) will produce E″ (p. 14).

[1] Cf. Strawson 1971b, where he argues that the notion of truth condition – if it is not taken as primitive – can be defined in terms of communication intention.

so that they range over features, modes of correlation and propositions respectively in a way which is co-extensive with a previously defined linguistic system. But if this linguistic system is to be used as a necessary part of the definition of what it means for a speaker to utter x, then sentence meaning can no longer be defined in terms of speaker-intentions since such a step would make the hypothesis circular and no longer explanatorily valid. Now it seems to me that the restrictions Grice places on his occasion-meaning are implicitly of the type I have suggested. In discussing how a speaker (U) might intend by a hand-wave (H-W) to indicate 'I know the route' Grice suggests that one condition of this being successfully communicated is that 'it is U's policy (practice, habit) to utter H-W if U is making an utterance by which U *means that* U knows the route'.[1] If this type of condition is applied to linguistic utterances, it seems that it can mean no more and no less than for an utterance x, to communicate one's belief as speaker (U) in a proposition p it must be 'U's policy (practice, habit)' to utter x if U is making an utterance by which U means that p. But unless U is idiolectal, his policy will be decided by the linguistic conventions of the language he is speaking. Thus the correlation between x and p reduces to a linguistic convention. If this interpretation is correct, then the claim that sentence meaning can be explained in terms of speaker-meaning cannot be maintained. Confirmation of this view is provided by Schiffer's (1972) criticism and extension of Grice's definition of meaning: in a refinement of Grice's account of the relation between speaker's meaning and natural language, Schiffer (chapter 6) incorporates a Tarskian definition of truth into the account of sentence meaning. But this is to admit the point made here, that sentence meaning cannot be explained in terms of speaker's meaning alone. I shall therefore assume that the stronger claim – maintained by Grice, Strawson and Schiffer – is not correct; and that the characterisation of what a sentence means for particular speakers on particular occasions is dependent on a prior definition of linguistic meaning independent of the use of sentences in communication.

7.1.2 The Co-operative Principle. Once the strong form of Grice's account of meaning is relinquished, this pragmatic definition can be

---

[1] Cf. Grice 1968a, pp. 232–3. In fact this definition is there dismissed in favour of the formulation 'U has in his repertoire a certain procedure' but the difficulties with this latter phrasing seem to be no different.

seen as a characterisation of the way in which speakers and hearers use a previously specified linguistic system. However Grice's analysis of communication has a second, quite different, aspect, and it is this other part of the account which is more familiar to linguists. Let me briefly summarise this aspect of Grice's theory for those to whom it is not familiar. A basic condition for a pragmatic theory is that it explains not only how speakers use sentences of the language in a way which corresponds to their meaning, but also how they succeed in using those sentences to communicate information which is not specified by the meaning of the sentences in question (for some examples, cf. R. Lakoff's examples of common topic discussed in chapter 4), and Grice's hypothesis of a Co-operative Principle between speakers provides a framework in which this is explained. This Co-operative Principle subsumes a number of maxims which specify the conventions which participants in a conversation should and normally do obey. These are as follows:

Quantity

1. Make your contribution as informative as is required (for the current purposes of the exchange).

2. Do not make your contribution more informative than is required.[1]

Quality

1. Do not say what you believe to be false.

2. Do not say that for which you lack adequate evidence.

Relation

Be relevant.

Manner[2]

This maxim has an over-all instruction 'Be perspicuous'. Grice subdivides this general instruction into four further maxims:

1. Avoid obscurity.
2. Avoid ambiguity.
3. Be brief.
4. Be orderly.

One striking characteristic of these 'rules' is that, unlike linguistic

[1] Cf. the equivalent 'platitudes' of Strawson 1964a – 'The Principle of The Presumption of Ignorance' and 'The Principle of The Presumption of Knowledge'.

[2] The maxim of manner is of less importance than the others, and I shall not consider it in detail. However, cf. 8.7 below.

rules in general, they are often broken. There are many liars and there are many conversations which change their subject abruptly as someone makes a statement quite irrelevant to what was said before. But these rules may also be deliberately and flagrantly broken, in such a way that the speaker knows and intends that the hearer shall recognise that a maxim has been broken. The hearer then has two alternatives: one is to say *You're a liar* or *That's irrelevant* or whatever, in which case the Co-operative Principle has broken down. But he may – and characteristically does – choose a second alternative. He assumes that the speaker is in general observing the Co-operative Principle and reasons in the following way: 'If he is observing the Co-operative Principle and if he is flouting a maxim in such a way that I shall notice the breakage, then he is doing so in order to convey some extra information which *is* in accordance with the Co-operative Principle, and moreover he must know that I can work out that information.' This extra information Grice calls an implicature. These 'conversational implicatures' of an utterance are by definition assumptions over and above the meaning of the sentence used which the speaker knows and intends that the hearer will make in the face of an apparently open violation of the Co-operative Principle in order to interpret the speaker's sentence in accordance with the Co-operative Principle. Grice's own characterisation (from the William James lectures) is as follows:

A man who, by (in, when) saying (or making as if to say) that p has implicated that q, may be said to have conversationally implicated that q, *provided that*: (1) he is to be presumed to be observing the conversational maxims, or at least the Co-operative Principle, (2) the supposition that he is aware that, or thinks that q, is required in order to make his saying or making as if to say p (or doing so in *those* terms) consistent with this presumption, and (3) that the speaker thinks (and would expect the hearer to think that the speaker thinks) that it is within the competence of the hearer to work out, or grasp intuitively, that the supposition mentioned in (2) *is* required.

Two examples of the type of phenomena explained by postulating such implicatures and the Co-operative Principle are examples (1), which obviously flouts the maxim of relation, and (2), which flouts the maxim of quality:

(1) The police came in and everyone swallowed their cigarettes.
(2) You're the cream in my coffee.

Someone hearing an utterance of (1) and not knowing about the illegality of marijuana might think that swallowing cigarettes is a stupid pastime and what did it have to do with the police anyway? However, anyone saying that in 1974 would assume that the hearer was able to work out that the second sentence is relevant if one assumes that the people would only swallow their cigarettes when the police came in if those cigarettes were illegal. Since people smoking illegal cigarettes are generally smoking marijuana (not opium, cocaine or other drugs) one interprets the sentence as implicating that everyone was smoking marijuana. (2) is an example of categorial falsity, and metaphor, and Grice's implicatures provide a natural explanation of how metaphor is interpreted (and why it commonly involves non-linguistic assumptions about the world). In order to interpret an utterance of (2) as not breaking the maxim of quality, the hearer must assume that the speaker is trying to convey something other than the literal meaning of the sentence. Since cream is something which is not only a natural accompaniment to coffee, but a perfect accompaniment, the speaker is perhaps saying that the hearer possesses similar attributes. He is therefore paying the hearer a great compliment.

Five characteristics of conversational implicature stand out.

1. They are dependent on the recognition of the Co-operative Principle and its maxims.

2. They will not be part of the meaning of the lexical items in the sentence since their interpretation depends on a prior understanding of the conventional meaning of the sentence.

3. The implicature of an utterance will characteristically not be the sole possible interpretation of that utterance. There may well be more than one possible assumption which will reinstate the Co-operative Principle in the face of an apparent breakage. Since these assumptions are not explicit, they are often indeterminate (for example, the interpretation of (2)).

4. The working out of an implicature will depend on assumptions about the world which the speaker and the hearer share (for example the interpretation of (1)). They will therefore not in general be predictable.

5. They are cancellable. That is, an interpretation which is not part of the conventional meaning of the utterance can be explicitly denied without contradiction. Thus, for example, one can say *The police came*

in and everyone swallowed their cigarettes though they were doing nothing illegal, or *You're the cream in my coffee but since I don't like cream, that's a dubious complement.*

So far I have assumed that there is a dichotomy between what is part of the conventional meaning of an utterance and what is super-imposed on that meaning on specific occasions. But Grice sets up not merely two distinct categories, but four: what is said, what is conventionally implicated, what is generally but conversationally implicated, and what is conversationally (occasion-specific) implicated.[1]

What is the justification for this classification – in particular for the distinction between conventional implicature and generalised conversational implicature? Grice argues that there is a range of examples which appear to contain implications that the speaker is committed to, without those implications being strictly what is part of the meaning. That is, they are determinable, non-contradictable and not dependent on the Co-operative Principle for their interpretation. His example is *John is an Englishman; he is therefore brave.* In saying this he suggests a speaker is certainly committed to there being a causal connection between the two statements but if it turned out that both statements were true but there was no connection, the speaker's statement as a whole would still be true. Moreover the speaker cannot say (if he is to retain his credibility) *John is an Englishman; he is therefore brave – though I don't believe there's any connection between the two.*[2] Conventional implicatures are thus those elements of meaning which are not truth-functional, but which are not contradictable. They are in effect an *ad hoc* way of labelling within a pragmatic framework counter-examples to the semantic framework I have argued for. General conversational implicatures on the other hand are common accompaniments to the meaning of a sentence but they can be contradicted. To make a statement of the form *P or Q* for example generally implicates that the speaker does not know which of *P* or *Q* is true. Thus the statement *It's either in your bedroom or the attic* said in response say to the question *Where's my book?* will generally imply that the speaker does not know exactly where the book is. But this implication is not a necessary part of the meaning: *It's either in your bedroom or the attic, and I'm not saying any more than that* does not have this implication, yet is clearly

---

[1] These distinctions are introduced briefly in Grice 1961 (section III), but they are not referred to there by the term implicature.
[2] Cf. chapter 9 for a discussion of the validity of this example.

not a contradiction. Moreover, this implicature has a natural explanation on the basis of the Co-operative Principle. Since the maxim of quantity militates that a speaker shall give as much information as is required, and the maxim of quality that he should have adequate evidence for what he claims, a speaker is or should be committed to making the strongest statement he can. A hearer of an utterance of the form *P or Q* will know (and know that the speaker knows) (*a*) *P or Q* is true just in case either of *P* or *Q* is true, and (*b*) that the speaker is making the strongest statement he can. If then he is complying with the maxim of quantity, the speaker must be uttering *P or Q* on the basis that he only has evidence for *P or Q* and not sufficient evidence to claim just *P* or just *Q* (to claim *P or Q* if one knows that P is to break the quantity maxim). Hence the speaker is implicating that he does not know which of *P* or *Q* is true. Since the calculation of such implicatures depends on a prior specification of the meaning of the sentence, it follows that general conversational implicatures – unlike conventional implicatures – are demonstrably not part of the representation of the meaning of sentences.

7.2 On criticisms of Grice

Before we can go further and consider the ways in which Grice's theory provides an account of the phenomena generally labelled *presuppositions*, there are two important factors to consider. First this formulation of the basis of communication must be extended to all forms of utterance, i.e. to imperatives and questions: otherwise the framework will not be sufficiently general. Secondly, and more importantly, it is essential that we take into account the various criticisms of Grice's theory. The most important of these are those which attack the theory in principle, since it is only if these can be rebutted that the use of Gricean principles to be given here will retain any explanatory value. I shall consider two such criticisms:

I: Grice's formulation of meaning involves an infinite regress of conditions. This being so, it is not statable in a finite form.

II: The conversational maxims are so vague and general that they allow the prediction of any implication whatever – specifically those which do not occur as well as those that do. The theory is therefore unfalsifiable, vacuous, and of no explanatory value.

7.2.1 Speaker's meaning and non-indicative utterances. Grice himself generalises the definition of meaning to include imperatives by defining meaning on an utterance 'x' signifying '*ψp' where *ψ is a dummy for a specific mood operator corresponding to the propositional attitude of ψ-ing (cf. Grice 1969, p. 171). Thus the definition I gave on p. 139 should be reformulated as:

For some specific occasion, a speaker S makes an utterance 'x' to a hearer H indicating '*ψp' if he intends that:

(1) H should think x has f (where f is a feature)

(2) H should think that he S intends H to think x has f

(3) H should think f is correlated in way c with the state of ψ-ing that p (where p is the propositional content)

(4) H should think that S intends that he (H) thinks f is correlated in way c with the state of ψ-ing that p

(5) H should think he S intends H (via (1) and (3)) to think that S ψ-s that p

(6) on the basis of (5), H should think that in fact S does ψ that p

(7) H should think that S intends (6)

(8) on the basis of (6) H should ψ that p.

If we define assertion and imperative as follows –

  '⊢p' is conventionally correlated with a belief that p

  '!p' is conventionally correlated with an intention (with respect to some audience) that that audience make p true –

Grice's definition of pragmatic meaning then provides an account of the basis on which a speaker will successfully convey his belief or intention that p.

The definition has however to be modified somewhat for questions (both *wh* and *yes-no*), since unlike imperatives or indicatives, the speaker is not indicating a positive attitude or intention with respect to *p*. Yet it is clear that a similar explanation must apply to questions. Suppose we characterise *yes-no* questions ('?p') as conventionally correlated with an intention (with respect to some audience) that that audience tell the speaker the truth value of *p* (equivalently, tell him either 'p' or '−p'). Then just as in the imperative case, where the speaker succeeds in conveying his intentions by virtue of the hearer's recognition of those intentions, so in the case of '?p', S intends

(A) that H should think '?p' has a feature f which is correlated in way c with intending with respect to some audience that that audience say either 'p' or ' −p' (the relation between f, c, and p, being given by the conventions of the language) (corresponding to conditions (1)–(3) of the definition)

(B) that H should think that S intends H to think via their common knowledge of the correlation c that S intends that H say 'p' or ' −p' (condition (5) of the definition)

(C) on the basis of this, that H should think that S does in fact intend that H say 'p' or ' −p' (condition (6))

(D) on the basis of knowing that H intends (C), H should form the intention to say either 'p' or ' −p'.

In other words the communication of meaning in *yes-no* questions can be described (as is intuitively correct) as no different in kind from the communication of any other utterance. This type of analysis extends naturally to *wh*-questions with slight modifications. In saying '?p' where *p* is made up of $(X \, wh\text{-}\beta Y)$, where X and Y are variables, S intends that H should think that $?(X \, wh\text{-}\beta Y)$ is correlated in way c with intending with respect to some audience that that audience say 'α', where α is a member of the set indicated by β. The process of deduction then goes through in exactly the same way, giving the conclusion that on the basis of S saying '$?(X \, wh\text{-}\beta Y)$' H forms the intention to say 'α'.[1] That is to say, each type of utterance is based on an intention on the part of the speaker which is itself based on an anticipation of the hearer's strategy on hearing that utterance (cf. the concept of 'co-ordination problem' outlined by Lewis, to be discussed in 7.2.2).

To what extent do the maxims apply equally to all types of utterance? Clearly just as statements have pragmatically to be uttered sincerely, so do imperatives and questions have to be uttered with a sincere intent to receive a response and the maxim of quality has to be generalised to apply equally to the three types of utterance. In addition, the maxim must apply to the implicatures of an utterance as well as what is stated. It is just as misleading to say *I'm tired* if you intend your hearer to construe from your utterance that you have a headache even though you do not have one as it is to say explicitly *I've got a headache* in the same circumstances. Thus the maxim must require that one not only

---

[1] The characterisation of *wh*-questions has only been given informally here, since it is not a central concern of this book. It is arguable that a pragmatic characterisation of questions should give an account which applies equally to *yes-no* and *wh*-questions. I shall leave this problem for another time.

believe or sincerely request one's utterance but one must believe (and have adequate evidence for) any implicatures consequent upon that utterance. The maxims of quantity and relation apply equally to all types of utterance even as they stand. In the case of the quantity maxim for example, as we shall see in more detail in 8.2, it is just as important to give sufficient information in asking a question or giving a command as it is in making a statement. Furthermore the maxim of quantity guarantees that questions be answered, and answered appropriately: at least one major interpretation of the first maxim is not that the speaker should merely give as much information as the situation requires, but more specifically that the speaker should give as much information as the hearer requires, should the hearer make a request for information.[1] It is this more narrow interpretation of the quantity maxim which applies in the case I have already discussed where an utterance of $P \ v \ Q$ will normally implicate that the speaker does not know which of P or Q holds. For example, suppose H asks *Where is my book?* and S replies *It's either in your bedroom or the attic* S knows that he is bound by the pragmatic convention on *wh*-questions and by the corresponding quantity maxim to provide a specification of the place where the book is. However he is also constrained to say only that for which he has adequate evidence. If therefore he gives a disjunction of two possible places, he knows and knows that H will recognise that he is not fulfilling the exact requirement on the question posed by H. On the assumption that he is in fact complying with the Co-operative Principle, he knows that H will deduce that he does not have adequate evidence to choose between the two possibilities he has put forward. He knows therefore that his utterance will be construed as indicating that he has evidence only for the disjunction *Either the book is in your bedroom or the attic*, and not for either disjunct.

In this section I have considered informally how Grice's account of meaning can be generalised to all forms of utterance, whether statement, imperative, *yes-no* question or *wh*-question. This has given us three (or possibly four) mood indicators '⊢', '!' and '?' (plus an operator for *wh*-questions, though cf. p. 148). With this generalisation, I take it that the limitation on Grice's account of pragmatics that it apply only to statements cannot be raised as a criticism of principle.

It might on the other hand be argued that this list of pragmatic

---

[1] For a discussion of an apparent counter-example to this interpretation of the maxim, cf. pp. 163–6.

mood operators is not long enough – that the phenomena of tag questions and negative exclamatory questions at least must be captured by separate pragmatic mood operators. Questions such as these I shall leave open,[1] though since in each case pragmatic mood operators correspond to different sentence types (cf. statement, question, imperative), any postulated pragmatic mood operator would have to have a syntactic reflex. Thus for example, in the case of tags and exclamatory negative questions, the evidence might include the distribution of *any*, which though it occurs freely in straightforward questions cannot occur either in positive tag questions (*She has done any good work hasn't she?*) or in negative exclamatory questions (*Hasn't she done good work* is ambiguous between a question and an exclamation, but *Hasn't she done any good work* is not). Of the possible additions to the list of sentence types, there is one putative operator which must however be excluded: a denial operator. Denial, I have argued already (5.2), is but one possible use of statements and does not constitute a separate sentence type.

7.2.2 The infinite regress problem.

Much more important than the problem that the theory has only been articulated to apply to statements are the accusations against it of infinite regress and vacuity. The first criticism has been pointed out by Grice himself as well as others (Grice 1969 pp. 156–9; Schiffer 1972; MacKay 1972),[2] though he suggests that the regress, if it exists, is not a serious one. I think he is correct in thinking the regress not serious, but not for the reasons he appears to hold. I take it however that the criticism of the harmfulness of infinite regress would be seriously eroded if it could be shown that this form of infinite regress was part of the very nature of convention, and hence of any analysis of the conventions for use of a linguistic system. This has been done by Lewis (1969), whose analysis of convention depends on such regress.

Briefly, this analysis depends on the notion of 'co-ordination problems',[3] and their solution. These are exemplified in the following way (to take Lewis' initial example). Suppose you and I both want to meet. It does not matter where – we each merely want to choose to go where

---

[1] Cf. 8.3.3 for a discussion of the interaction of exclamations and Grice's maxims.

[2] MacKays' claim of infinite regress alternating with a claim that the conditions are quite *ad hoc* is based on a mistaken notion of justification and a misunderstanding of the central nature of the Gricean definition of meaning. I shall therefore not consider it in detail. In any case, the first of two conditions which he objects so strongly to, does not appear in the 1967/8 lecture version I have adopted here.

[3] The term is Lewis' own, but the problems are also developed by Schelling 1960.

the other is most likely to go. Co-ordination is achieved if we succeed in meeting. In order to do this, each of us has to work out a strategy, and each of us knows that if one succeeds in his strategy then the other will also have done so, since we are both planning to the same end (namely to succeed in meeting). This being so, I shall try to work out where to go on the basis of what you will do; and the way to work out where to go is therefore to replicate your reasoning. Like me, you will work out where to go on the basis of where you think I shall go. Since where I go is determined by where I think you will go, it follows that you will be trying to anticipate where you think I think you will go. But since where you go depends on where you think I shall go, it follows that you will be trying to anticipate where you think I think you think I shall go, etc., etc. This attempt to replicate the expectations of the other member in a co-ordination problem automatically sets up an infinite chain of expectations.[1] Given only this overly brief exemplification of a co-ordination problem, one might wonder why communication (or more specifically a Gricean theory of meaning$_{nn}$) should have anything to do with co-ordination problems. The answer, as Lewis suggests, is that all conventions involve the solution of co-ordination problems.[2] More formally,

a regularity R in the behavior of members of a population P when they are agents in a recurrent situation S is a *convention* if and only if in any instance of S among members of P

1. everyone conforms to R
2. everyone expects everyone else to conform to R
3. everyone prefers to conform to R on condition that the others do, since S is a coordination problem and uniform conformity to R is a coordination equilibrium in S [= the best strategy for successful coordination] (p. 42)

Thus a convention is in effect a standard solution to a co-ordination problem. Having sophisticated this definition of convention and given a definition of a conventional signalling system on the basis of this definition, Lewis then goes on to give a proof that Grice's definition of meaning is a consequence of his own definition of conventional signalling – i.e. is a solution to a co-ordination problem (the problem in the case of statements being roughly the transmission of a certain

---

[1] It is important to note that this is a chain of implications, not of steps in anyone's actual reasoning. Cf. p. 152.
[2] This is disputed by Schiffer (1972, p. 151).

belief by uttering a certain signal – co-ordination is only successful if the hearer does in fact gain the belief in question).[1] He does this by showing that Grice's definition of what it is for a speaker to mean$_{nn}$ something by a symbol * can be derived by examining the reasoning that justifies his saying '*': this reasoning replicates exactly the characteristic structure of an agent's justification within a conventional signalling system (cf. Lewis 1969, pp. 152–9). Since conventions of meaning$_{nn}$ are shown to constitute a conventional signalling system, it follows that any analysis of the basis of these conventions will by definition involve infinite regress in the way that all solutions to co-ordination problems do. Furthermore, this regress is not, as the original Gricean regress seemed to be, a serious one, since there is no claim that anyone's actual reasoning to a co-ordination equilibrium involves an infinite number of steps. The infinite regress concerns rather a chain of implications which follow from any finite (and normally very limited) number of steps. As Lewis points out, there is therefore nothing improper about its infinite length (p. 53). On the basis of Lewis' arguments (which I have presented here regrettably in a highly impoverished form for reasons of exegesis), I shall therefore assume that any attempt to explain what a speaker does in using his conventional (linguistic) system is bound to set up a regress which is in principle infinite, though in practice it never exceeds more than three or four steps. The characteristic of infinite regress in Grice's theory of meaning does not therefore raise objections in principle to the theory, but is part of the very essence of convention itself.[2]

7.2.3 The vacuity of the maxims.

That the maxims of the Co-operative Principle are too vague to be anything but vacuous has been argued by Kroch (1972), who provides two examples which purport to demonstrate that the maxims can in the one case and must in the other generate contradictory implicatures. On these grounds, he concludes that the theory is unfalsifiable.

His first and main consideration is with time adverbs. He points out that there are adverbials which are sometimes interpreted as synonymous, sometimes not.

---

[1] The position is not in fact this simple. Cf. Lewis 1969, pp. 179–80.

[2] The arguments of Lewis do however suggest the correctness of the position adopted here, that Grice's theory of meaning can only be a basis for a pragmatic theory and not for a linguistic theory of semantics – it is hardly the burden of the semantics of any conventional system to explain not only the interpretations to the elements of the system, but also the nature of convention *per se*.

(3a) Before the arrival of the army, the government controlled the town.

(3b) Until the arrival of the army, the government controlled the town.

(4a) During one period before the arrival of the army, the government controlled the town.

(4b) ?During one period until the arrival of the army, the government controlled the town.

(5a) John died before dawn.

(5b) ?John died until dawn.

That *until* and *before* clauses cannot have the same semantic representation is demonstrated by the contradiction inherent in (4b) and (5b), though they clearly are synonymous in (3). On the basis of these examples, Kroch analyses *until* and *before* as:

until   = at all times prior to NP
before = at some time(s) prior to NP
(where NP is the object of the adverb phrase)

To these definitions, he adds a rule of interpretation (a putative general conversational implicature) that adverbs containing an existential quantifier will be interpreted universally when the action modified is durative, given that the context does not prohibit it. Hence the synonymy of (3a) and (3b). He points out however that if there is an explicit existential quantifier in the time adverbial, then there is no such implication.

(6) At some time before the arrival of the army, the government controlled the town.

Unlike (3a), (6) is not normally interpreted with *some* read as *all*. On the contrary, there is an opposite implication that the government did not control the town for the entire period before the arrival of the army. Yet, Kroch argues, the only difference in the meaning of (6) and (3a) is that there is an explicit quantifier in (6). Since they have the same basic meaning, these sentences should have the same conversational implicatures. These examples therefore appear to constitute a case where either the theory must allow for two contradictory implicatures, or we have to admit an implication which is not predictable by implicature.

Notice however that Kroch's argument only goes through on the assumption that (6) and (3a) have the same semantic representation.

If they do not, then the theory has a natural basis for predicting different implicatures. Kroch's analysis of *before* I shall at the moment accept as containing an existential quantifier, since parallel to the interpretation of '∃', it allows for the entire range from one moment in the time specified (e.g. (5a)) to every moment in the time specified (e.g. (3a)). I suggested earlier however (following Bierwisch – cf. pp. 119–20) that the interpretation of noun phrases in general should not be based on the existential and universal quantifiers of predicate calculus, and it seems not unreasonable to suggest along the lines put forward by Bierwisch (1971) that the *some* of natural language should be described in terms of a subset of some whole (where the notion of set is taken as primitive) rather than in terms of a collection of one or more individuals (in the formalisation of predicate calculus).[1] Thus, while (3a), containing *before*, correctly involves a paraphrase 'at least one time prior to NP', (6), containing *some*, does not. The distinction is I suggest analogous to the following pair:

(7a) They took some of the girls.
(7b) They took at least some of the girls.

Notice that (7b), with *at least*, allows the implicature that they took more than some girls, namely all, whereas (7a) does not. More generally, any sentence containing *at least* will carry an implicature which we must somehow capture as 'one or more notches up the scale in question'.[2] Thus for example *Her jewels cost at least two thousand pounds* implicates that they probably cost more. By contrast, sentences without *at least*, such as (7a) and (6), which are to be interpreted as involving a subset of the members of the whole set in question, implicate that that subset is not co-extensive with the whole set.[3] While I grant that these observations are informal, and I have no suggestions to make here as to their formalisation, they seem to provide a natural basis for the distinction between (3a) and (6). I take it then that there is some evidence to suggest that (3a) and (6) should have semantic representations which differ at least in that (3a) will have a representation which relates it to other sentences containing *at least* explicitly.

Kroch's other attack on the maxims is his claim that they have the

[1] For a more formal and much more detailed discussion of some other aspects of plural noun phrases, cf. Bierwisch 1971, pp. 414–16.
[2] This implicature is straightforwardly deducible on the basis of the maxims of quantity and quality.
[3] Cf. fn. 2 above.

power to predict on the same utterance both the implicature which does not exist and the one which does. Thus for *John ate the apple*, he gives two parallel arguments:

(A) If the speaker had meant that the whole apple was eaten, then he would have said, 'John ate all of the apple' in order not to violate the maxim of quantity...by giving too little information. Since he left out the word 'all', he must have been obeying the maxim of quality...and avoided saying more than he knew. Therefore, all that the speaker was saying is that at least part of the apple was eaten.

(B) The speaker would have said 'John ate at least some of the apple' if that were all he knew [by the maxim of quality]. Since he left out the qualifying phrase, he must have meant to convey that the whole apple was eaten. Otherwise he would have been giving too little information.

However only (B) exists as an implication of *John ate the apple*. From this he concludes that the theory, in allowing both for the case which does and for the case which does not exist, is in principle unfalsifiable and therefore vacuous.

Unfortunately his example is not a good one. If the interpretation of *John ate the apple* corresponds roughly to 'There is some specific apple which John chewed and swallowed', it is not obvious that *John ate his apple but only some of it* is not a contradiction.[1] Compare *John has eaten his food but not all of it* which seems a clear case of contradiction. This being so, the semantic interpretation of the sentence will predict that the interpretation that Kroch aims to predict by (A) is not a possible interpretation of this sentence.

Nonetheless I grant that answers of the kind just given to attacks in principle are merely fending off the day when a better example will be thrown up (cf. 8.3.3 for a discussion of further examples which appear to suggest the same conclusion). To disagree over data does not alter the force of the criticism. The objection remains an important one: if Grice's Co-operative Principle is to provide a substantive explanation of the basis on which communication is conducted, we must restrict it in such a way that it constrain the nature of communication processes as narrowly as possible. Otherwise the apparent naturalness with which the framework appears to explain the varying phenomena is merely a

---

[1] I assume that it is not a linguistic matter that in eating objects there is a convention that only certain edible parts are relevant. Thus the fact that *James has eaten his cake though there are a lot of crumbs on the floor* and *John has eaten his apple but he's left the core* are not contradictions does not alter the point being made here.

consequence of the vacuity of the framework. Since, as I shall argue, the Gricean maxims seem to allow a natural explanation both of occasion-specific implications on utterances (such as Robin Lakoff's speaker-presuppositions) and also of more general implications such as arise in the use of definite noun phrases and factive verbs), one of my chief concerns in the following chapter will be to consider to what extent the maxims can be given a greater degree of content.

My main concern in this chapter has been the exposition of the two facets of Grice's theory – his concepts of meaning$_{nn}$ and the Co-operative Principle. We have not yet considered how Grice's theory can be used to explain the apparent anomalies which have arisen during the course of this study. Yet clearly its validity as part of an over-all linguistic theory depends on whether it can provide a natural explanation of these apparent anomalies. Since this explanation, as we shall see, rests on the concept of the Co-operative Principle, its maxims, and the consequent implicatures, I shall restrict my attention in the remainder of this study to the maxims and shall not consider the details of meaning$_{nn}$ further.

8 *The application of Grice's theory*

We saw in chapter 7 that Grice's theory of meaning and communication provided a potential basis for a theory of pragmatics. In 7.2, I defended Grice's theory against specific criticisms of infinite regress and vacuity. Our troubles would not be over however, even if it were certain that Grice's hypothesis could be presented in a testable way. The general problem that remains is to explain how Grice's framework can capture the insights which presupposition has been used by linguists in the past to capture. This can be broken down into six parts:

(i) We have to be able to explain the concept of a natural interpretation as opposed to an unnatural one – viz. why some interpretations of negative sentences are so much more likely than others. Connected with this problem is a second problem, which has so far not been discussed at all. In general, linguists arguing for presupposition have claimed that in negation *and* questions the presuppositions of a sentence will be preserved. Since the basis for presupposition was in terms of the truth-value assignment to statements, my discussion of linguists' use of the term was restricted to negative sentences. Yet questions share with negation the property that certain entailments of the corresponding positive statement are normally assumed to be true when that statement is questioned. Thus *Does John regret going?* implies in isolation that he went, and *Is The King of Rumania coming to the coronation?* implies that there is a King of Rumania. However, as in negation, this implication can be cancelled without creating a contradiction: in (1)–(7) there is no assumption either of the truth of the factive complement or of the existence of the referent corresponding to the particular definite noun phrase.

(1) Does John regret going or didn't he go in the end?
(2) Did Pete regret doing an MA – I didn't think he was accepted for the course.

(3) Was the teacher annoyed that Sue was late or did she manage to get there on time?

(4) Was the teacher annoyed that Sue was late – I thought she got there on time.

(5) Is the King of Rumania coming to the coronation, or doesn't Rumania have a king?

(6) Is the King of Rumania coming to the exhibition – I thought Rumania was a republic.

(7) Did the Duke of Plazitoro come to the opening ceremony – I didn't think there was such a place as Plazitoro, let alone that it had a Duke.

So it seems that in both negation and question, we have to be able to explain how an implication which normally appears to be part of the meaning of the sentence can be cancelled out without contradiction, a possibility which is by definition not open to central core meaning of sentences. Since this problem arises only within an over-all theory which does not incorporate a logical concept of presupposition, I consider this one of the chief remaining tasks of this book.

(ii) We have a heterogeneous collection of lexical problems to explain – viz. the non-truth-conditional idiosyncrasies of *the* (cf. 5.5), *but* (cf. pp. 56–7), *and* (cf. p. 56), and *even* (cf. pp. 83–4).

(iii) We have to be able to characterise presupposition in the sense of Chomsky (1971) and others – i.e. what is assumed in an utterance of a sentence, as opposed to what is asserted.

(iv) We should be able to predict why stress assignment and the interpretation of sentences are interdependent.

(v) There must be some explanation of R. Lakoff's suggested constraint of common topic on co-ordination.

(vi) Finally there is a somewhat different problem which, like the problem of questions, I have not considered in detail so far – the status of Austin's concept of illocutionary force. Since I have argued (pp. 39–40) that, semantically, performative statements are no different in kind from other statements, the burden of explanation of such concepts as illocutionary force must fall on a pragmatic theory.

8.1 The concept of relevance

Since it is evident that the validity of a Gricean pragmatics depends initially on giving the theory sufficient content to render it non-vacuous, the first hurdle to overcome is to see to what extent Kroch's criticism (cf. 7.2.3)[1] can be answered more generally. Since it is the maxims of relation and quantity which are largely responsible for the Co-operative Principle's enormous power of application, it is these for which I shall attempt to give a more precise definition. I shall turn initially to R. Lakoff's concept of common topic, which concerns the problem of relevance.

To recapitulate, she argued that no sentences could be conjoined unless they shared a common topic, and she pointed out that the harder the topic was to construe, the more various became the interpretations informants found. However I argued (4.1) that every conceivable sentence containing two conjuncts could be construed as having some common ground and that the constraint was therefore vacuous. Moreover it appeared that any sentence containing two conjuncts could be given more than one interpretation. Each of these characteristics is predicted if the interpretation of the specific common topic is analysed as a consequence of the conversational implicatures of an utterance. Thus for example our speaker (S) says *John owns a yacht and Bill has a house in Knightsbridge* and he knows that the hearer (H) will reason in the following way: 'S has said both that John owns a yacht and that Bill has a house in Knightsbridge, and since he is biding by the Co-operative Principle he must be assuming that the second sentence is relevant to the first, despite the fact that it appears not to be. But S knows and knows that I know that yachts are very expensive and so is property in Knightsbridge, particularly houses. John and Bill must therefore be rich, and this – together with the two assumptions necessary to reach this conclusion – is what S is implicating.' But this interpretation depends on the assumption of shared knowledge made by S and H. If our speaker and hearer operate with a different set of assumptions, then the interpretation of the sentence will, as we saw in chapter 4, be different. Along similar lines, every conjoint sentence can both be construed as having some common point of relevance and as having more than one interpretation. And this is the result that our analysis should predict: implicatures by definition are open-ended, different assumptions providing different interpretations (cf. the third characteristic listed on p. 144), and hence the interpretation of common topic is unpredictable in isolation (cf. condition (4) on p. 144). Prediction of the shared know-

[1] Echoed by many colleagues informally.

ledge of speaker and hearer is not possible without knowing both participants. Furthermore these results follow only if such implicatures are analysed as quite separate from the lexically specified meaning of the sentence.

Now it is clear I think that Robin Lakoff's concept of common topic can be extended to discourse structure in general. From her account I argued that given a sentence containing S_1 and S_2, the hearer must be able to deduce some form of (partial) identity if the two con- juncts are to be seen as possessing a common relevance (cf. R. Lakoff 1971, pp. 118–19) – either by virtue of the semantic interpretation of the two conjuncts, or if not, via some extra assumptions or implicatures. Thus in our example above, the hearer deduced that the speaker was implicating that yachts are very expensive, that Knightsbridge is an expensive area, and hence that both John and Bill are rich. A more general form of the constraint would be that in order for any S_i to be relevant in a given conversation, it must carry at least one implicature or entailment that is implicated by S_{i-1}. To see that this is at least in part correct,[1] consider a conversation between A and B:

A: John has a yacht
B: Bill has a house in Knightsbridge
A: Which do you think is the richer?

Parallel to the conjoint sentence, A implicates that John is rich. On the basis of this implicature, B makes a statement which implicates that Bill is rich. This common topic is then made explicit in A's question. Alternatively, to give a case where the second utterance entails the implicature of the first, consider the following discourse: A says 'John's late' implicating that he's rude, and B replies 'He takes great pleasure in being rude'. Thus as we would expect, the apparent constraint on co-ordination seems to be a property of discourse structure in general, and the maxim of relation can be reformulated with this in mind as:

Only say any sentence S_i made up of '$*\psi p$', if p either entails or implicates some proposition q which is also implicated by S_{i-1}

This characterisation of relevance in conversation is of course only a first approximation, and is in any case absurdly limited. In any detailed account of conversational relatedness, it is clear that the interdependence

---

[1] Cf. the parallel definition of relevance given by Apostel 1971, p. 18: 'p is relevant if the belief in p is held to be logically connected with some statement that occurred not too long before or that will occur not too much later'.

between implicature and entailment must be specified. Notice first for example that it is not a sufficient condition of relevance that a sentence S_i should share at least one entailment with the preceding sentence S_{i-1} in the discourse, since both the sentences *John went to London yesterday* and *John's mother has got cataract* entail the sentence *There is someone called John* yet the latter could only be seen as relevant to the former on the basis of some further assumption, for example that John's mother lives in London. Thus we do not want to say that any sentence S_1 which entails S_2 will also implicate S_2.[1] However one might reasonably hypothesise that a relation of implicature does hold between two sentences S_1 and S_3 when S_1 is used to implicate a sentence S_2 which entails S_3. This would predict that *John doesn't regret running until he was sick* (S_1) normally implicates that John went until he was sick (S_3) since S_1 normally implicates that John ran until he was sick (S_2) (cf. 8.5), which in its turn entails that John went until he was sick (S_3).

But this is only the tip of the iceberg. There are undoubtedly many such relations which must be formalised in any pragmatic account which makes reference to both entailment and implicature. Moreover, this is particularly important in view of the tentatively proposed definition of relevance since the definition – if it is even approximately correct – now allows that any sentence S_1 will be relevant in a discourse if an entailment of any one of the propositions it may be used to implicate is also implicated by the preceding utterance of the discourse.

I shall not go further into this area here, since my main purpose has been merely to consider a possible way of constraining the notion of relevance so that it become open to empirical investigation. We shall see in any case in 8.6.1, that it is not obvious that the notion of relevance can be so constrained, if our pragmatic constructs are to account for the whole range of data (particularly problems of stress).

8.2 The maxim of quantity: some preliminaries

Having taken a few tentative steps towards making the maxim of relation more specific *via* a consideration of R. Lakoff's data, I shall now consider the maxim of quantity, for discussion of this maxim is a necessary preliminary for the pragmatic account I shall give of definite noun phrases, factive-verb complements, and the assertion-presupposi-

[1] Cf. chapter 4, pp. 61–2, where examples such as these were seen to provide problems for Lakoff's mechanism predicting sentence-presupposition pairs.

tion contrast. This maxim has in Grice's formulation two subparts:

(i) Give as much information as is required.
(ii) Do not give more information than is required.

Grice himself suggested (in his 1967/8 lectures) that the second part of the maxim is either unnecessary (since it is not a violation of the Co-operative Principle to say too much, merely a waste of time) or it is covered by the maxim of relation since if you give more information than is required, this additional information will of necessity be irrelevant. For these reasons I shall restrict my attention to the first part of the maxim.

There are several problems with the maxim 'Give as much information as is required'. Like the maxim of relation, its formulation allows for an extremely wide interpretation. First the agentless passive form of 'as is required' allows for an interpretation so open that it is almost entirely without content, since it allows the requirement to be forced by either the semantic or pragmatic content of the previous discourse, or by the hearer, or by more general elements of the situation. Secondly, the constraint of 'being informative' seems to need two quite different statements (as we shall see), and as it stands, the maxim is simply neutral between these, allowing in fact the addition of any further interpretation which may be required in the face of counter-examples.

While I am by no means certain that the following analysis is anything more than an interim measure,[1] I shall argue for the need of at least two separate sub-maxims of quantity to cover: (i) the requirement that one answer questions appropriately, (ii) the requirement of presenting sufficient information in questions and imperatives to enable one's requests to be successfully carried out, (iii) the general requirement of not saying what is familiar. Since in each case, the requirement of informativeness can be stated with at least a certain amount of precision, the specification of further maxims would appear to go some way towards increasing the content of the Co-operative Principle.

I have already suggested (p. 149) that one interpretation of the maxim is that the speaker should 'give as much information as the hearer requires', and I argued that this was equivalent to an instruction that one answer a *wh*-question according as the semantic interpretation of the question (or a corresponding imperative) determines. One appar-

---

[1] One would presumably wish ultimately to give a unified account of informativeness where this has two separate parts.

ent counter-example to this is provided by comparing the two following conversations, which let us assume take place in Regent Street, London:

(8) A: How long does it take by taxi to Piccadilly Circus?
   B: One minute.
(9) A: How long does it take by taxi to Piccadilly Circus?
   B: You don't need a taxi – it's only two minutes' walk.

According to the above interpretation of the maxim, the conversation in (8) is well-formed (and informative) whereas that in (9) is not. Yet clearly the conversation in (9) is the more informative one: in (8) B is being, under all normal circumstances, misleading or at least unhelpful. It thus might seem that one cannot constrain the concept of 're-quired information' to anything less general than elements of the situation. However this conclusion is not I think warranted. In the situation created by A's utterance in Regent Street, B is faced with a conflict between the given maxim of quantity and the maxim of quality that one believe one's utterance and its implicatures. A's utterance implies that one goes by taxi to Piccadilly Circus. If therefore B answers the question in the way it strictly requires, he will also be implicating that one goes by taxi to Piccadilly Circus. But he knows that this is false, and to answer thus would therefore violate the maxim of quality. Since this is the fundamental maxim on which all the others depend, the maintenance of the maxim of quality over-rides the maxim of quantity, thus predicting that the only communicatively helpful answer to a question in which the questioner makes a mistaken assumption is one which corrects the assumption. Examples such as these are therefore not counter-examples to this analysis, since they can be naturally explained in terms of a conflict between the proposed maxim and the maxim of quality.

However this is not the only counter-example. Assume that you are standing at a cross-roads in Salisbury and someone drives up in a car and asks you *How long does it take to get to London?* Now clearly the answer you should give is one which incorporates information from the situation (viz. that the questioner is in a car) – something like *Three hours* being an appropriate answer. Yet the maxim merely makes reference to the content of the question. So, according to the maxim, a perfectly straight answer would be *A week*. Moreover, it might be a true answer, on the basis that one was walking. Thus there appears to be no violation of either the maxim of quantity or the maxim of quality on the part of the hearer. What has gone wrong? Is this evidence that we cannot constrain the maxim of quantity so that it apply only in terms of responding to the request strictly made by the question? Again I think the answer is 'No', though the reason is not the same as before. What I suggest is the basis of the difficulty here is that the questioner has provided too little information to allow his question to be answered without making further assumptions. That is, he knows (and knows that the hearer knows) that a *wh*-question is a request for information with respect to a certain variable, in this case of time.[1] Moreover, he knows (and knows that the hearer knows) that the time an action takes is dependent on the speed of the action.[2] Since his question makes no mention of how he is getting to London, he knows that the hearer will not have sufficient information offered him to make a proper answer. The hearer might thus construe that he the speaker is violating the maxim of quantity. However he knows that the hearer knows that he is in a car and will therefore be able to work out that since he is in a car he is likely to wish to drive to London. Since if H makes this assumption S's utterance no longer violates the maxim of quantity, S therefore assumes that if he utters the sentence *How long does it take to get to London?*, H will take him to be implicating that he will be going by car. This form of analysis suggests that the reliance on facts of situation is not part of the definition of the quantity maxim but an implicature which arises from apparent violation of the maxim. That this is correct is suggested by the fact that the utterance of *How long does it take to get to London?* allows for differently appropriate answers according as different assumptions are made. The variability of interpretation by virtue of changing assumptions is as we have seen (p. 144) a defining criterion of conversational implicature. It therefore seems at least the analysis is on the right lines.

But what version of the quantity maxim has been invoked? What is involved in being constrained to give sufficient information to enable your question to be answered? The problem is not restricted to questions: it also arises with imperatives. If A, a business man, asks B, his secretary, *Please get Smith on the phone* and at the end of the day she has still not done so, he will no doubt round on her and say *Why haven't you got Smith on the phone?* But she is technically in the right if

---

[1] Cf. p. 148 for an informal discussion of *wh*-questions.
[2] I assume that this fact should at least follow as a consequence of the semantic representation of duration adverbials. However the formal semantic representation of duration adverbials is quite unclear to me, and I shall not give further details.

she says *But you didn't tell me when to get him on the phone – I was going to do so tomorrow*. However, in fact A knows that she will recognise that he has given insufficient information for her to know exactly in what way she should obey the command and on the basis that he is in fact obeying such a quantity maxim, she will make the further assumption that he wants it carried out at the time of utterance. Thus it is only on the basis of an implicature that the command be carried out now that A can be construed as obeying the quantity maxim that he give sufficient indication to enable his hearer to know exactly how to meet his request. So it seems that with both imperatives and questions we must be able to state what constrains speakers to give sufficient information for hearers to obey them. How is this constraint to be stated? Is it covered by 'Give as much information as the hearer requires'? In one sense it is: the hearer *does* require a certain minimum of information in order to be able to reply to a question or respond to an imperative. The problem is that the maxim does not apply in the same way that it did in the case of answering questions. In the earlier case, the maxim covered the fact that speakers must answer questions appropriately by supplying information with respect to the variable already indicated by the questioner. Now we have the converse, that questioners must give information which will enable their hearer in the one case to provide information solely on the variable in question, and in the other case to carry out the command precisely. The question then arises: are these two forms of explanation correctly collapsed into one maxim? If the maxim applies to both these cases, the problem of over-generality raises its ugly head again. Is the notion of 'what the hearer requires' any less all-embracing than 'what the situation requires'? If it is not, then any explanation which depends on the maxim of quantity is in danger of being no more explanatory than the maxim itself. If however the concept of what the hearer requires can be explained in terms of the semantic and pragmatic content of either the speaker's utterance or preceding utterances, then it would seem that hearer-requirements can be given a reliable degree of content. I think in the case of imperative and question, the requirement of informativeness can be traced to the interpretation given to commands and *wh*-questions. In the former case, since propositions can only be true relative to a specific state of affairs at a specific point in time, it is arguable that a command to make some proposition true is pragmatically inadequate unless a specification of the time at which it should be made true is included. *Wh*-questions, on the other hand, as requests for information with respect to a particular variable, are pragmatically inadequate if they do not imply the truth of propositions which must be believed in order to give a value to the variable in question. Thus in the case of *How long does it take to get to London?*, the question itself gives no implication of the manner of travel. Yet the semantics of duration is such that the hearer must know the manner of travel if he is to provide a specification of duration.[1] So the only way to construe the questioner as not breaking the maxim of quantity is to make some further assumption which would reinstate the maxim. Hence the implicature that the speaker is travelling to London by car. It seems then that if we wish the maxim of quantity to be maximally specific, we should add separate maxims of quantity guaranteeing that inadequacies of this type do not arise. Since all of this is extremely tentative I shall not give further specification to the maxim here. What I hope however to have indicated is how in principle the concept of hearer's requirement of informativeness (whether as a questioner or questionee) can be defined in terms of the semantic or pragmatic content of the discourse.

8.3 The maxim of quantity and the Pragmatic Universe of Discourse

Constraints on informativeness are not however fully covered by the maxim 'Give as much information as the hearer requires'. In addition, there is a more general constraint of informativeness which applies to all forms of utterance. I pointed out earlier (p. 142) in a footnote that the maxims demanding that the speaker's contribution be as informative as required but not more so corresponded to Strawson's 'Presumption of Ignorance' and 'Presumption of Knowledge' (Strawson 1964a, pp. 97–8). These 'presumptions' capture on the one hand the assumptions on the part of the speaker that the hearer does not already know what the speaker is telling him and on the other hand the speaker's assumption that the hearer knows certain 'empirical facts relevant to the particular point to be imparted in the utterance' (p. 97). What this latter presumption suggests is that there is a certain body of facts which in any discourse a speaker will presume that his hearer knows. Now if we are to give any content to the maxim of quantity construed in a general sense and give an account of the oddity of uttering tautologies

[1] Cf. p. 164 fn. 2 above.

or statements which are generally recognised to be true, we must give an explicit characterisation of the concept of 'assumed knowledge'; since if a sentence is to be informative it must not merely tell that hearer what he already knows nor what both the speaker and the hearer already know each other knows. And more importantly perhaps for the specific hypotheses presented in this book, we shall see that a formal definition of 'assumed knowledge' provides a natural basis for explaining the assertion-presupposition distinction and its interaction with stress assignment. Moreover such a definition plays a part in accounting for the pragmatic behaviour of definite noun phrases and factive comderments, which is one of our chief remaining concerns.

8.3.1 The Pragmatic Universe of Discourse.

What we have to capture is that in any conversation, there is a body of facts which both speaker and hearer believe they agree on and which is therefore not in dispute: this set of propositions constitute their shared knowledge – knowledge which they believe they share. That is, for any individual S, there is a fund of knowledge which may be represented as a set of propositions K_i. When this arbitrary individual communicates to any other individual H, who also possesses a fund of knowledge K_j, there will generally be a subset of K_i which is also a subset of K_j. More formally we can say that for every conversational exchange in which S is the speaker and H the hearer, the set of propositions which constitute the knowledge which two such speakers will believe they share must meet the following four conditions:

(1) S believes P_i
(2) S believes H knows P_i
(3) S believes H knows S believes P_i
(4) S believes H knows S believes H knows P_i

I shall call this set of propositions the Pragmatic Universe of Discourse.[1] For any proposition P_i, if it fulfils these conditions it will constitute a proposition which both speaker and hearer will (or will expect each other to) assume. Moreover, if a proposition P_i fulfils these conditions then the entailments of P_i must also fulfil these conditions. This follows from the general rule of doxastic logic (logic of belief statements cf.

---

[1] This concept of a Pragmatic Universe of Discourse is close to the concept of 'mutual knowledge' defined independently by Schiffer 1972, pp. 30–1: S and A mutually know* that p iff K_SP, K_AP, K_SK_AP, K_AK_SP, $K_SK_AK_SP$, $K_AK_SK_AP$, $K_SK_AK_SK_AP$, $K_AK_SK_AK_SP$,...

Hintikka 1962): that for any speaker S, if he believes that p and p entails q, then he is committed to the belief that q.[1] Notice furthermore that by this rule condition (1) of the definition follows from condition (2), since *H knows* P_i entails P_i.

The Pragmatic Universe of Discourse is not, as this formulation might suggest, a static one. On the contrary it changes (increases) its membership as a conversation progresses. This changing content of the Pragmatic Universe of Discourse is a consequence of the information-bearing nature of making a statement. Once you have made a statement S_i, there are two options open to the hearer. By the definition of meaning$_{nn}$ and the quality maxim, he is bound at least to believe that you believe S_i. But he may consider your saying S_i sufficient evidence for believing S_i himself. In this latter case, if he makes known his belief by asserting some S_j which entails S_i,[2] he will thereby cause you to believe that he believes S_i. This being so, S_i will be a statement you both share knowledge of. But our definition of the Pragmatic Universe of Discourse predicts exactly this process of enlargement: according as the conversation progresses from $S_1, S_2, \ldots S_n$, S_1 (and its consequent commitments) can become a proposition which fulfils all four of the defining conditions. That is, the speaker believing S_1 (condition 1) tells it to the hearer. If his intention in communicating S_1 is successful and is explicitly shown to be successful, he is then in a position to believe the hearer knows S_1 (condition 2) and moreover he believes (by the quality maxim) that the hearer knows he believes S_1 (condition 3) and similarly that the hearer knows that he believes the hearer knows S_1 (condition 4).

---

[1] This rule of Hintikka's needs to be restricted by some concept of immediate conse-quence, since it is possible for someone to have inconsistent beliefs as long as he doesn't believe that he does. Such a concept was first discussed by Rescher 1968, pp. 40–53, who points out that included in the set of immediate consequences would be all those which follow by virtue of the rules of the language. Since I shall be re-stricting myself to this form of entailment, I shall ignore this problem.

[2] It is insufficient in this case for the speaker's utterance S_j merely to implicate S_i since implicatures are cancellable. For example, only the first of the following discourses commits B to a belief in the existence of a referent to the definite noun phrase in question: the other two only commit B to a belief that A believes there is such a referent.

  I A: Deep structure is replaced by the empty node convention.
      B: OK. The empty node convention is a necessary constraint in any case.
  II A: Deep structure is replaced by the empty node convention.
      B: Is the empty node convention a necessary constraint?
  III A: Deep structure is replaced by the empty node convention.
      B: The empty node convention is not a necessary constraint.

It may seem that the definition of the Pragmatic Universe of Discourse is unnecessarily unwieldy and that the two conditions (1) and (2) are sufficient to characterise what will constitute the assumptions made by two speakers at any one point in a conversation and will therefore not be part of their conversation at that point. But this is not always so. There are cases in which the Co-operative Principle is being maintained. and conditions (1) and (2) hold, but the propositions in question are not part of what we want to say are the assumptions of that utterance. Take for example a situation in which an examiner says to a student *What is a transformational rule?* Now the student may assume that the examiner knows that a transformational rule is a rule which states a relation between two phrase markers, but he may still say *A transformational rule is a rule which states a relation between two phrase markers.* This is not assumed to be part of the Pragmatic Universe of Discourse of that conversation. For what the student does *not* believe is that the examiner knows he knows that a transformational rule is as described (i.e. condition (3) is not fulfilled). Likewise a personnel officer talking to a new man in the firm may believe that the new man knows that no information about the firm may be given to outsiders (condition 2) but he does not believe that the man knows that he the personnel officer knows that the man knows this (condition 4) – the new man may therefore think he can break the rule. Thus the personnel officer may say *No information about the firm may be given to outsiders.* The failures of conditions (3) and (4) are clearly not the normal reasons why a proposition is not part of the Pragmatic Universe of Discourse, but rather what is stated. The general condition on saying something is that you believe that the hearer does not know what you are telling him – that is, condition (2) is not met. And if condition (2) is not met, then it is not possible that condition (4) be fulfilled. If condition (1) is not met, then clearly the proposition in question cannot, trivially, be part of the Pragmatic Universe of Discourse since the speaker does not believe it.

8.3.2 The maxim of quantity II. My initial aim in delimiting the Pragmatic Universe of Discourse was to incorporate into the maxim of quantity some general constraint on being informative. I suggest the following maxim as a first approximation:

> Do not assert[1] any proposition p which is a member of the Pragmatic Universe of Discourse

[1] Cf. 8.6 for a discussion of assertion.

or, more generally:

For any proposition p, and any mood operator '$*\psi$' (i.e. '⊢', '!' or '?'), do not say '$*\psi p$' if p is a member of the Pragmatic Universe of Discourse.

But p will only be a member of the Pragmatic Universe of Discourse if sufficient conditions for the truth of p are themselves members of that Pragmatic Universe of Discourse. Equivalently, if p is known to be true, the conditions which guarantee the truth of p will also be known to be true. The maxim can thus be given the further specification:

For any proposition p whose truth is minimally guaranteed by n conditions, and any mood operator '$*\psi$', only say '$*\psi p$' if $\leqslant n-1$ of those conditions are members of the Pragmatic Universe of Discourse.

As a first indication of how this maxim might operate, let us look first at positive assertions, imperatives and questions. The maxim was defined to exclude as conversationally inadequate saying what is mutual knowledge between speaker and hearer.[1] It also excludes ordering one's audience to carry out some action which is already clearly true. Thus one should not tell someone to shut the door if it is already shut.[2] Along similar lines, one should not ask a question to which one knows the answer if moreover one knows that the hearer knows the answer. The position is further complicated here by the fact that '?p' indicates a request for either the utterance 'p' or the utterance '$-p$'. Unlike imperatives which indicate a simple intention, '?p' expresses a complex intention (containing a disjunctive *or*) and it is therefore conversationally inadequate to say '?p' if either p or $-p$ are members of the Pragmatic Universe of Discourse. How do negative statements obey this maxim? We have seen in previous chapters that the semantic representation of some statement $-p$ is a disjunct of semantic features, say,

$$[A/M] \text{ v } [A/N] \text{ v } [A/P] \text{ etc.}[3]$$

---

[1] Notice that this does not exclude the possibility of repeating, recapitulating or summarising what one has said, since not all one's utterances of the discourse become part of the Pragmatic Universe of Discourse – only those which are explicitly agreed by the hearer to be true.

[2] In fact the constraint is stronger than the maxim indicates, since a generalisation of the maxim of quality should forbid one to command something if it is already known to be true (whether or not this is also known by the hearer).

[3] A/M_i is the antonymy operator for a member M_i of a set $M_1, M_2, M_3, \ldots$ such that $A/M_i \equiv M_1 \text{ v } M_2 \text{ v} \ldots M_{i-1} \text{ v } M_{i+1} \ldots \text{ v } M_n$ (cf. p. 12).

Any one of these disjuncts is a sufficient condition for the truth of $-p$ but no one of them is a necessary condition. What the maxim claims is that if any one of these disjuncts is a member of the Pragmatic Universe of Discourse, it will be otiose for any speaker to inform his hearer of the statement $-p$. And this is what we find. As an example, let us assume a very approximate schematic representation of *John didn't kill Mary*[1] to be

$$[A/J]X_1 \text{ v } [A/M]X_2 \text{ v } [CAUSE]X_1([A/DIE]X_2) \text{ v}$$
$$(a) \qquad\quad (b) \qquad\qquad\qquad (c)$$
$$[A/CAUSE]X_1([DIE]X_2)$$
$$(d)$$

If it is common knowledge between any speaker and hearer either that someone other than John killed Mary (cf. (a)) or that John killed someone other than Mary (cf. (b)) or that Mary died but John definitely was not the cause of it (cf. (d)), or that John raped Mary but she did not die as a result (cf. (c)), then the maxim predicts that the utterance of this sentence will flaunt the Co-operative Principle and therefore be conversationally inadequate, in just the way that *John killed Mary* constitutes an inadequate utterance if the speaker and hearer both know that this is so.

8.3.3 Exclamations and the requirement of informativeness. In all the discussion of the maxims of the Co-operative Principle so far, I have restricted my attention to statements, questions and (briefly) imperatives. There remains however a further class of utterance – exclamations.[2] Utterances such as *Isn't she clever! Isn't the view lovely! Didn't she sing beautifully!* appear to constitute clear counter-examples to the constraint that speakers should not say what is known and known to be known by the participants in a conversation. There is little doubt that two people can stand in front of the Mona Lisa and knowing both that it is a beautiful painting and that the other knows it is a beautiful painting still naturally turn to each other and say *Isn't it a beautiful painting!*.

These examples are interesting for a further, and potentially more

---

[1] This representation is misleading in that all problems of quantification are ignored. These details do not however affect the point being made, so I have excluded them for the sake of clarity. For a fuller representation of negative sentences of this type, cf. pp. 130–3.

[2] These examples were pointed out to me by Dick Hudson.

damaging, reason. Unless the maxim of quantity is given greater content than is provided by Grice, examples of this type show up its vacuity since the maxim enables one to predict either that they should be deviant or that they are not. If the maxim 'Give as much information as is required' insists, as it suggests, that all utterances must have some information content, where information is measured in terms of what is not agreed between speaker and hearer (corresponding to the definition of the Pragmatic Universe of Discourse: cf. p. 167) then since these utterances neither offer nor seek information, they are predicted to be conversationally deviant. If however the maxim allows for a situation in which no information being required, no information need be given then the theory predicts that exclamations of this type do not violate the maxim. However if this interpretation of the maxim is allowed, it is not clear what conceivable situation it could exclude. It is therefore vacuous, and without content. This criticism does not however extend to the reformulation of the maxim I have given; but the examples instead become counter-examples.

One possible explanation of such exclamations is that they are not mere statements of fact but are communications of the strength of the speaker's commitment to the statement in question. It has been pointed out by Quirk *et al.* (1972; p. 400)[1] that exclamatory questions of this type are only possible if the question contains a gradable term, the interpretation always being that the speaker is committing himself to an assessment of the gradable term as at the extreme end of the scale of gradation. Thus *Isn't she lovely? Didn't she sing badly? Didn't she sing a beautiful song?* can all be exclamations, whereas *Isn't he coming tommorrow?, Wasn't she your secretary last year?* and *Didn't he do the washing-up?* can never be. Though the speaker may know that the statement itself is known by the hearer to be agreed by him and the speaker, what the speaker does not assume is that his hearer knows the strength of his commitment. Hence part of the information conveyed by such utterances is not mutually agreed by the participants. The problem with this form of explanation is its informality, an informality which seems unavoidable given the problems involved in stating a predictable interpretation for negative questions of this kind. They are unique in being sentence forms which do not allow a cumulative interpretation of their constituent parts. The interpretation of *Isn't she lovely!* is not a questioning of the negative proposition *She is not*

[1] Cf. also Hudson 1973.

lovely.[1] Thus it bears no relation either to its sentence operator, the negative element, or to its pragmatic operator, the question element. It seems clear that until we have a non-*ad hoc* way of giving an interpretation to such utterances, we have no means of testing the validity of explaining their message-content in terms of a considerable degree of commitment on the part of the speaker. With reservations of this sort, I shall accept this explanation *pro tem.*

In this section, we have seen how a formal characterisation of the notion of 'assumed knowledge' (in terms of a Pragmatic Universe of Discourse) can be used to give greater specification to one of the central maxims, the maxim of quantity. This now contains two subparts:

(i) Give as much information as the hearer requires
(ii) Only say '$*\psi p$' if p is not a member of the Pragmatic Universe of Discourse.

Both the maxims of relation and quantity are now at least partially defined in terms of the semantic and pragmatic content of the utterance and, in being restricted in this way, are less open to universal application. One large problem however remains: should they be restricted in this way? As we shall see in 8.6.1, there is evidence that at least the maxim of relation cannot be restricted merely to the content of the utterance since the interpretation of stress depends not merely on utterance content but on its form. Furthermore the problem is not restricted merely to predicting the available data. As I shall consider in the final chapter, the question of how the maxims should be specified may depend on the theoretical status of pragmatics within an over-all theory of language. For the moment however I shall simply assume that the restriction of the maxims to the pragmatic and semantic content of utterances can only be beneficial in giving them greater content and thus greater explanatory value.

8.4 The pragmatic interpretation of definite noun phrases

We are now in a position to tackle the most important remaining problem – how to account for those properties of definite noun phrases which I dismissed earlier as not semantic. In chapter 5 I

---

[1] This is unlike true negative questions such as *Isn't she coming?* which can be analysed as querying *She isn't coming.* Indeed these are characteristically uttered in the face of their corresponding statement (or an implication of it).

argued that there are two such implications in the use of definite noun phrases. These are for any object described with the use of *the* that there is such an object, and that the hearer knows of the existence of the object (in so far as he can uniquely identify it for the purposes of the particular discourse). I argued however that only the first of these implications was semantic, since to say *the x* does not entail that the hearer be able uniquely to identify the object referred to by *the x*, though this is a normal implication of its use (cf. 5.5). So this latter implication we have to characterise in pragmatic terms. This is not the only problem which definite noun phrases present. In addition we have to explain the natural interpretation of definite noun phrases in questions and negatives that they be protected from the scope of negation.

In chapter 7 I defined two categories of standard implicature, conventional implicature and generalised conversational implicature, and we can now assess the explanatory value of these categories. As a preliminary to doing so, let me briefly recall examples which demonstrate the central properties of general conversational implicature and conventional implicature. The first was exemplified by *P or Q*, an utterance of which normally implicates in response to a *wh*-question that the speaker does not know which of *P* or *Q* holds, since by virtue of the maxim of the Co-operative Principle that one must give the information that the hearer requires (cf. 8.2), the hearer deduces that if the speaker knew that *P* was true he should be committed to stating that P: the speaker will therefore be taken to be implicating that he does not know which of *P* or *Q* is true. The reasons why this category is not a conventional implicature are (*a*) that the implicature is cancellable either explicitly or by virtue of the situation in which it is uttered and (*b*) it is deducible from the maxims of the Co-operative Principle in conjunction with the linguistic specification of the sentence in question. Conventional implicature by contrast fails both these criteria – it is not cancellable and it is not deduceable from the Co-operative Principle. It is thus in effect not explicable by means of the pragmatic constructs. One of Grice's standard examples of conventional implicature is the implication in *but* of a contrast between its conjuncts (cf. Grice 1961), which I suggested in chapter 4 was not formalisable in semantic terms since it was not possible to predict any contrast (either semantic or syntactic) which was a necessary pre-requisite of *but*'s occurrence. This implication of contrast seems to carry all the hallmarks of conventional implicature: it appears not to be part of the word's meaning for reasons already given,[1] but it seems in some sense always a consequence of the word's use – to utter the sentence *X but Y, but I don't mean to imply there's any contrast between the two* is indefensible in the same way as it is indefensible to say *X but I don't believe it*: and it is not dependent on the Co-operative Principle for its interpretation.[2] Since in the case of *but*, the semantic argument against distinguishing *but* and *and* are arguably fairly strong ones, the *ad hoc* nature of the pragmatic mechanism guaranteeing that *but* conveys a particular implication does not provide a serious flaw in the theoretical framework. However it seems clear that unless the use made of the concept of conventional implicature is extremely restricted, the over-all explanatory value of the pragmatic framework could be cast seriously in doubt. Thus though in principle we have two possible ways of explaining the pragmatic implications of definite noun phrases, it would be a reasonable criticism to suggest that if these implications had to be analysed as conventional implicatures, they would constitute much more serious counter-examples than *but* to the general position adopted in this book.

We have already seen that the relationship between *I saw the Lord Mayor of Bristol* and a statement such as *You know who I am referring to by the phrase 'the Lord Mayor of Bristol'* is not one of entailment, since *I saw the Lord Mayor of Bristol* can be true whether or not the hearer knows of the existence of such a man. And the relationship between *I didn't see the Lord Mayor of Bristol* and *There is a Lord Mayor of Bristol* is not a truth dependence either. Is the second sentence of each of these pairs of sentences a general conversational implicature of the first? If so, we should be able to derive them from the first member of each pair by an argument based on an apparent violation of the Co-operative Principle unless an assumption corresponding to the second sentence of the pair is made (cf. p. 143). Let us take the anaphoric use of the definite noun phrase first. In saying the sentence *A dog was given*

---

[1] Cf. however pp. 215–18 for a further consideration of this possibility.

[2] One might try to interpret a speaker saying *X but Y* as reasoning '(1) H knows I am obeying the Co-operative Principle and making the strongest statement possible; (2) since I am not saying *X and Y* I must be implicating something further; (3) therefore I am implicating that *X* is in contrast to *Y*.' This is not however a valid deduction (even using such weak forms of the maxims), since there is no justification for the jump from (2) to (3). The only means of making this step is to know that *but* indicates a contrast. But this means that in order to predict the contrastiveness of *but* by means of the Co-operative Principle, we have to assume that *but* is contrastive. This implicature is therefore not dependent on the Co-operative Principle.

to my son for his third birthday and the dog bit him, a speaker (S) might reason that his hearer (H) knows and knows that S knows (*a*) that both *A dog was given to my son for his third birthday* and *The dog bit him* entail *There was a specific dog,* (*b*) the syntactic convention that [+Def] is a feature which occurs automatically on a noun phrase when it is in an environment which contains a preceding coreferring noun phrase (cf. pp. 103–4), and (*c*) the pragmatic convention (of meaning$_{nn}$) that S will only say a sentence meaning that P if he intends H to believe P on the basis of recognising that he S believes that P. In addition, both S and H assume the maintenance of the Co-operative Principle, and S is therefore in a position to reason that H will assume that he, S, is obeying the quality maxim and hence that H will believe not only that S believes that the utterance is true but also that S believes its entailments (or immediate consequences: cf. p. 168 fn. 1 above) are true. Thus S knows that H will believe that he S believes both that there was a specific dog which was given to S's son for his third birthday and that there was a specific dog which bit him. Moreover on the basis of their mutual knowledge of the rule of definitisation, S can deduce that H will recognise that he, S, believes that the dog which bit his son is identical to the dog which his son was given for his third birthday. But this guarantees that H knows the referent of the definite noun phrase subject in S's utterance, since it follows that H knows that the reference of the noun phrase in question is the dog which S believes was given to S's son for his third birthday (cf. Hintikka (1970) who gives as a logical form for *a knows who b is,* '($\exists$x) (a knows that b = x)'). Thus the implication on anaphoric definite noun phrases that the hearer knows who the speaker is referring to is a direct consequence of the pragmatic definition of meaning, the quality maxim, and the condition for application of the rule of definitisation. The deduction for negative sentences containing anaphoric definite noun phrases proceeds identically, except that the commitment of the speaker (S) to a belief in the existence of the referent in question is not deduced directly from an entailment on the negative sentence (as it is in positive statements) but from the contradiction that would arise with the preceding sentence if S did not believe that there was such an object (cf. pp. 104–5). In these cases then the implication that the hearer knows who is being referred to is not an implicature according to Grice's definition (cf. p. 143), since it is not deduced *via* an apparent violation of the maxims of the Co-operative Principle. Rather it is parallel to the relation between *P* and *I believe that P* – an automatic consequence of the way the pragmatic framework is defined.

From this implication in the anaphoric use of the definite article, we can predict that those environments where the definite article is not anaphoric will also be interpreted as implying that the hearer knows who is being referred to, though in this case the implication is not a (pragmatically) necessary one. We have seen that [+Def] occurs obligatorily for formal syntactic reasons in an environment where, as a joint consequence of the characterisation of the linguistic conventions, the pragmatic definition of meaning and the quality maxim, the object to which the noun phrase refers is automatically construed as being known to (identifiable by) the hearer. Now recall that in chapter 6 (6.1–6.2) I argued that definite and indefinite noun phrases are syntactically and semantically identical at deep structure except that the syntactic feature [+Def], which has no semantic interpretation, may be arbitrarily assigned by optional rule (cf. p. 124). Despite this semantic identity, we know that if the speaker (S) is obeying the Co-operative Principle, he must be intending to convey some extra information by the use of the feature [+Def] where it is optional. But [+Def] has no semantic interpretation. So S can only be interpreted as conveying extra information if he is deliberately seeking to convey that implication which is an automatic consequence of the obligatory use of the definite article.

Take for example the sentence *I met the Lord Mayor of Bristol*. In saying this sentence, our speaker S might argue 'I know and I know that H (the hearer) knows that (*a*) *I met the Lord Mayor of Bristol* entails *There is a Lord Mayor of Bristol*, and (*b*) [+Def] occurs both optionally on noun phrases, and obligatorily just in case it is in an environment which contains a preceding coreferring noun phrase. Moreover I know that H knows that where [+Def] occurs obligatorily it always carries an implicature that H knows what I am referring to. In addition I know that H will expect that I use the feature [+Def] where it is not obligatory only if I intend to convey some extra information. But both H and I know that the feature has no semantic interpretation, and that it can therefore only be construed as offering extra information if it is used to convey the same information as its obligatory use. I therefore know that H will take my utterance of *I met the Lord Mayor of Bristol* as implicating that he knows who I am referring to.' Now in this case, if S believes the implicature that H knows who he, S, is referring to – as he must if he is to conform with the quality maxim – he must also believe that H believes that there is a referent of the definite noun phrase in question, since there is no other (linguistically anaphoric) basis for H's knowledge of the referent. (This is unlike the previous anaphoric case, where S believed H knew who S was referring to on the basis solely of knowing the rule of definitisation.) But if the utterance of *I met the Lord Mayor of Bristol* implies that both S and H believe that there is a Lord Mayor of Bristol, and that both believe that they both know this, the proposition that there is a Lord Mayor of Bristol is implied to be a part of the Pragmatic Universe of Discourse they share.

A similar form of explanation applies to negative sentences containing definite noun phrases. In these cases, on the basis of the speaker's and hearer's mutual recognition of the Co-operative Principle and the conventions of the language, S will deduce, and intend that H will deduce, that his utterance of, say, *I did not meet the Lord Mayor of Bristol* will carry (as implicatures) the implications carried by the anaphoric use of the definite noun phrase in the same environment (on the assumption, as before, that H will know that S would not be using the definite noun phrase if he did not wish to convey extra information). But the relation between the anaphoric and non-anaphoric definite noun phrases in negative sentences is not the same as in positive sentences. Though both anaphoric and non-anaphoric uses of definite noun phrases in positive sentences entail the relevant existence claim, this does not carry over to negative sentences. There is a relation of entailment between the conjunction of a statement entailing the existence of some object with a second, negative, statement containing a definite noun phrase which corefers to the noun phrase in question in the first conjunct, and a statement asserting the existence of the object in question. But a negative sentence, on its own, which contains a definite noun phrase, does not entail the existence of any object. These properties of the language both S and H know (and know that they know) by virtue of knowing the language. So S knows (and intends) that H will deduce that in using a definite noun phrase in the negative sentence *I did not meet the Lord Mayor of Bristol*, he S must be wishing to convey some specific extra information not carried by the semantically identical indefinite article. But S knows that H knows that the definite article can only be construed as offering extra information if it is used to convey the same information as its obligatory (anaphoric) use. On this basis, S knows that H will take his utterance as implicating the two implications which are a necessary consequence of a parallel statement involving anaphoric definite noun phrases: viz. (i) that H knows the referent to which he is referring (the Lord Mayor of Bristol), and (ii) that there is a Lord Mayor of Bristol. But if S believes that H knows the object (the Lord Mayor of Bristol) to which he is referring independently of information given by S's utterance, it follows that S believes that H believes that there is a Lord Mayor of Bristol. So on the basis of the maxims of the Co-operative Principle, we can naturally predict that an utterance of a negative sentence containing a non-anaphoric definite noun phrase will generally imply (*a*) that the speaker believes that there is an object to which the noun phrase refers, (*b*) that the speaker believes that the hearer believes that there is an object to which the noun phrase refers, and (*c*) that the speaker believes the hearer knows which object is referred to. That is to say, negative and positive statements containing a non-anaphoric definite noun phrase both imply (though not on an identical basis) that knowledge of the object referred to is part of the Pragmatic Universe of Discourse the speaker and hearer share (strictly speaking the Pragmatic Universe of Discourse the speaker believes he and his hearer share).

There is one problem in the over-all pattern of deduction: in what way do the maxims apply to demand that the speaker offer extra information in his use of the definite article? If we invoke the maxim of quantity, then it appears to be applying in its most general form. Certainly nothing the hearer has said or will say affects the speaker's choice of the definite article, so the revised form of the maxim of quantity (cf. 8.2) does not apply. And in the form adopted in 8.1, the maxim of relation also concerns preceding utterances of the discourse and this is not relevant to the problem we have here. However I indicated there (p. 161) that the maxim of relation would have to be extended to accommodate problems of stress. To anticipate what is argued for in detail in 8.6.1, it appears that the maxim of relation needs a separate submaxim which applies to the relation between form and content for any utterance, viz: 'Make the form of your utterance relevant to its content'. Now if this maxim is justified – and I argue in 8.6.1 that it is the only way to accommodate stress phenomena without reducing the maxims to vacuity – it has a natural application in the case of definite noun phrases. If the speaker uses a noun phrase whose syntactic and semantic specification is identical to that of an indefinite noun phrase except that it bears the feature [+Def] arbitrarily assigned (by optional rule) at deep structure (cf. p. 124), he will be breaking this maxim of relation unless he intends the use of this feature [+ Def] to be relevant to the content of his utterance. And the only way to construe it as having relevance is to deduce that the speaker must be deliberately invoking that implication which is an automatic consequence of the obligatory use of the definite article. So it seems that where the use of the definite noun phrase is non-anaphoric, the deduction of its implicatures depends on the linguistic conventions, the pragmatic definition of meaning (Grice's meaning$_{nn}$), the quality maxim, and a not yet justified extension of the maxim of relation.

This account of the pragmatic implications on definite noun phrases extends naturally both to other types of sentence and across utterance boundaries. In a conversation in which H says *I met a man yesterday* and S responds with the question *Did the man speak to you?*, S will argue 'I know that H knows the linguistic conventions of entailment between *I met a man yesterday* and *There was a specific man* and of definitisation. Moreover I know that on the basis of these and the deductions already given (pp. 177–9) that H will deduce that definite noun phrases in effect occur obligatorily when a speaker wishes to convey that the hearer knows what object he is intending to refer to. Since I am using the definite article, H will therefore deduce that I am implicating that he knows the man to which I refer (and also that there is a specific object to which I am referring). But if I were referring to some man other than the one H has just alluded to, I would be breaking the maxim of relation,[1] since my question would have nothing to do with his utterance. Since to do so would therefore be to break the pragmatic maxims, and since H will assume that I am obeying these, H will take my question as referring to the same man as his utterance.'[2] As this example demonstrates, we now appear to be able to account for cases of coreference not only within and across sentence boundaries, and within different sentence types, but even between sentences with different speakers.

---

[1] This invocation of the maxim of relation refers to the maxim defined in 8.1: 'Give as much information as the hearer requires.'

[2] Notice that in such cases as these, where a question – from which there is no entailment of existence – contains an anaphoric definite noun phrase, the speaker of that question is only necessarily committed to a belief that his hearer believes in the existence of the relevant object, because as the hearer of the original *I met a man yesterday* he need only believe that his hearer, the speaker of this previous claim, believes in the existence of the man in question (cf. p. 168 fn. 2 above, and pp. 184–5).

The pattern of explanation in all cases except coreference within a single utterance has depended on three factors characteristic of implicatures: (i) the prior specification of the linguistic system, (ii) the maxims of the Co-operative Principle and the pragmatic definition of meaning, and (iii) a deduction process *via* these maxims in the face of an apparent violation of them. However in this account of non-anaphoric definite noun phrases, the assumptions necessary to re-instate the maxims were not context-specific. On the contrary, they were the general assumptions that there be an object referred to by the noun phrase in question, and that the hearer knows the object referred to. This suggests that these implicatures on non-anaphoric definite noun phrases are indeed general conversational implicatures.

Such an analysis would further predict that these implicatures are cancellable. We have already seen that they are. One of the main arguments against a semantic concept of presupposition centred around the fact that the implication of existence was only a necessary consequence of using a definite noun phrase in non-opaque environments. In negative and other related environments, it was not, because it could be cancelled. So these sentences also provide evidence for a pragmatic account of definite noun phrases in terms of general conversational implicature. In this connection, consider such examples again.

(10) The King of Ruritania didn't visit the exhibition because there isn't a King of Ruritania.
(11) Ruth's husband didn't come to meet her – she's not married.
(12) The swimming pool at Ely wasn't closed – there isn't a swimming pool there.

In all these cases, there is no assumption of the existence of the object in question. So the other implicature, that the hearer knows of the existence of such an object, is simultaneously cancelled. This is not however the only environment in which this latter implicature can be cancelled. My analysis has claimed that this was also an implicature of positive non-opaque sentences. And predictably it can be cancelled in these environments too, either explicitly or by virtue of the situation:

(13) The King of Ruritania came to my exhibition, though I don't suppose you knew I was having one, let alone that there was a King of Ruritania – did you?
(14) Situation: A does not know Bill, who is a friend of B's. In

particular he does not know that Bill is married. B knows that
A does not know this.

A: How's your friend Bill these days?

B: His wife has just left him.[1]

In neither of these cases is the speaker assuming that the hearer knows
the object he is referring to. In addition, this assumption can be cancelled in negative sentences independently of the assumption of
existence:

(15) The King of Ruritania never showed up at my exhibition,
     though I don't suppose you knew there was such a person,
     did you?

Now while the labelling of these implications as general conversational
implicatures predicts the distribution correctly, it is not *prima facie*
obvious that it does so in an explanatory way. I have so far not accounted
for the fact that in (10)–(12) both implicatures are simultaneously
cancelled, nor for the fact that the implicature of hearer's knowledge
can be cancelled independently of the implicature of existence, as in
(15). Furthermore, there is the additional unexplained fact that (10)–
(12), which explicitly cancel the assumption of hearer's knowledge,
characteristically imply that the hearer believes in the existence of the
object in question, though the speaker does not. But these phenomena
are all naturally accounted for if we recall the pragmatic consequences
of analysing non-anaphoric definite noun phrases as implicating the
existence of the object in question and the hearer's knowledge of this
object. If he is observing the Co-operative Principle, the speaker is
committed by the quality maxim to believe the information he is
conveying and hence any implicatures of his utterance, together with
their consequences. So in using a definite noun phrase, a speaker will
generally be taken to be implying: (i) that he believes there is an object
that he is referring to, and (ii) that he believes the hearer knows what
he the speaker is referring to. However, I have argued that since, in
cases of the non-anaphoric definite noun phrase, the speaker believes
the hearer only knows the object that he the speaker is referring to
independently of this utterance, he is also committed to a third implication, (iii), that he believes the hearer believes that there is such an
object (cf. p. 178). Equivalently, in using a non-anaphoric definite
noun phrase, a speaker will generally be taken to be implying that the

[1] I am grateful to Edward Keenan for this example.

existence of the object in question is a member of the Pragmatic Universe of Discourse he and the hearer share.

Now these three commitments on the part of a speaker are not independent. For example, (i) is a consequence of (ii) (cf. pp. 167–8), and so is (iii) (cf. p. 177). Thus by a line of argument which should by now be familiar, this analysis predicts that if either (i) or (iii) are cancelled, (ii) cannot be implied. Conversely, a cancellation of (ii) should be consistent with either a commitment to or a cancellation of (i), and similarly (iii). Furthermore, since (i) is independent of (iii), a cancellation of (i) – though it necessitates the cancellation of (ii) – should allow (iii) either to be retained or cancelled. And this is exactly what we have found. (13) and (15) present cases where there is no implication of any knowledge on the part of the hearer as to the existence of the King of Ruritania: the speaker does not believe that the hearer believes there is a king of Ruritania and therefore cannot believe H knows the object he S is referring to (schematically '⊢(i) −(ii) −(iii)'). In (10)–(12), representing the central cases of this book, the speaker is denying the existence of the object, so since he is committed to the belief that there be no such object, he cannot also believe that the hearer knows the object he is referring to, and the implication of the hearer's knowledge is bound also to fail. However the common implication in such cases is that the speaker believes the hearer believes there is some object of the appropriate kind (i.e. schematically '−(i) −(ii) ⊢(iii)'); and this our analysis predicts since the cancellation of (iii), but not (ii), is independent of the cancellation of (i). Yet even this implication is cancellable, as in (16), where we have '−(i) −(ii) −(iii)'.

(16) Let's start the meeting with some points of agreement. First of all, I take it that we all agree that the Queen of Mombasa didn't visit our exhibition, because there's no such woman.

And so we find that the analysis of these implications as general conversational implicatures, taking into account the dependencies between them, thus correctly predicts all the aspects of the behaviour of definite noun phrases under negation.[1]

[1] The only prediction from the dependencies between (i)–(iii) which is not matched by the data is that the implicature of hearer's knowledge of the referent, (ii), can be cancelled without also cancelling the hearer's belief in the existential, (iii). The concept of knowledge of objects has been discussed by Hintikka 1970, who analyses 'a knows who b is' as '(∃x) (a knows that b = x)'. It follows from this account that if this is denied, then it is not possible also to maintain that a knows that there is an object b. Though the dependency here deserves much more investigation, the lack

In addition, this analysis provides an automatic explanation of the marked nature of negative sentences containing definite noun phrases where the implication of a specific referent of the noun phrase in question is included within the scope of negation. For the theory predicts that any cancellation of a general conversational implicature constitutes a marked case. And in the case of marked interpretations of negative sentences, two general implicatures are simultaneously cancelled – a doubly marked case. Hence the unlikelihood of such sentences providing the normal interpretations of negation. Since moreover the deduction of the implicatures is directly dependent on the syntactic property of the definite noun phrase as a coreference marker, it follows that the markedness of the particular interpretations of negative sentences which have been central to my arguments can be traced not to the semantic properties of definite noun phrases (as one might at first expect) but to the pragmatic interpretation given to the syntactic feature [+Def].

An exactly parallel explanation extends to questions, as we have already partly seen (p. 180). Again both the existence of the referent and the hearer's knowledge of the referent (and belief in its existence) are normally assumed; but they can be cancelled out in a way similar to negative sentences, as witness (17)–(20):

(17) Is the King of Rumania coming to the coronation, or doesn't Rumania have a king?

(18) Is the King of Rumania coming to the exhibition – I thought Rumania was a republic.

(19) Did the Duke of Plazitoro come to the opening ceremony – I didn't think there was such a place as Plazitoro, let alone that it had a duke.

(20) Is the Society of Ignored Minorities represented in our directory, or didn't you know there was one?

Examples (17)–(19) (repeated here for convenience from p. 158) do not imply that there is a specific referent corresponding to the definite noun phrase in question and therefore they cannot be taken to imply that the hearer knows such a referent. Moreover, while (18)–(19) may imply that the hearer believes that there is a referent corresponding to the definite noun phrase, (17) does not; and this variability is what the analysis predicts. Finally (20) cancels the implication that the hearer

of clarity in this particular prediction is not essential to the over-all analysis of definite noun phrases.

knows the object referred to, but maintains the implication of (i.e. the speaker's belief in) its existence. Thus the pragmatic account of definite noun phrases in negative sentences seems to extend to questions without any additional problems.

In general terms, what this section has – hopefully – demonstrated is that an independently motivated pragmatic framework appears to provide a natural explanation of those properties of definite noun phrases which we have already seen from semantic evidence are different in kind from other semantic properties of such noun phrases. Since in addition this pragmatic explanation of definite noun phrases automatically predicts (*a*) the possibility of negative and interrogative sentences in which the existence of the referent of a noun phrase is denied or questioned respectively, and (*b*) that such interpretations are extremely marked, I think we can reasonably conclude (as long of course as the explanation is correct) that it provides reassuring confirmation of the semantic and pragmatic frameworks adopted here.

8.5 The pragmatic interpretation of factive complements

We saw in chapter 6 that there was semantic evidence for an interpretation of factive sentential complements in a way that corresponds to specific noun phrases, and that there was syntactic evidence that the underlying syntactic structure of such factive complements should contain an explicit definite noun head such that the sentences *The King regretted the fact that the Queen was sick* and *The King regretted that the Queen was sick* possessed the same deep structure. Two consequences follow from this analysis which are relevant to the problem we face here of explaining the marked status of negative sentences and questions incorporating the complement of factive verbs within the scope of negation or question. First, in giving factive verb complements a specification at deep structure which contains the feature [+Def] (cf. p. 135), one is committing oneself to a specific prediction about the pragmatic behaviour of these complements – since the pragmatic behaviour of definite noun phrases is triggered by the syntactic feature [+Def], factive complements should have the same pragmatic properties as definite noun phrases. This first prediction leads to the second. There are verbs which entail the truth of their complement but which do not share many of the syntactic characteristics of factives. Take for example *prove*. This cannot take the full range of gerunds, and it allows both the *for-to* construction and the accusative plus infinitive construction.[1] If we distinguish between *Jones regretted that Einstein was right* and *Jones proved that Einstein was right* by assigning only to the former a deep structure definite noun head, our formal mechanism will automatically lead to a prediction that the pragmatic behaviour of *regret* and *prove* should be different, since it is the feature [+Def] on the head noun of the complement sentence which causes the pragmatic interpretation of factives. Both these predictions are matched by the evidence.

We have already seen in part that the first prediction is fulfilled. Both factives and definite noun phrases have occupied a central part in my arguments here because they share the property of having certain logically possible but highly marked interpretations in negative environments. Moreover this shared property carries over to questions (cf. examples (1)–(7) pp. 157–8). Secondly there is an implication in the use of factives to which I have not yet drawn attention. An utterance of (21) and (22) would characteristically imply that the speaker assumes that the complement is true (hence the common use of presupposition) – in other words the speaker believes the hearer knows that the complement is true.

(21) John regretted that Mary was sick.

(22) Edward realised that his mother was dying.

But this implication on factives parallels the implication on definite noun phrases that the speaker believes the hearer knows the referent to which the noun phrase refers. Now the implication on definite noun phrases was, I argued, based on a general conversational implicature that the hearer knows the referent in question, since – among other things – it was cancellable. The implication on factive complements behaves in exactly the same way: it can be cancelled, either explicitly as in (23)–(24), or – in the case of negative and interrogative sentences such as (25) and (26) – just in case the truth of the complement is also denied or doubted. Thus corresponding to examples (10)–(15) (pp. 181–2) we have:

(23) I didn't regret going to see your mother, though you never knew until now that I ever went to see her, did you?

(24) I regretted having been a secretary for two years, though I don't suppose you knew I had ever been one, did you?

(25) John didn't regret that Mary was sick because she was not sick.

---

[1] These are among the criteria specified by the Kiparskys 1970.

(26) Does Felicity regret taking a BBC audition – I thought she'd always refused to take one.

Thus (23) does not imply that the hearer knows that the speaker went to see his mother, though it does imply that he did so; (24) similarly; (25) neither implies that the hearer knows that Mary was sick nor that Mary was sick, though it allows the possibility that the hearer believes that Mary was sick; and similarly (26). And as with definite noun phrases, this further implication can also be cancelled out, as in

(27) Let me start this evening's discussion with something which we all agree about. At least we agree that our chairman does not regret spending too much money on entertainment, because he knows he has never spent enough money on entertainment.

Notice moreover that like the implication on anaphoric definite noun phrases, there is no implication of assumed independent knowledge on the part of the hearer if such sentences are part of a co-ordination of the type *Belinda went to the party and Jim regretted that Belinda went to the party*. So it seems that the prediction made by the theoretical account of factives given here is correct: both pragmatic properties of definite noun phrases – that in negative sentences and questions the implication of existence of the noun phrase will not be included within the scope of the operator, and that in all sentences there is a general implicature that the speaker believes the hearer knows the referent in question – appear to stand in a one-to-one correspondence with the pragmatic properties of the complements of factive verbs.

Our second prediction was that by virtue of the different syntactic analyses of *prove* and *regret*, the pragmatic behaviour of these verbs would be correspondingly different. And so it is. As we would expect, two properties distinguish verbs such as *prove* from the factive set. Unlike factives, the complement of *prove* is normally interpreted as falling within the scope of negation if the verb itself is. Though the natural interpretation of *John didn't regret that Mary was sick* is not that given in (25) but is that Mary was sick, there is no such parallel in (28):

(28) Jones didn't prove that Einstein was wrong.

Here there is no indication of whether or not Einstein was wrong. Similarly the natural interpretation of questions containing *prove* is that the complement of *prove* is being questioned. Thus in (29) there is certainly no assumption that Generative Semantics is vacuous – rather this is just what is being questioned.

(29) Has Chomsky proved that Generative Semantics is vacuous?

Secondly, the complements of *prove* carry no implication of assumption of their truth on the part of the hearer. That is, a sentence such as *John proved that Einstein was wrong* does not carry an implication that the hearer already knows that Einstein was wrong. All these predictions are exactly consonant with the analysis given and they provide independent confirmation not only of the semantic and pragmatic account offered here but also of the syntactic analysis accorded to factives by the Kiparskys.

It thus appears that in collapsing the pragmatic account of factive verbs with that of definite noun phrases, we have to hand a natural means of explaining marked and unmarked interpretations for a large range of negative and interrogative sentences. And in a more general perspective, this joint account of factive complements and definite noun phrases together with the pragmatic constructs independently defined by Grice provides an automatic explanation of the apparent discrepancy between the semantics of negation and its use.

8.6 The assertion-presupposition contrast

So far in this chapter, I have been pursuing my two chief aims: firstly to reformulate Grice's maxims so that they can reasonably be said to have explanatory value; second to use these maxims to explain why it is that some interpretations of negative sentences are 'natural' and unmarked while others are highly 'unnatural' and marked. I wish to turn now to the notion of assertion, since in predicting the relationship between what a speaker assumes (presupposes) and what he asserts, queries, etc., where this correlates with stress assignment, we shall see that there is evidence to suggest that the maxims cannot be restricted solely to message-content. We shall therefore be forced to reconsider the problem of the extreme power of the maxims.

Up to this point in the book, the term *assertion* has been used in two different ways. First I introduced (cf. p. 44) a pragmatic assertion mood operator, which conventionally indicates a belief in the truth of the proposition it attaches to. But then, in chapter 3, I argued that there were two uses of presupposition, one associated with statements and one associated with the speaker of an utterance, of which the latter stood in contrast to assertion in the sense of what the speaker is actually asserting. The first use of the term assertion, as a mood operator, applies to a sentence as a whole, the second, in contrast to presupposition, applies to some subpart of an utterance. In chapter 5, I argued that it was a confusion between these two separate senses of assertion that underlay the disagreement between Strawson and Russell. It might therefore seem that these two constructs should be distinguished not only theoretically but terminologically, as say entailment and implicature are.

There is however a parallel problem with imperatives and questions, as Searle has pointed out (1969, p. 162). In ordering someone to visit the King of France, you are not ordering him to cause the existence of the King of France, and in asking whether the King of France is married you are not (normally) querying the King of France's existence. In both cases, the command and the query respectively are restricted to a subset of the conditions necessary for the truth of the proposition in question. In the one case, the scope of the imperative is restricted to the relation between your audience and the King of France, viz. that your audience visit the King of France; in the other, the scope of the question is restricted to whether the man in question has the property of being married. If then we proliferate terminology for the two senses of assertion, we shall have also to do so for command and for question. But in this way, we shall not be providing any explanation of the homogeneous behaviour of the three utterance types. If we are to give any general account of this phenomenon, we must provide a uniform explanation of the varying scope interpretations associated with the three mood operators.

The explanation can be found in the concept of the Pragmatic Universe of Discourse and the associated maxim of quantity. In 8.3 I argued firstly that the Pragmatic Universe of Discourse was defined as a set of propositions which the speaker believed the hearer knew the speaker believed the hearer knew (the other three conditions being derivable from this) and that secondly, the maxim of quantity should be given greater content by adding a further maxim:

Only say '$*\psi p$' if, of n conditions minimally guaranteeing the truth of p, $\leqslant n-1$ conditions are members of the Pragmatic Universe of Discourse.

The relation between the mood operators as applied to the proposition as a whole and the part of the utterance which is in fact being asserted/queried/commanded is deducible from this maxim. The speaker believes the hearer knows (and knows that the speaker knows) a certain body of propositions (i.e. there is a Pragmatic Universe of Discourse) and in making a certain utterance '*ψp' he believes that the hearer, knowing the conventions of the language and hence the conditions for the truth of the proposition in question, will recognise a subset of those conditions as being part of that Pragmatic Universe of Discourse and hence neither assertible, deniable or queriable (without violating the quantity maxim),[1] and a second mutually exclusive subset of the conditions as being outside the Pragmatic Universe of Discourse. This latter set, he will interpret as being asserted, denied, commanded or queried. Thus what the speaker asserts in making some statement '⊢p' will be precisely those conditions of p which he believes are not in the Pragmatic Universe of Discourse since he believes the hearer does not know (or does not know that he knows) them. What he commands in saying '!p' will be those conditions of p that he believes are not currently true, and hence by definition are not part of the Pragmatic Universe of Discourse. What he questions in saying '?p' will normally be those conditions which he believes are not members of the Pragmatic Universe of Discourse, in this case not because the hearer does not know their truth value, but because he, the speaker, does not (though cf. p. 169). In each case, because the body of propositions which makes up the Pragmatic Universe of Discourse varies from context to context, the assertion-presupposition (or question-presupposition or command-presupposition) distribution for any sentence will vary according as the context varies (given the limits imposed by the semantic structure of the sentence in question). What now becomes self-evident is why the entailments on factive verbs and definite noun phrases (for example) were mistakenly construed as being necessarily part of what the speaker assumes (presupposes) as opposed to what he asserts. Since, as we have seen, both factive verbs and definite noun phrases generally implicate respectively that the proposition expressed by their complement and the proposition claiming existence of a specific referent are members of the Pragmatic Universe of Discourse except in particular co-ordinate environments, it follows by definition that in any assertion (whether negative or positive), question, or command, these propositions

[1] This subset may be empty.

would generally be assumed to be true. The mistake of presupposition supporters lay in setting down a requirement that such an assumption necessarily hold. As we have seen in much of the earlier discussion, this implication is context-dependent, and as such is not a semantic property of the sentence in question. On the contrary, the fluctuating nature of the assertion-presupposition, question-presupposition distribution in different utterances of the same sentence is a characteristic of pragmatic generalisations and is predicted naturally under this analysis. Furthermore the discrepancy in the presuppositional account of such pairs as *John is sick and Bill regrets that he is* and *Mary is coming to the party and Bill regrets that John is sick* (where only in uttering the latter would the speaker normally presuppose the truth of the complement – cf. 4.3.2) is naturally captured, since in the first sentence the proposition that John is sick is not part of the Pragmatic Universe of Discourse the speaker and hearer share. It is merely believed by the hearer to be believed by the speaker.

8.6.1 Speaker-presupposition, stress assignment and the maxim of relation. To have given a working definition of the utterance phenomena of assertion-presupposition, question-presupposition, etc., is not however the end of the story. As many writers have pointed out, there is a conventional correlation between stress assignment and the interpretation of the assertion-presupposition (positive or negative) and question-presupposition distribution. The stressed item is (roughly) interpreted as the sole item falling within the scope of the mood operator, everything else being assumed to be true. The problem as we have seen earlier (pp. 50–1) is that this phenomenon cannot be truth-conditional since it has no effect on the truth value of a statement in the positive case.[1] It therefore lies outside the domain of what I have argued is semantics. Yet Chomsky (1971) has argued that focus (or scope) of the question or negation is entirely predictable given the stress assignment, both in the case of normal and contrastive stress assignment. Two

[1] Actually this is a simplification, since in all opaque contexts, stress can lead to a change in the truth value of a statement (cf. Dretske 1972). I assume however that interpretations of opaque environments are like negation and contain a disjunct set of conditions (cf. 1.3.3), and that stress does not alter meaning in these cases. Rather, I shall argue, it provides a pragmatic means of drawing attention to those conditions which are construed as falling within the scope of the operator in question: cf. pp. 192–6. However, as Deirdre Wilson has pointed out to me, of the following two sentences, only the first is contradictory: *Like MOST bachelors, my husband likes chatty girls*; *Like most BACHELORS, my husband likes chatty girls*. These sentences stand as counter-examples to the analysis given here.

questions then arise: is this claim correct, and if so what is the nature of the rule which encapsulates it?

The claim Chomsky makes is that the presuppositions of the sentence can be read off by replacing the focused item (where the focus is any phrase containing the intonation centre) by a variable. Thus for example the presuppositions of the assertion *John didn't meet Mary in the garden* (with normal stress assignment on *garden*) are either that John met Mary somewhere (*in the garden* being the focus of negation), or that John met someone somewhere (*Mary in the garden* being focus), or that John did something (the entire verb phrase being the focus). I have already argued (pp. 22–3) that this claim is inadequate if stress is normally assigned on the grounds that the full range of scope possibilities is available with normal stress assignment and this range cannot be predicted by considering the phrase containing the intonation centre. However, if stress is contrastive (i.e. not placed on the final lexical item in a sentence), then the interpretation of the scope of negation or question is not in general left open, but is restricted to the lexical item (or phrase containing the lexical item) which is stressed. Since this phrase is often not the end-placed item, contrastive stress assignment will not therefore allow an interpretation in which every part of the sentence is interpreted as falling within the scope of negation, question, etc. Thus Chomsky's formulation of focus–presupposition correctly predicts that *The man in the GREEN coat didn't ask a question* has the following possible interpretations: either that *A man in some sort of coat asked a question* is presupposed (focus = Adjective), or that *Some man asked a question* is presupposed (focus = Prepositional Phrase) or that *Someone asked a question* is presupposed (focus = Subject). But these possibilities represent only a subset of the scope possibilities for this sentence, and do not include for example verb or verb phrase scope (where respectively the presuppositions would be *The man in the green coat did something with a question, e.g. answer one*, or *The man in the green coat did something, but not ask a question*). Presupposition in this sense is, as we have seen, that part of the semantic interpretation of a sentence which corresponds to propositions which are in the Pragmatic Universe of Discourse.

Now Chomsky's generalisation could be incorporated directly into the pragmatic framework elaborated here in the form of a pragmatic instruction:

For any utterance '*$*\psi p$', only assign stress within that syntactic construct which corresponds to conditions for the truth of p which are not in the Pragmatic Universe of Discourse.

Thus in the case of a question such as *Did JOHN kill Mary?*, if stress is assigned to *John*, the rule predicts that *John* will be the only constituent corresponding to conditions not in the Pragmatic Universe of Discourse assumed to be shared by the speaker and hearer, the remainder (viz. that *kill Mary* is true of someone) thus being construed as within it and hence assumed to be true. The same phenomenon applies, though more weakly, in the case of imperatives. *Play with the ball in the GARDEN* implies, as the rule predicts, that the fact that the hearer plays with the ball somewhere is assumed and not in question, but what is commanded is the place in which the audience is to play. Finally, negation. Take by way of example the utterance of *JOHN didn't kill Mary* with an approximate schematic semantic representation:

$$[A/J]X_1 \text{ v } [A/M]X_2 \text{ v } [A/CAUSE]X_1([DIE]X_2) \text{ v}$$
$$\quad (a) \qquad\quad (b) \qquad\qquad (c)$$
$$[CAUSE]X_1([A/DIE]X_2)^1$$
$$\qquad\qquad (d)$$

The rule says only assign stress to a condition (in the case of this utterance, (a)) which does not correspond to a member of the Pragmatic Universe of Discourse. One might thus assume that the other conditions in the representation (viz. (b)–(d)) are members of this Pragmatic Universe of Discourse, a result which would be counter to the actual interpretation of the sentence. However we already have a maxim 'Only say "$*\psi p$" if $\leqslant n-1$ of n sufficient conditions for the truth of p are members of the Pragmatic Universe of Discourse.' And if any one of the conditions (b)–(d) are members of the Pragmatic Universe of Discourse then this maxim is violated (since each is a sufficient condition for the truth of the utterance). On the assumption that the speaker is not violating this maxim, it thus follows that in obeying our new rule, a speaker would by saying *JOHN didn't kill Mary* be implying that all other sufficient conditions for its truth (viz. (b)–(d)) are not met and that therefore someone killed Mary.

As it stands, this rule is *ad hoc*: it does not fit in any natural way into the theory. It clearly is not a maxim of behaviour. So if such a rule is to be explained naturally within this pragmatic framework, either it

---

[1] Cf. pp. 131–3 for a more detailed representation of negative sentences containing *kill*. Cf. also p. 171 fn. 2 above.

should be deducible from the maxims and as such be a generalised conversational implicature, or it has to be listed as a conventional implicature. As we have already seen in the case of negation, compliance with this rule depends on complying with the maxims, and this suggests that the rule itself is derivable from the maxims. Notice moreover that contrastive stress has a second characteristic which is a criterion of conversational (as opposed to conventional) implicature. The implicatures consequent upon contrastive stress are cancellable. There is no contradiction in the following utterances, where the standard implicatures are contextually cancelled out:

(30) Though I don't wish to imply that Mary was necessarily hurt, what is absolutely certain is that JOHN didn't hurt Mary.
(31) Though we do not as yet know whether the mayor was murdered, what is absolutely certain is that his WIFE didn't kill him.
(32) Though we cannot be sure Smith was even in the hospital that night, the question we need the answer to is 'Was he at any time in the OPERATING theatre?'
(33) Though we cannot be sure that anyone was cheating, what we have to check is whether any LAW students had books with them in the exam room.

The evidence of these examples suggests that the implication derived from contrastive stress cannot be considered to be an inherent one in any case, since it is not a necessary part of the interpretation of sentences with contrastive stress assigned. On the contrary, however, such variability is a defining characteristic of a general conversational implicature.

How then could an implicature consequent upon stress assignment be derived from the maxims? There are two ways in which this could be done: either via a combination of the maxims of relation and quantity, or by setting up a new maxim. The problem with the first alternative is that in the reformulation I have given to the maxim, the notion of relevance relates solely to the pragmatic and semantic content of the utterance (and that of the preceding discourse). But stress is not part of the semantic or pragmatic content of the utterance and moreover its relevance relates only to the utterance itself and not (or not necessarily) to the preceding discourse. Yet if we loosen the restrictions imposed on the maxims and resurrect the old maxims, we face yet again the problem that they have very little content and therefore correspondingly little explanatory value. Suppose that we seek to demonstrate the conversational nature of implications consequent upon stress assignment by deducing them from an assumption of the maintenance of the old maxim of relation and the maxim of quantity. This could be done in the following way if we merely assume that stress is a conventional means of emphasis. Thus if a speaker S says *A MAN hit Mary*, he knows the hearer H will deduce that since stress is a conventional means of emphasising and since he S is committed to asserting *A MAN hit Mary* only if at least one of its conditions is not in the Pragmatic Universe of Discourse, his emphasis will only be relevant to his utterance of *A MAN hit Mary* if he is seeking to draw H's attention to one of these conditions. Since H assumes that S is obeying the maxim of relation, he therefore assumes that *man* corresponds to conditions (a set of conditions), one of which is not in the Pragmatic Universe of Discourse he and S share. Since moreover S has not drawn his attention to any other part of the utterance,[1] H will further deduce that S must be implying that that is the only part of the utterance which is not in the Pragmatic Universe of Discourse. H will therefore deduce that S is implicating that the remainder of the utterance *does* correspond to propositions in the Pragmatic Universe of Discourse. S will therefore be taken to be implicating that H knows that someone hit Mary, and that H knows that S knows that someone hit Mary.

The problem with this form of deduction is that the umbrella maxim 'Be relevant' in its most general interpretation does not strictly speaking apply to the concept of relevance here. 'Be relevant' is normally construed as the relation between utterance and event, or between utterance and utterance; but the notion of relevance used here is an intra-utterance notion, relating utterance form to utterance content. Thus if we are to claim an explanation of stress assignment in terms of the maxim of relation, not only do we have to return to the highly general original form, but we have to construe it as applying more generally still. I take it that in view of what I have argued earlier (pp. 155–6), this analysis is not therefore a possible one.

However, if we admit that the choice of the form of utterance may be relevant to an interpretation of that utterance (given that the choices

---

[1] Contrastive stress is not merely uniquely assignable within one sentence. Consider *BILL didn't KISS Mary* which implies (*a*) that someone kissed Mary, and (*b*) that Bill did something to Mary. Since it seems that in principle, any item could be contrastively stressed, the fact that an item is not stressed in an environment containing contrastive stress is adequate evidence for the hearer to deduce that anything which is not stressed corresponds to a proposition which is in the Pragmatic Universe of Discourse.

range only over those options which do not alter the meaning)[1] then a plausible alternative is to maintain the maxim of relation in its strict form, viz. 'Only say a sentence S_i if it either entails or implicates some sentence S_n which is also implicated by S_{i-1}' (cf. p. 160), and to add a further maxim of relation 'Make the form of your utterance relevant to its content.' With this second maxim of relation, the deduction of the implicature goes through exactly as before, but we have not reduced the predictive content of the other maxim of relation. A similar explanation will apply in the case of negation and question. Thus if S asks *Did a MAN hit Mary?* he knows that H knows that by the maxim of quantity he must be assuming that at least one of the propositions entailed by *A man hit Mary* is not in the Pragmatic Universe of Discourse and is the focus of S's query. Moreover, his emphasis on *man* will only be relevant to the content of his question if it corresponds to a condition which is being questioned. Since moreover, it is the only stressed item, S knows that H will deduce that it is the only item in question and that *hit* and *Mary* correspond to conditions which are part of the Pragmatic Universe of Discourse and hence not in question. H therefore takes it that by his utterance of *Did a MAN hit Mary?* S is implicating that H knows both that someone hit Mary and that S knows he knows this. On the basis of this form of explanation, I shall assume the existence of an additional Relation maxim, 'Make the form of your utterance relevant to its content.'

To see how this form of explanation has a natural general application, let us look at the sentences which G. N. Lakoff (1971b) posed as problem sentences for anyone not incorporating a notion of pragmatic pre-supposition into the grammar:[2] *John called Mary a lexicalist and then SHE insulted HIM.* As Lakoff points out, these are normally interpreted as implying to call someone a lexicalist is to insult them, and within the framework here we would expect that such an implication be derivable as a conversational implicature. And a deduction of this implication *via* the newly extended list of maxims is indeed possible, using the pattern of deduction necessary for an interpretation of more straightforward contrastive stress examples. In saying the sentence *John called Mary a lexicalist and then SHE insulted HIM*, S knows and intends that H will consider the following line of deduction. 'In saying any sentence of the form *P and Q* I know that S knows that by the maxim of relation, *P*

---

[1] Cf. its application in the case of the syntactic feature [+Def], pp. 179–80.
[2] Cf. p. 61 above.

and Q must bear some relation to each other (minimally that Q must implicate some proposition entailed by P – cf. 8.1). Moreover I know that in saying *SHE insulted HIM*, S is intending to imply (in accordance with the maxims of relation and quantity) that I already have prior knowledge that somebody was insulted, since *insult* is the only unstressed item in that conjunct. Yet I know that S believes I have no knowledge of this. Thus he appears to be breaking the maxims of relation and quantity in assigning contrastive stress in this way, since he knows the implication required is not satisfied. All these anomalies are however solved if I make one assumption – that to call someone a lexicalist constitutes an insult. Because on this basis I know that in saying *John called Mary a lexicalist* S would intend me to believe not only that John called Mary a lexicalist and someone called someone a lexicalist, but also that John insulted Mary. But *John insulted Mary* entails *Someone insulted someone*. S would therefore be intending that *John called Mary a lexicalist*, *Someone called someone a lexicalist*, *John insulted Mary* and *Someone insulted someone* should all become part of our common stock of knowledge – our Pragmatic Universe of Discourse. On this basis I would know that he intends that I shall further work out that of the propositions entailed by *Mary insulted John*, *Someone insulted someone* cannot be part of what he is asserting, since he would have intended by his previous utterance to guarantee that this proposition be part of our Pragmatic Universe of Discourse. But this is what S's stress assignment indicates. Thus if I make this assumption, S's stress assignment becomes entirely predictable and no longer constitutes a violation of the maxims of quantity and relation. I take it therefore that S is implicating that to call someone a lexicalist constitutes an insult.' Thus Lakoff's examples seem to have a natural explanation within this framework. The implication between *John called Mary a lexicalist and then SHE insulted HIM* and *To call someone a lexicalist is to insult them* will, accordingly, not have to be accounted for at the semantic level.

We have now seen how stress assignment and the consequent interpretation of questions, negative and positive assertions can be predicted within a Gricean framework, with the addition of one maxim. Since the addition of this maxim preserves the content of the other maxim of relation, I assume that taking this step strengthens the explanatory power of the theory. This is presumably preferable to allowing a generalisation of the single maxim of relation, which would guarantee a reduction in the explanatory adequacy of the concept of the Co-operative

Principle on which all my explanations have depended. I do not of course wish to imply in giving these Gricean deductions that no problems remain in providing an explicit pragmatic explanation of the phenomena considered in this section. In particular, there remain some examples of contrastive stress assignment (cf. p. 191 fn. 1 above) which appear to resist the type of analysis offered here. But at least it seems clear in principle that the interaction of stress and different sentence-types can be accounted for naturally along these lines.

8.7 *And* and the maxim of manner

I have so far restricted my attention to problems arising with the maxims of relation and quantity. In explaining the pragmatic behaviour of *and* however, I shall have to refer to the maxim of manner which has an over-all instruction 'Be perspicuous' (cf. p. 142). In chapter 4 I argued (against R. Lakoff) that the sequence of time implied in such sentences as *The police came in and we swallowed our cigarettes* was not a presuppositional implication and indeed not an inherent property of *and* at all since sentences not joined by *and* carried the same implication (cf. pp. 55–6). What explanation would such an implication have within a Gricean framework? It clearly cannot be a conventional implicature since this construct characterises inherent non-truth-functional properties of linguistic items, and we have already seen that this is not merely a property of *and*.[1] But it cannot be a conversational implicature either since in order to be so, it must be deducible from the maxims, and there is no obvious way in which this could be done. What solution is there? One possible solution is to suggest that the implication of time sequence is analogous to the implication on every statement that the speaker believes the proposition it expresses. On this view it would not be an implicature but a direct consequence of preserving the maxims straightforwardly. In the case of time sequence, the maxim one might invoke is the submaxim of manner 'Be orderly'[2] with the interpretation 'Unless you explicitly mark the time relation, make your narration of events reflect their sequence.' If such an interpretation of the maxim is justified, then the implication in many sentences of the form *P and Q* is automatically predicted. Moreover since sentences

[1] Cohen argues (1971, pp. 54–9) that this implication is not merely an inherent property of *and* but a truth-conditional one. His examples however conflate causality and time sequence, making the case appear stronger than it is.

[2] Cf. Cohen's report of the 1967/8 lectures by Grice (Cohen *ibid.*, p. 55).

joined by *or* or *if-then* do not constitute the 'narration of events' they will, predictably, not carry the implication in question.

Is this solution entirely *ad hoc?* The answer seems to be that in some respects it is, but others not. First, let us look at its disadvantages. The chief of these is that unlike the other maxims, it is not clear that a flagrant violation of this maxim would lead to a re-interpretation of the sentence uttered. Take as an example (34):

(34) Rob Roy rode away and jumped on his horse.

An utterance of this sentence could not I think be re-interpreted in such a way as to give the utterance a plausible interpretation (in the way that *You're the cream in my coffee* can). If this criticism is right, we thus have a maxim which does not take part in the interpretation of implicatures (at least by flagrant violation of the maxims). To this extent it is *ad hoc*. On the bonus side however, such a maxim provides an automatic explanation of the oddity of both (34) and (35).

(35) Rob Roy rode away. He jumped on his horse.

In both cases, S_1 entails that at time Q (such that Rob Roy was riding away) Rob Roy was on some animal (or at least some moving object). S_2 entails that at time P immediately prior to the time when he jumped on his horse, Rob Roy was not on his horse. If the maxim of manner ensures that utterances with no explicit time dependence between them will be interpreted as reflecting the sequence of events, then it ensures that (34) and (35) will be interpreted as contradictions. This is because S_2 entails that at a time P before the event at time Q that it describes, Rob Roy was not on his horse. But S_1, which by the maxim depicts the event at time P, describes Rob Roy as on some animal at that time. Thus at time P, Rob Roy is implied to be both on his horse and not on his horse. Hence the contradiction.

Like all the other maxims we have considered, this interpretation of 'Be orderly' raises yet again the two problems of (i) the power of the maxims, (ii) whether the maxims should in principle be so stated as to apply solely to the linguistic instances of communication (cf. p. 173). At every point, we seem to have found that it is possible to stretch the maxims so that they apply to anything, and yet with each extension of their predictive power, we reduce the chances of their possessing any explanatory power. In this particular case I have resisted this temptation, and have on the contrary interpreted a maxim so narrowly that it apply to a specific problem. But in doing so, I have given it a linguistically specified interpretation which it could be argued is too narrow. I shall return to these problems briefly in the final chapter. For the moment I assume that the implication of time sequence on certain utterances can be predicted without any difficulty by a particular specification of the maxim of manner.

8.8 *Even* remains

There is just one more problem left if the general Gricean framework is to provide some sort of explanation for all the non-truth-conditional 'presuppositional' phenomena which have emerged during this study – the problem of *even*. Let me briefly recapitulate the problem it creates. As Fraser points out in his discussion of *even* (Fraser 1971), a sentence such as *Even Max tried on the pants* has two implications specifically due to the presence of *even:*

(i) Other people tried on the pants.
(ii) One would not expect Max to try on the pants.

Neither of these is logically related to *Even Max tried on the pants* since if the sentence were uttered on an occasion in which neither (i) nor (ii) were true, it might still be true (even though odd) to say *Even Max tried on the pants*. But if this is so, then it appears that the conditions for the truth of *Even Max tried on the pants* and *Max tried on the pants* (and too *Max even tried on the pants*) are identical. Thus the theory of semantics outlined in previous chapters would predict that these three sentences are synonymous, and that *even* is a meaningless particle (since it does not affect the truth conditions of sentences it occurs in). Intuitively this seems unfortunate.

In one sense, however, this prediction is correct. It is correct in so far as it predicts that whatever contribution *even* makes to the sentences in which it occurs, this contribution is different in kind from the contribution most words make to sentence meaning. This is certainly so. In fact the properties of *even* are so odd that they do not naturally fit into the Gricean pragmatic framework either. One might expect that implications such as (i) and (ii) would constitute conventional implicatures – they certainly are not derivable in any natural way *via* the maxims. But these implications have a further characteristic which seems to militate against such an analysis – they are to some extent cancellable. Consider the following utterance:

(36) All the kids tried on something. Mary tried on a pair of trousers, Sue a long shawl. Even Max tried on a fancy tie. But then it's not really surprising. Now that his mother has married again, he joins in with things much more.

What does *even* contribute to this utterance of *Even Max tried on a fancy tie?* It is not at all clear. The utterance certainly does not imply that the speaker assumes that other people tried on a fancy tie. But nor is the speaker assuming that one would expect him not to try on a fancy tie. He is rather making the weaker assumption that some people (including the hearer?) might expect him not to try on a fancy tie. This type of problem can arise with every case of *even*. (37) presents a similar case.

(37) Each member of the group did one thing towards getting publicity: May wrote to her bank manager, Bill to his local newspaper. Adrian even wrote to the Prime Minister. But then I suppose it's not surprising when one considers how adventurous he is.

Here too, the speaker is clearly not intending to imply that Adrian did a number of things including writing to the Prime Minister. Nor is he implying that it is surprising that he did so. All he is implying is that his audience might expect Adrian's action to be surprising. Yet this implication is not itself a necessary property of *even*. There is nothing odd in saying (38).

(38) I know you won't find this surprising since you know John better than anyone but he's even read Aristophanes of Byzantium.

In this case, what seems to remain is the implication that John has read other things and that other people might find it surprising that John has read Aristophanes of Byzantium. Thus what we appear to be faced with is a disjunction of properties: *even* either implies that the constituent to which it is prefixed should be construed as one of a group[1] or that there is some element of surprise involved (either on the part of the speaker or on the part of the hearer or someone else). However if *even* is correctly characterised as having a disjunction of properties, it is then not obvious that this disjunction is not truth-conditional. On

[1] This statement is over-simplified. For a discussion of scope phenomena and *even*, cf. Fraser 1971, Anderson 1972, and also p. 18 fn. 1 above.

this view a sentence such as (39) would be a contradiction since it cancels out each of the possible interpretations.

> (39) I know neither you nor anybody else will find this surprising (and I certainly don't) but having never achieved anything ever before and without having done any work at all, John has even managed to pass the exams.

But is it? If it is, then an account of *even* can be stated within a truth-conditional framework. Moreover such an account would characterise why *even* was exceptional since it would be one of a small class of items[1] which have a disjunctive semantic representation. If it is not, then it constitutes an anomaly to the framework, and has to be listed as one of the few examples of conventional implicature. At this point, I must leave the conclusion open, but we shall return to it shortly when we assess the status of pragmatics within an over-all linguistic theory.

8.9 Illocutionary force: its status within pragmatics

Finally there is one general problem which I have more or less ignored throughout this book – that of illocutionary force. My earlier suggestion (pp. 41–2) that illocutionary force and the analysis of speech acts did not form part of semantics was on the ground that they provide all the problems of indeterminacy which render semantics non-predictable. But if concepts such as illocutionary force are to form part of a pragmatic theory, then we must be able to demonstrate that they are compatible with the pragmatic framework given here. Otherwise they will be problems which have merely been swept under the pragmatic carpet, and left there.

While I do not intend to give a detailed characterisation of this very large area, it can be quite straightforwardly shown that an analysis of illocutionary force is dependent upon a knowledge of what the speaker is (non-conventionally) implicating and therefore must be part of pragmatics. We have already seen that a sentence such as *Are they leaving soon?* may be used to convey either a command, a threat or a statement (cf. p. 41). For a further example, consider *I've got a headache*. This sentence can be used at least as a warning, a request (for advice or sympathy) or an apology. In order for an utterance of this sentence to constitute a warning for example, the speaker must reason that the

[1] For some other cases which might be handled this way, cf. chapter 9.

hearer will work out the relevance of the utterance on the basis that both speaker and hearer know, say, that when the speaker has a headache, he is normally very disagreeable and on the basis of this common assumption, the hearer will work out that the speaker is implicating that his company may be unpleasant and is thus giving the hearer prior warning. While this analysis is informal, it demonstrates none the less that the calculation of whether the statement is a warning is dependent on the implicatures of the utterance. This must be so since the illocutionary force relates directly not to the semantic content of the sentence used, but to the content of the message which the speaker is seeking to convey. At the very least then, it seems certain that the prediction of illocutionary force for any utterance can only be part of a pragmatic theory.

There is however a stronger claim possible which naturally accounts for the dependence of illocutionary force on the Co-operative Principle, as we shall see immediately. Both Cohen (1964) and Searle (1968) have pointed out that the distinction between illocutionary force and utterance meaning is not clear cut. While the utterance of *I've got a headache* construed as a warning may be said to have two distinguishable facets, its meaning and its illocutionary force, the performative statement does not: the utterance of *I warn you that I've got a headache* has the intention of warning the hearer as part of its meaning. Moreover, as Searle points out (p. 271) 'for every illocutionary act one intends to perform, it is possible to utter a sentence the literal meaning of which is such as to determine that its serious literal utterance in an appropriate context will be the performance of that act'. On the basis of this, both argue that the distinction between illocutionary force and utterance meaning is not well-founded and should be given up.[1] In the light of the deduction of warning that I gave on an utterance of *I've got a headache*, we can see why this distinction is so tenuous. Compare the first formulation with the following. S reasons in uttering *I've got a headache* that since both he and H know that when he has a headache he is very disagreeable, H will deduce that S is wishing to convey to H that his company is likely to be unpleasant and he is therefore implicating the statement *I warn you that I am likely to be unpleasant*. The only difference between the two formulations I have given is that in the first, the warning is not itself said to be an implicature, whereas in the latter the speaker is said to be implicating the performative statement *I warn you that*. . . Is the

[1] The solutions they offer are not however compatible.

difference between the two substantive? I think not, for reasons which are stated in detail by Cohen and Searle. Briefly, there is little justification for claiming that *I warn you that I've got a headache* is a specification of the illocutionary force of the utterance of *I've got a headache* rather than a specification of one part of the pragmatic meaning of that utterance, particularly since in the utterance of a full performative, the specification given is unquestionably part of the meaning of that utterance. If this is so, and the intended deduction of illocutionary force of the speaker's utterance is merely one type of implicature,[1] then it follows automatically that an account of the illocutionary force of utterances is part and parcel of an account of the pragmatic properties of a language.

This is not to suggest that the concept of illocutionary force is necessarily redundant, and few would be foolish enough to suggest that re-analysing illocutionary force in terms of implicature did more than re-label the problem. In any case such an account raises extra problems for the Gricean framework. It is not obvious that the implication of warning (or request, apology, etc.) is dependent on the Co-operative Principle in the sense that its deduction depends on an apparent violation of the maxims.[2] However it seems reasonably clear that implicatures in general arise even when maxims are not violated. There seems no reason to doubt for example that the implicature of the speaker's likely unpleasantness in the utterance of *I've got a headache* is just as plausible in answer to the question *How are you?* (when it would certainly be relevant and there need be little reason to suppose it untrue) as if it were uttered with flagrant disregard for relevance (for example in response to the greeting *Hello*). Thus the relation between the concept of implicature and the conversational maxims is not a problem specific to the incorporation of illocutionary force as one type of implicature but applies to the entire model.

Whatever problems this re-analysis of illocutionary force gives to the general concept of the Co-operative Principle, the general tenor of the argument remains unaltered. Both the arguments given by Searle and

[1] An argument against this conclusion is given by Schiffer 1972, p. 89, who claims that in order to know the illocutionary force of an utterance it is not enough to know what was meant by the sentence uttered, one must also know what it was meant *as*. If however I am right in saying that for every case where an utterance is construed 'as a warning' there is an equivalent analysis in which a performative statement (of warning) is construed as part of what is meant, then Schiffer's distinction falls to the ground.

[2] Cf. p. 143 for Grice's own characterisation of implicature.

Cohen and the close affinity between the deduction of illocutionary force and the deduction of implicatures suggest that illocutionary force on utterances is but one of the aspects of implicated meaning of utterances and is not different from it in kind.

8.10 Summary

In the course of chapters 7 and 8, I have concentrated on two main problems: (*a*) whether Grice's Co-operative Principle can be given sufficient constraints to constitute a non-vacuous theory of communication; (*b*) whether the framework so specified can account for the wide range of phenomena which have been given by various people at various times the label of presupposition.

What I hope that chapter 8 has unequivocally shown is that the phenomena often incorporated into semantics under an umbrella label of presupposition can naturally be explained within a framework which depends on a logically prior system of linguistic conventions and that these phenomena are thus not themselves part of the semantics of that system. The more tentative part of these chapters concerns the constraints on that pragmatic framework. It seems clear that there must be such constraints and what I have put forward can be seen as a first attempt to provide them.

There are in any case serious problems for a Grican theory of pragmatics, even in its most general form. One of these I have touched on: can the concept of implicature be defined as an assumption necessary to preserve the assumption of compliance with the pragmatic maxims? If the examples I considered in the preceding section are correct, then it seems that implicatures need not be restricted to apparent violations of the maxims. There is also the problem of how the subject of any conversation can legitimately be changed. If a Gricean theory is to be accepted as the only serious contender for a pragmatic theory, then problems such as these will have to be solved. I have not gone into them here simply because there have been more immediate and pressing problems.

More important perhaps than all these points of detail is the question of what status a pragmatic theory has within an over-all theory of language. It is this question that I shall take up in the final chapter.

9 Pragmatics and the competence–performance distinction

The main tasks of this book are now all complete. These were to set out as a preliminary a linguistic framework to provide a perspective within which all consequent arguments would be considered, and then to argue: (i) that the semantics of a natural language involves a statement of the conditions for the truth of all the sentences of that language (by a recursive finite procedure), (ii) that concepts pertaining to speakers' beliefs in uttering sentences are correctly excluded from that semantics by virtue of very general requirements on semantic theory, (iii) that the logic required within such a truth-conditional semantics is two-valued (containing the values true and false) and is not a presuppositional three-valued logic, (iv) that apparent counter-examples to these three hypotheses are naturally explained at a separate theoretical level, that of pragmatics, and thus do not in fact constitute counter-examples.

There would however be no justification whatever for assuming that there are now few remaining problems, even if my arguments are correct. Many, quite fundamental, problems remain at every stage. Within the semantic framework for example, even assuming that the Bierwisch semantic representation constitutes a justified linguistic level,[1] the problems of stating the inter-relation between this level and a model-theoretic semantics along the lines of Montague, Lewis, etc., remain entirely untouched. And within the pragmatic framework outlined by Grice, we have already seen that large problems remain. In any case, not all the data have been taken into account – I have not given a pragmatic explanation for some of the examples raised by Keenan. Since I could not pretend to solve all these problems within the bounds of a single book, I have concentrated my attention on those which seemed of primary importance. The others remain in need of a solution.

[1] Jerry Fodor argued in a lecture in London in May 1974 that there is no level of semantic representation.

There is, however, one further problem which must be taken up. Though I have considered in some detail the nature of a theory of pragmatics, I have not yet broached the question of what status such a theory should have within an over-all linguistic theory. In order now to be able to discuss this, let us first recapitulate the whole range of phenomena for which an explanation is demanded. First there is the central ('referential' or 'cognitive') meaning of sentences and words, which can, I have argued, be stated – with very few exceptions – in terms of truth conditions on sentences (or in the case of words, the contribution they make to such sets of truth conditions). The few putative exceptions are words like *but, even*, and *therefore* (but cf. pp. 213–18), whose contribution to sentence meaning does not appear to affect the truth conditions of sentences. Then there are the very general implications on sentences which I have argued cannot be seen as an inherent or necessary part of sentence meaning in the same way as truth-conditional properties, since these implications can be cancelled out without resulting in a contradiction. Finally there are the occasion-specific implications which depend on assumptions shared by particular speakers and hearers, and which may run counter to the standard message conveyed by utterances of that same sentence.

It seems to me that this range of data could be incorporated into a formal linguistic model in one of seven possible ways.

I (equivalent to the Lakoffs' position) The distinction between semantics and pragmatics could be disputed and the entire theory of sentence interpretation based on a number of different procedures within the semantic component of the competence model. Implicit in this formulation would be the claim that the disparity of the evidence just listed should be reflected directly in a non-homogeneous account of natural language semantics.

II (equivalent to the Kiparskys' and Fillmore's positions) Occasion-specific implicatures would be explained as performance phenomena; but all general implicatures, whether contradictable or not, would be predicted within the semantic component. This could be done in two ways: (*a*) by recognising the non-homogeneity of semantics (similar to the view I above), and predicting strict entailments and general implications by two separate procedures (cf. the Kiparskys' distinction between assertion and presupposition, 1970); (*b*) by generalising the concept of implication so that it apply regardless of whether the implication is cancellable or not (cf. Fillmore's use of presupposition, 1971). The distinction between semantics and pragmatics as I have drawn it is still disputed on both these positions: under position (*b*) semantic relations, though defined univocally, are not defined in terms of truth dependencies, and under position (*a*) the concept of natural language meaning is not defined univocally. As a consequence, in both cases, many implications which I have explained pragmatically fall under the domain of semantics.

III The distinction between semantics and pragmatics is maintained as I have defined it and a pragmatic component (in the form of a model of Grice's theory) is incorporated into the competence model (with inputs from all three components, syntactic, semantic, and phonological).

IV Semantics and pragmatics, as I have defined them, are formulated respectively within a competence and within a performance model – but with one important exception. Conventional implicatures, such as might be suggested for *but* and *even*, which are not cancellable in the same way as those of conversational implicatures, are listed in the lexicon (which otherwise specifies truth conditions for lexical items) with an *ad hoc* device indicating that they are not themselves truth-conditional.

V Pragmatics, along Gricean lines, is altogether formalised as a subpart of a theory of performance and the sole function of the semantic component of the competence model is to predict truth conditions on sentences and consequent entailments between sentences. This position can be maintained in two ways. Either conventional implicatures on *but* and *even* can be explained within performance (v*a*), or the problem which these items present is solved by claiming despite *prima facie* evidence to the contrary that their interpretation can be handled within a truth-based theory of meaning (v*b*). On the latter view, alternative v*b*, there is no need for a category of conventional implicature and the dichotomy of semantics and pragmatics corresponds exactly to that of competence and performance.

Now it is evident that the choice between the last three alternatives will depend solely on the status of items such as *but* and *even*. But before considering the category of conventional implicature, to which they seem to belong, let me take up each of the preceding alternatives. Since I discussed the consequences of adopting alternative I in some detail in chapter 4, I shall not consider this position further other than to reiterate what I said there that since such a theory has no predictive power, it cannot provide an acceptable solution.

What of the two alternatives listed under II? Alternative II(*a*) is similar to alternative I in so far as the non-homogeneity of the data is reflected in the semantic statement. Rather than disagree with this argument directly, let us consider how such non-homogeneity could be written into the theory. The performance model would presumably incorporate the Gricean maxims to explain occasion-specific implicatures, and these would therefore play no part in the competence model. The problem would thus concern phenomena such as the interpretation of *but, even, the* (as distinct from the indefinite article), factive verbs (in positive and negative environments) and stress assignment. In a Gricean framework, the first two of these have conventional (non-contradictable implicatures),[1] the last three general but contradictable implicatures. One possibility is to specify such implications as part of the lexical entry. Thus *but* might have an entry indicating that it always conveys some form of contrast between the two elements it conjoins. However there has to be some explicit indication that entries such as this are different in kind from other semantic components since setting up this form of semantic component must not make any standard predictions about the behaviour of the item in question. Thus, for example (as was pointed out in 4.1), no contradiction arises if *but* conjoins two sentences which are entirely non-contrastive (a combination which would be contradictory if the component in question were truth-conditional). Furthermore in the case of *the* or the factive verbs involving implications which are cancellable, there will have to be some *ad hoc* statement that these implications are normal but not necessary implications.

One way round these problems is to postulate a distinction for cases such as these between their meaning and conditions for their use. Thus *but* could have two subsections to the semantic specification of its lexical entry: a statement of its meaning and a statement for conditions on its use – viz. that the speaker imply that there be some form of contrast between the two conjuncts. But this formulation not only meets exactly the same difficulties that face a separate theory of pragmatics, but appears to be no more than a terminological variant of it. Notice that within this partially truth-conditional framework, if *even* has no

---

[1] Though cf. pp. 201–21 and pp. 216–18 for a discussion of the possibility of a truth-conditional account of these items.

truth conditions associated with it, it will have no meaning assigned to it in this framework either; it merely has conditions for its use. Both formulations would therefore predict that *John was there* and *Even John was there* do not differ in meaning. It thus seems that none of the problems for pragmatics is avoided. Moreover, there is no explanation whatever within this putative partially truth-conditional semantics for the fact that some of these non-truth-conditional properties (such as those on *the*) are cancellable while others are not. And it is not obvious how this could be captured. It therefore seems reasonable to conclude that the non-homogeneity of sentence interpretations is captured by setting up the distinction between semantics and pragmatics and it is therefore redundant to introduce such non-homogeneity into the semantic formalisation itself.

Alternative ii(*b*) constitutes a more radical criticism of the views I have put forward. On this view, the central importance of entailment is doubted and a weaker relation (to cover entailments and sentence-pairs such as *I didn't regret going, I went*; *Even John hit Mary, Other people hit Mary*; etc.) is defined in its place. A supporter of this view might argue that in certain crucial cases I have distorted the evidence so that the issue appears more clear-cut than it in fact is. For example, in chapter 4 I pointed out that sentences containing *pretend* such as *John pretended that he was sick* did not entail *John was not sick* despite a very general implication that this was so. Since the argument in chapters 4 and 5 did not depend on the nature of this implication, I did not pursue the matter further there. But it might be argued that this is one of many implications which linguistic semantics should wish to predict and if this relation is not reducible to a truth dependence, so much the worse for truth-dependent semantics. Verbs such as *criticise* and *accuse* provide further examples, and it is no coincidence that Fillmore chose this group of examples in seeking to attack a componential approach to semantics. I argued in 4.2 for example that a sentence such as *John criticised Mary for taking his books* did not presuppose that she took them, but rather entailed the weaker statement *John was assuming that Mary took his books*, whether or not she in fact did, and whether he believed it or not (cf. examples (18) and (20)). Now such a claim might be countered by the criticism that the inclusion of assumptions (as a primitive?) in the formal statement of *criticise* is merely an *ad hoc* device to avoid recognising the need for a weaker implication between sentence pairs such as *John criticised Mary for taking his books* and

Mary took his books. On this view, to formalise this relation as an entailment between *John criticised Mary for taking his books* and *John was
assuming that Mary took his books* is a confusion of a metalinguistic
statement and a statement of the object language. Confirmation of this
general view might be sought by pointing out that *even* provides no
anomaly in a system based on a weak (undefined?) form of implication.
Even only provides a problem if entailments are to be predicted, since
it is precisely the set of entailments of a sentence to which it is attached
that *even* appears not to affect.

   This form of criticism is not, however, I think justified. Notice that
by seeking to confirm or refute hypotheses of meaning by the evidence
of contradictions, we successively refine our analyses of meaning so
that they make exactly the predictions required. So for example the
observation that the sentence *John pretended that Mary was sick* does
not entail that Mary was sick merely indicates that the analysis of
pretend is more complicated than the initial hypothesis suggested. A
similar procedure applied in the case of *criticise* and *accuse*. In contrast
to this, a theory of meaning based on some loosely defined umbrella
term of implication would either not be able to make predictions of any
sort since it would not distinguish between necessary and possible
implications, or it would be of such general application (cf. the various
uses of the term *presupposition* in chapter 4) that its explanatory power
would be nil. Furthermore, and more seriously, to base analyses on
general implications rather than on necessary implications leads
inevitably to shoddy results since as in the case of *accuse*, and *criticise*
(and indeed *pretend*), general implications lead to approximate and
untestable analyses (verifiable only by speakers' hazy intuitions as to
what constitutes part of a sentence's meaning) rather than exact and
testable ones. Thus the existence of implications on utterances which
do not extend to all uses of that sentence does not seem to me to provide
any evidence for the need to incorporate some looser form of implication
into semantics, either in the form of alternative II(*a*) or the stronger
alternative II(*b*) – particularly since, as we have already seen, the general
implications on negative factive sentences, on definite noun phrases,
etc., can be given an explanation by reference to pragmatic constructs
such as the Co-operative Principle and its maxims which are, by definition, logically posterior to a linguistic system.

   There remain alternatives III, IV and V, each preserving much more
closely the dichotomy that I have assumed in previous chapters of this

thesis. Alternative III must, I think, be dismissed for the following reason. If a competence model was envisaged as containing a pragmatic component (dependent on information from the other three components of the grammar) then it would automatically become a matter of one's linguistic knowledge that people generally speak the truth and stick to the point. In other words, 'Do not say what you believe to be false' and 'Be relevant' would become rules of one's competence. But the content of these rules and the way in which they apply are quite unlike any rules of either the syntactic, semantic or phonological component. In particular, the interpretations the maxims provide may have an indeterminacy which is quite unlike the outputs of the three existing components of the model. On the contrary, the model is committed to providing a fully determinate syntactic, semantic, and phonological specification to the sentences it generates. In fact, all the problems which necessitated the delimitation of semantics to exclude speaker-belief constructs – the most important being the loss of predictive power – immediately return if pragmatics is incorporated into the model of competence. These reasons suggest that the pragmatic maxims are not part of the central competence model but must rather be part of a theory of performance.

One rejoinder might be made to this conclusion. In chapters 7–8 I went to considerable lengths to constrain the notions of informativeness and relevance so that the Gricean maxims might acquire at least some predictive power. It might however be argued that in doing so I have committed myself to incorporating some Gricean concept of pragmatics into a linguistic competence model, since the revised maxims make reference largely to the specific semantic and pragmatic content of messages and not to more general concepts (cf. in particular the postulation of a second maxim of Relation on p. 196 to account for stress phenomena and the interpretation of the maxim of Manner in connection with *and* on pp. 198–9). Thus the maxims only apply to linguistic behaviour and no longer constitute conventions on social behaviour in general as Grice appears to have intended them to. This rejoinder is not I think valid. Remember – the point of the increased specificity of the maxims was to increase their content so that they became less vacuous. If the rejoinder suggested here were correct, it would seem that a necessary condition on performance theories is that they be so general as to guarantee vacuity. In any case there is no *a priori* reason why performance constructs should not refer to linguistic constructs. On the contrary, there is evidence that they must. If as Bever suggests (Bever 1970) there are perceptual strategies associated with the understanding of constructions, and if his formulation of such strategies is even partially correct, then it seems certain that whatever form an over-all theory of performance might take, it must make reference to specific linguistic constructs.[1] The assumption behind such a criticism of the revised maxims thus seems to be false.

In suggesting that the maxims must be part of a theory of performance rather than the exclusively linguistic model, I have still not closed the door on alternative IV, though it may seem so at first glance. What is at issue here is not the general but contradictable implications on definite noun phrases or factives discussed in chapter 8. The three alternatives IV, v*a* and v*b*, are agreed that anything which can be explained by virtue of the maxims must be part of the domain of performance, since the maxims do not constitute linguistic rules. And so we must now take up in more detail the problem of those implications which are apparently inherent properties of the word in question but which appear not to be truth conditional. We have already seen (p. 145) that not only do these seem to be counter-examples to a truth-conditional semantics but they are also, in effect, counter-examples to a Gricean pragmatics since they neither fall within the domain of his meaning$_{nn}$ nor are they explicable by reference to the maxims of the Co-operative Principle. These then are the examples which do not fit satisfactorily into the semantics-pragmatics dichotomy and which in addition cause pragmatics (if they be part of pragmatics) to apply across the competence-performance distinction.

In assessing these examples, the first question to ask is 'How big is the list?' Of the problems which have arisen in all that precedes, just three appear to constitute possible conventional implicatures – the implications of *but*, *even*, and *therefore*. The last, *therefore*, was used by Grice as a standard example of this form of implication and I bowed to this judgement in using it in chapter 7 (p. 145). However the validity of this analysis is questionable. Consider what a statement of the meaning of *therefore* would have to indicate. To give the meaning of *P and therefore Q* one would have to give the set of conditions guaranteeing the truth of *P and Q* together with a condition specifying, roughly, that *Q* follows from *P*. If this last condition is not truth-

[1] Cf. also Katz and Bever 1974.

conditional, it should not affect the truth value of two sentences it conjoins. But consider the following:

(1) If Bill hit Mary and therefore she was covered with bruises, she will have won her suit for damages.

Presumably we are agreed that this statement will be true if both antecedent and consequent have the same truth value, whether true or false, and false if the antecedent is true and the consequent false. Now suppose we envisage a situation such that (i) Bill did hit Mary, (ii) Mary was covered in bruises but none of them caused by his hitting her – she got them from falling off her bicycle in the rush hour, (iii) she did not win her suit for damages. That is to say, each of the separate claims made by the antecedent is true except for the condition expressed by means of *therefore*. Now if *therefore* does not contribute to the truth conditions of the sentences in which it occurs we would expect (1) to be false in the situation specified. But if on the contrary it does affect the truth-value assignment, then since the causal connection asserted is not fulfilled in the particular state of affairs, we would expect (1) to be true. And so, I think, it is. Consider also (2)

(2) If it's not true that Bill hit Mary and therefore she's covered in bruises, then she will have given up her suit for damages.

in conjunction with a situation in which (i) and (ii) hold as before – Bill hit Mary but the bruises she has have nothing to do with his hitting her – and this time, she sues him. That is, the claim made by the conjuncts in the antecedent are both true though they are not causally connected. Thus if *therefore* has no contribution to make to a truth-conditional statement, the antecedent is false, since the conjunction is preceded by negation. If, however, *therefore* makes a contribution to the statement's set of truth conditions, then the conjunction of *P and therefore Q* will in this case be false, and so the whole antecedent true. The consequent is false. If the implication on *therefore* is truth-conditional, we would predict that in this state of affairs, (2) will be false. If *therefore* only provides a conventional implicature on the other hand, we would predict that (2) will be true (both antecedent and consequent being false). Though one's intuitions have to work hard at this level of logical complexity, it seems certain that given the state of affairs outlined, (2) is false.

This example is interesting for a different reason. (2) provides an example in which the implication induced by *therefore* falls within the scope of negation. If this property is truth-conditional as statements (1) and (2) suggest, this is just as one would expect, since the rule interpreting negatives is a semantic rule. If, however, the implication were pragmatic, then one might expect that such a property should not be subject to a semantic rule such as negation. This therefore provides independent confirmation of the truth-conditional nature of *therefore*.

So the list of exceptions brought up during the course of the book is reduced at least to two – *but*, and perhaps *even*. Are there any other exceptions to a truth-conditional account which should be added to this list? Wilson (forthcoming) argues that there are several. She suggests for example that the pair *deprive* and *spare* differ only in that one has a general non-truth-conditional implication that it is bad to withhold the object in question, and the other the contrary implication that it is good.

(3) She deprived her children of love.

(4) She spared her students a lecture on Generative Semantics.

Thus (3) implies that it is bad not to give one's children love, (4) that it is good not to give students lectures on Generative Semantics. That such implications are not truth-conditional she argues on the strength of their being cancellable in positive sentences. Moreover this cancellation has the peculiar property that an alternative implication immediately replaces the cancelled implication. Thus if a speaker claims (3) but explicitly denies that he believes it to be bad to withhold love from one's children, the implication will be that the hearer, or the object deprived, or any interested party, will believe that it is a bad thing to deprive one's children of love. In this connection, notice the difference between (3) and (5) which does not imply that the speaker holds the relevant opinion nor that the subject of the sentence does, nor that the hearer does. Rather it implies that the object of the sentence does.

(5) She deprived her children of sweets because she knew, like us, that sweets were bad for them.

This type of phenomenon she argues is not an isolated one, but turns up in several cases, including *but*. If a belief in the contrast between *P* and *Q* is denied by some speaker claiming *P but Q*, then an alternative implication that someone else believes that there is such a contrast immediately takes the place of the original implication.[1]

Now we have already seen evidence of this kind in connection with

[1] For a much fuller discussion, cf. Wilson (forthcoming).

even (8.8). Since the phenomenon seems to be more widespread than at first appeared, it is arguable that it must be accounted for within a truth-conditional framework if the claim that the semantics of natural language is exclusively truth-conditional can be maintained. There is I suggest one possible solution. In all sentence semantic representations that we have considered so far, the interpretation of the argument is bound in the manner of variable-binding in standard logic. But in these cases here, the interpretation of who the particular predicate applies to is open: it can be the speaker, the hearer, the subject of the sentence, the object (where these are relevant), or some other interested party, or even merely the public at large. One might therefore suggest that the level of semantic representation requires the use of a device parallel to the use of empty nodes in syntax, in this case the use of unbound variables in the semantic representation of sentences. The statement made by any sentence containing such variables would then be true if, other conditions being satisfied, there were any arbitrary individual who met the required condition. On this view, one of the truth conditions of (3) would be that 'X believes that it is bad not to give children love.' It would then be a pragmatic matter to interpret that variable appropriately. If this were a possible analysis of this range of phenomena, notice that *even* and *but* need no longer constitute counter-examples to the general restriction of semantics to the statement of truth conditions. *P but Q* for example would not be semantically identical to *P and Q* since it would have the extra condition that 'X believes *P and Q* contrast.' And *even P* would have an analogous condition that 'X believes *P* surprising.' I shall not attempt to give the details of the account more formally since, as Wilson has herself pointed out to me, there is at least one serious problem associated with it: open formulae are not standardly well-formed formulae and are not therefore assigned a truth value within a formal logic. This being so, it would seem that sentences whose semantic representations involve an open formula cannot be assigned truth conditions either. It is not entirely clear to me whether this is a fundamental objection or whether it constitutes a potential point of divergence between standard logic and the requirements on the logical form of natural language. I shall therefore leave the position open.

Notice, however, that the predictions made by such an analysis are at least partially confirmed. As one would anticipate of a truth-conditional element, the implication on *deprive* (and *spare*) can undoubtedly be included within the scope of negation:

(6) She didn't deprive her students of a lecture on Generative Semantics – she spared them it.

(7) She didn't deprive her children of sweets – sweets aren't good for them.

The interpretation of *even* in negative sentences is more complicated, though the observation also holds here. Recall that in 8.8 I suggested that *even* be analysed as a disjunction of the interpretation that the item to which *even* is attached[1] be construed as one of a group and of the interpretation that somebody find the proposition stated surprising. Now the former of these implications does appear to interact with negation (and question):

(8) The Vice-Chancellor didn't even resign.

(8) has two possible interpretations:[2] one in which the interpretation that the Vice-Chancellor did other things is unaffected, one in which it is – equivalent respectively to 'It is not the case that the Vice-Chancellor even resigned' and 'It is even not the case that the Vice-Chancellor resigned'. Compare (8) with (9).

(9) Did Bill even hit Mary?

This can either be interpreted as assuming that he did other things to her and asking whether one of the things was hitting her, or it can be interpreted as asking whether he so much as hit her. This disjunction of interpretations is brought out most clearly with items which induce opposite likely interpretations:

(10a) John didn't even torture his brother's wife.

(10b) John didn't even flirt with his brother's wife.

(11a) Did John even torture his brother's wife?

(11b) Did John even flirt with his brother's wife?

Since this implication on *even* does interact with the truth-based rule of negation, it seems plausible to suggest that it is itself a truth-conditional component of meaning. Similarly with the implication that 'X believes it is bad not to give students a lecture on Generative Semantics' in *Joan deprived her students of a lecture on Generative Semantics*. The status of 'X believes *P* surprising' as a possible condition for the truth of *even P* is less clear-cut. If (8) is true by virtue of the Vice-Chancellor having done nothing, not even resign, then there is an accompanying

---

[1] Cf. p. 201 fn. 1 above.
[2] There are of course other possible interpretations, but these are not relevant.

possibility of its being surprising to someone that he has not done so. In the other interpretation – a straight denial of *The Vice-Chancellor even resigned* – the interpretation of surprise does not seem to arise at all. This pattern repeats itself in (10a)–(11a). While this might be taken as evidence of the truth-conditional basis of the implication (the claim being that when there is no interpretation of surprise, this implication lies within the scope of negation), it can hardly be said to be strong evidence. With *but*, the evidence is even more difficult to evaluate. Can $-(P\ but\ Q)$ be interpreted as 'It is false that $P\ and\ Q$, and it is false that X thinks $P\ and\ Q$ contrast'? It certainly cannot be interpreted as 'It is true that $P\ and\ Q$, and it is false that X thinks $P\ and\ Q$ contrast'. Consider in this connection (12).

(12) It's not true that John hit Bill but Bill didn't hit John – Bill did hit John.

Can we say in this case, on the ground that the element of contrast between the conjuncts (positive-negative) is denied, that the implication of contrast is included within the scope of negation? If we can, then this suggests that even this implication is after all truth-conditional. If not, then it is not. The evidence in these cases is therefore far from unambiguous – either in favour of a truth-conditional analysis or against it. And until we can solve the problems associated with a formal representation of the implications in question, I see no immediate hope of any more substantial conclusions.

There is however yet another problem which I have not tackled at all in this book, which Wilson argues is a particularly important case of a non-truth-conditional implication – the problem of counterfactuals. It is well-known that counterfactuals generally imply the falsehood of both antecedent and consequent; but, as Karttunen (1971d) and Thomason (1973) have pointed out, these implications are not truth dependencies since they can be cancelled out. Wilson argues that though not truth-conditional, these implications are undeniably semantic. I am not however sure that this issue is at present a decidable one either. The difficulty posed by the semantics of counterfactuals rests, I suggest, at least to some extent on our ignorance about the semantic analysis of tense: until we have some means of deciding what analysis a sentence such as *The singer would have been a success* should have, there is very little decisive that we can say about sentences such as *If the accompanist had been competent, the singer would have been a success*. Given this state of ignorance, almost any analysis is possible. Thus a Gricean account of the implication on counterfactuals might run as follows. A speaker knows that an implication of future action and of perfected action cannot be simultaneously attributed to the same action. Yet the consequent of a counterfactual contains a tense form (*will* + past + perfect) which implies just such a contradiction. This being so, the speaker knows that the hearer will assume that he must be trying to convey some other information, additional to that inherent in the logical conditional, which will resolve this anomaly. But tense contradictions, unlike lexical contradictions, are not interpretable metaphorically. So the only possible implication that the speaker could be conveying in using a contradictory tense specification is that the consequent is indeed false. On the assumption that this is so, the only way the speaker can be committed to the truth of what he is saying is if he also believes the antecedent is false. With the extra assumption that the consequent is false, there is no longer any contradiction in what the speaker intends to convey and since moreover if this is so then he must by the maxim of quality be implying that the antecedent is false, the speaker knows that in uttering a counterfactual conditional, his hearer will – other things being equal – interpret his utterance as implying that both antecedent and consequent are false. Now I do not wish to claim that there is any special merit in this Gricean form of deduction. What it does suggest however is that before the problem of counterfactuals can be solved, a great deal of work needs to be done on the problem of tense. In the meantime counterfactuals remain a problem for everyone. The over-all conclusion from Wilson's examples is therefore I suggest an open one. Given the various solutions which can be put forward, it is by no means obvious that the list of conventional implicatures needs to be extended. On the contrary the discussion has tended to show that at least a plausible case can be made for the view that the set of conventional implicatures does not contain any members at all. But if this is so, then the distinction between the alternatives IV, VA, and VB listed at the beginning of the chapter simply evaporates.

So we are finally left with a measure of uncertainty. Given the present lack of any real understanding about the relevant phenomena, the evidence remains ambivalent between three alternatives. Either the properties of items such as *but* and *even* are only explained at the performance level and not as an inherent part of the formal system at all (VA). Or these properties are merely arbitrarily listed in the grammar with some *ad hoc* characterisation of their exceptional nature (IV). Or we have to justify a truth-conditional account of these properties, which are ones that have proved most troublesome to such an account (V*b*). Now the first of these three alternatives, alternative V*a*, is not I think a serious competitor for independent reasons. Performance conventions and constraints are in general not arbitrary in the way that linguistic conventions are: it is not the case that in some societies people generally tell lies as a basis for communication, and it would indeed be surprising to find a society which found centre-embedded constructions easier to understand than co-ordinated constructions. Yet the conventions for the use of *but* and *even* are arbitrary in just the same way as any other linguistic sign: it is hardly a function either of the structure of the English brain or of our society that *even* and *but* have the interpretations they do. If then we were to include the interpretation of items such as *even* and *but* within the umbrella of performance, we should have to distinguish this type of implication from all other performance conventions. For this reason, I think the choice is restricted to a decision as to whether or not the phenomena which do not fit easily into a truth-conditional framework are in fact exceptions or merely constitute areas where our knowledge of the semantic properties in question is insufficient to enable us to unravel the complexity of the truth-conditional account required.

Which of these two solutions will turn out to be correct, I now leave the reader to lay bets on for himself. To leave this one conclusion open is not of course to suggest that no conclusions can be drawn. On the contrary, what is agreed in both alternative solutions is that any phenomena which can be explained by the maxims of the Co-operative Principle, however intuitively conventional they may seem, must be seen as determined by conventions of performance, and thus not part of the competence model. So, despite the difficulty presented by a few border-line cases, the evidence accumulated through this book leads unerringly to two conclusions: (*a*) that Grice's explanation of communication, as extended and modified here, provides at least a first formulation of some data that a theory of performance will have to account for, and at most the first steps towards a theory of pragmatics as part of a theory of performance; and (*b*) that many of the phenomena often thought to be explicable in terms of the internal properties of the formal system of a linguistic model – such as scope variation in negation and question, and the interdependency of scope and stress – are in fact naturally accounted for only as a subpart of a theory of performance incorporating the Gricean theory of communication. It remains to be seen what formal representation can be provided to give serious content to the theory of pragmatics I have been pressing for here. In particular, for example, I have said nothing about the initial translation from a truth-conditional semantic statement into a Gricean pragmatic statement (of meaning$_{nn}$) (cf. 7.1). But problems such as this, and indeed many others, I must leave for another time.

Bibliography

Alston, W. P. (1964). *Philosophy of Language*. Englewood Cliffs, N.J.

Anderson, S. R. (1972). 'How to get *even*', *Language*, **48**, 893–906.

Annear, S. (1965). 'English and Mandarin Chinese: definite and indefinite determiners and modifying structures'. In *Project on Linguistic Analysis Papers*. University of Ohio.

Apostel, L. (1971). 'Further remarks on the pragmatics of natural languages'. In Bar-Hillel, Y. (ed.) *Pragmatics of Natural Languages*, 1–34, Reidel, Holland.

Austin, J. L. (1962). *How to Do Things With Words*. Clarendon Press, Oxford.

Baker, A. J. (1956). 'Presupposition and types of clause', *Mind*, **65**, 368–78.

Baker, C. L. (1966). 'Definiteness and Indefiniteness in English'. Unpublished M.A. thesis. University of Illinois.

Bar-Hillel, Y. (1954). 'Indexical expressions', *Mind*, **63**, 359–79.

Barrett, R. B. and Stenner, A. J. (1971). 'On the myth of the exclusive "or"', *Mind*, **79**, 116–21.

Bartsch, R. and Vennemann, T. (1972). *Semantic Structures*. Athenäum Verlag, Frankfurt.

Bendix, E. H. (1966). *Componential Analysis of General Vocabulary*. Mouton.

Bever, T. G. (1970). 'The cognitive base for linguistic structures'. In Hayes, J. R. (ed.) *Cognition and the Development of Language*, 279–362. Wiley and Sons.

Bierwisch, M. (1969). 'On certain problems of semantic representation', *Foundations of Language*, **5**, 153–84.

(1970). 'Semantics'. In Lyons, J. (ed.) *New Horizons in Linguistics*, 166–84. Penguin.

(1971). 'On classifying semantic features'. In Steinberg, D. D. and Jakobovits, L. A. (eds.) *Semantics*, 410–35. Cambridge University Press.

Bloomfield, L. (1933). *Language*. Holt, Rinehart & Winston.

Cassin, C. E. (1970a). 'Russell's discussion of meaning and denotation: a re-examination'. In Klemke, E. D. (ed.) *Essays on Bertrand Russell*, 256–72. University of Illinois Press.

(1970b). 'Russell's distinction between the primary and secondary occurrence of definite descriptions'. In Klemke, E. D. (ed.) *Essays on Bertrand Russell*, 273–84, University of Illinois Press.

Caton, C. E. (1959). 'Strawson on referring', *Mind*, **68**, 539–44.

Chomsky, A. N. (1957). *Syntactic Structures*. Mouton.

(1965). *Aspects of the Theory of Syntax*. MIT Press.

(1969). 'Remarks on nominalization'. In Jacobs, R. A. and Rosenbaum, P. S. (eds.) *Readings in English Transformational Grammar*, 184–222. Ginn & Co.

(1971). 'Deep structure, surface structure and semantic interpretation'. In Steinberg, D. D. and Jakobovits, L. A. (eds.) *Semantics*, 183–216. Cambridge University Press.

(1972). 'Some empirical issues in the theory of transformational grammar'. In Peter, P. S. (ed.) *Goals of Linguistic Theory*, 63–130. Prentice-Hall.

Clark, M. (1971). 'Ifs and hooks', *Analysis*, **32**, 33–9.

Cohen, D. (1973). 'On the mis-representation of presuppositions', *Glossa*, **7**, 21–38.

Cohen, L. J. (1964). 'Do illocutionary forces exist?', *Philosophical Quarterly*, **14**, 118–37.

(1971). 'Some remarks on Grice's views about the logical particles of natural language'. In Bar-Hillel, Y. (ed.) *Pragmatics of Natural Languages*, 60–8. Reidel.

Curry, H. B. (1953). 'Mathematics, syntactics and logic', *Mind*, **62**, 172–83.

Davidson, D. (1967). 'Truth and meaning', *Synthese*, **17**, 304–23.

Dretske, F. I. (1970). 'Epistemic operators', *The Journal of Philosophy*, **67**, 1007–23.

(1972). 'Contrastive statements', *The Philosophical Review*, **81**, 411–37.

Dummett, M. (1958/9). 'Truth', *Proceedings of the Aristotelian Society*, **59**, 141–62.

(1973). *Frege Philosophy of Language*. Duckworth.

Fillmore, C. J. (1968). 'The case for case'. In Bach, E. and Harms, R. (eds.) *Universals in Linguistic Theory*, 1–88. Holt, Rinehart & Winston.

(1969). 'Types of lexical information'. In Kiefer, F. (ed.) *Studies in Syntax and Semantics*, 109–37. Dordrecht.

(1971). 'Verbs of judging: an exercise in semantic description'. In Fillmore, C. J. and Langendoen, D. T. (eds.) *Studies in Linguistic Sematics*, 273–89. Holt, Rinehart & Winston.

Fodor, J. (1970). 'Three reasons for not deriving "kill" from "cause to die"', *Linguistic Inquiry*, **1**, 429–37.

Fodor, J. and Garrett, M. (1966). 'Some reflections on competence and performance'. In Lyons, J. and Wales, R. J. (eds.) *Psycholinguistics Papers*, 135–54. Edinburgh University Press.

Fodor, J. and Katz, J. J. (eds.) *The Structure of Language*. Prentice-Hall.

Fraser, B. (1971). 'An analysis of "even" in English'. In Fillmore, C. J. and Langendoen, D. T. (eds.) *Studies in Linguistic Semantics*, 151–78. Holt, Rinehart & Winston.

Frege, G. (1892). 'Über Sinn und Bedeutung'. Translated in Geach, P. and Black, M. (1966). *Translations from the Philosophical Writings of Gottlob Frege*, 56–78. Blackwell, Oxford.

(1918–19). 'The thought: a logical inquiry'. Translated by Quinton, A. M. and M. (1956). *Mind*, **65**, 289–311.

Gale, R. M. (1970). 'Negative statements', *American Philosophical Quarterly*, **7**.3, 206–17.

Garner, R. (1971). '"Presupposition" in philosophy and linguistics'. In Fillmore, C. J. and Langendoen, D. T. (eds.) *Studies in Linguistic Semantics*, 23–42. Holt, Rinehart & Winston.

Geach, P. T. (1958–9). 'Russell on meaning and denoting', *Analysis*, **19**, 69–72.

(1965). 'Assertion', *The Philosophical Review*, **74**, 449–65.

Geach, P. T. and Black, M. (eds.) (1966). *Translations from the Philosophical Writings of Gottlob Frege*. Blackwell, Oxford

Geiss, M. L. and Zwicky, A. M. (1971). 'On invited inferences', *Linguistic Inquiry*, **2**, 561–6.

Gordon, D. and Lakoff, G. N. (1971). 'Conversational postulates'. In Adams, D. *et al.* (eds.) *Papers from the Seventh Regional Meeting of the Chicago Linguistic Society*, 63–84. University of Chicago.

Green, G. (1968). 'On *too* and *either*, and not just on *too* and *either*, either'. In Darden, B. J. *et al.* (eds.) *Papers from the Fourth Regional Meeting of the Chicago Linguistic Society*, 22–39. University of Chicago.

Grice, H. P. (1957). 'Meaning', *The Philosophical Review*, **62**, 377–88.

(1961). 'The causal theory of perception', *Proceedings of the Aristotelian Society* Suppl. Vol. **35**, 121–52.

(1968a). 'Utterer's meaning, sentence-meaning, and word-meaning', *Foundations of Language*, **4**, 225–42.

(1968b). 'Logic and conversation'. Mineo.

(1969). 'Utterer's meaning and intentions', *The Philosophical Review*, **78**, 147–77.

Hall-Partee, B. (1970). 'Negation, conjunction and quantifiers: syntax *vs.* semantics', *Foundations of Language*, **6**, 153–65.

(1971). 'On the requirement that transformations preserve meaning'. In Fillmore, C. J. and Langendoen, D. T. (eds.) *Studies in Linguistic Semantics*, 1–21, Holt, Rinehart & Winston.

(1972). 'Opacity, coreference and pronouns'. In Harman, G. and Davidson, D. (eds.) *Semantics of Natural Language*, 415–41. Reidel.

Hasegawa, K. (1972). 'Transformations and semantic interpretation', *Linguistic Inquiry*, **3**, 141–59.

Heidolph, K. E. (1970). 'Zur Bedeutung negativer Sätze'. In Bierwisch, M. and Heidolph, K. E. (eds.) *Progress in Linguistics*, 86–101. Mouton.

Heny, F. (1973). 'Sentence and predicate modifiers in English'. In Kimball, J. P. (ed.) *Syntax and Semantics* 2, 217–44. Seminar Press.

Herzberger, H. G. (1970). 'Truth and modality in semantically closed languages'. In Martin, R. L. (ed.) *The Paradox of the Liar*, 25–46. Yale University Press.

Hintikka, J. (1962). *Knowledge and Belief*. Cornell University Press.

(1968). 'Logic and philosophy'. in Klibansky, R. (ed.) *Contemporary Philosophy*, **1**, 3–30. Cornell University Press.

(1969). *Models for Modalities*. Reidel.

(1970). 'Objects of knowledge and belief: acquaintances and public figures', *The Journal of Philosophy*, **67**, 869–83.

(1972). 'The semantics of modal notions and the indeterminacy of ontology'. In Harman, G. and Davidson, D. (eds.) *Semantics of Natural Language*, 398–414. Reidel.

Hochberg, H. (1970). 'Strawson, Russell, and the King of France'. In Klemke, E. D. (ed.) *Essays on Bertrand Russell*, 309–37. University of Illinois Press.

Horn, L. (1969). 'A presuppositional analysis of *only* and *even*'. In Binnick, R. L. *et al.* (eds.) *Papers from the Fifth Regional Meeting of the Chicago Linguistics Society*, 98–107. University of Chicago, Chicago.

(1972). 'On The Semantic Properties of Logical Operators in English'. Unpublished Ph.D. thesis. University of California Los Angeles.

Hudson, R. A. (1973). 'The meaning of questions'. Mimeo.

Jacobs, R. A. and Rosenbaum, P. S. (1968). *English Transformational Grammar*. Ginn & Co.

Jacobson, A. (1970). 'Russell and Strawson on referring'. In Klemke, E. D. (ed.) *Essays on Bertrand Russell*, 285–308. University of Illinois Press.

Jackendoff, R. (1969). 'An interpretive theory of negation', *Foundations of Language*, **5**, 218–41.

(1971). 'Modal structure in semantic representation', *Linguistic Inquiry*, **2**, 481–514.

(1972). *Semantic Interpretation in a Generative Grammar*. MIT Press.

Jackson, L. A. (1971). 'A Transformational Theory of Context'. Unpublished Ph.D. thesis. London.

Karttunen, L. (1971a). 'Implicative verbs', *Language*, **47**, 340–58.

(1971b). 'Some observations on factivity', *Papers in Linguistics*, **4**, 55–70.

(1971c). 'Definite descriptions with crossing coreference', *Foundations of Language*, **7**, 157–82.

(1971d). 'Counterfactual conditionals', *Linguistic Inquiry*, **2**, 566–9.

(1973). 'Presuppositions of compound sentences', *Linguistic Inquiry*, **4,** 169–93.

Katz, J. J. (1964). 'Analyticity and contradiction in natural language'. In Fodor, J. and Katz, J. J. (eds.) *The Structure of Language*, 519–43.

(1966a). *The Philosophy of Language*. Harper & Row.

(1966b). 'Mr Pfeiffer on questions of reference', *Foundations of Language*, **2,** 241–4.

(1967). 'Recent issues in semantic theory', *Foundations of Language*, **3,** 124–94.

(1970). 'Interpretative semantics *vs.* generative semantics', *Foundations of Language*, **6,** 220–59.

(1972). *Semantic Theory*. Harper & Row.

(1973). 'On defining "presupposition"', *Linguistic Inquiry*, **4,** 256–60.

Katz, J. J. and Bever, T. G. (1974). 'The fall and rise of empiricism'. Mimeo.

Katz, J. J. and Fodor, J. (1963). 'The structure of a semantic theory', *Language* **39,** 170–210.

Katz, J. J. and Postal, P. M. (1964). *An Integrated Theory of Linguistic Descriptions*. MIT Press.

Keenan, E. L. (1971). 'Two kinds of presupposition in natural language'. In Fillmore, C. J. and Langendoen, D. T. (eds.) *Studies in Linguistic Semantics*, 45–54. Holt, Rinehart & Winston.

(1972). 'On semantically based grammar', *Linguistic Inquiry*, **3,** 413–61.

Kempson, R. M. (1973). 'Review of Fillmore, C. J. and Langendoen, D. T. *Studies in Linguistic Semantics*', *Journal of Linguistics*, **9,** 120–40.

Kiefer, F. and Ruwet, N. (eds.) (1972). *Generative Grammar in Europe*. Reidel.

Kiparsky, P. and Kiparsky, C. (1970). 'Fact'. In Bierwisch, M. and Heidolph, K. (eds.) *Progress in Linguistics*, 143–73. Mouton.

Klima, E. S. (1964). 'Negation in English'. In Fodor, J. and Katz, J. J. (eds.) *The Structure of Language*, 246–323. Prentice-Hall.

Kroch, A. S. (1972). 'Lexical and inferred meanings for some time adverbs', *Quarterly Progress Report no. 104 of the Research Laboratory of Electronics MIT*, 260–7.

Kuroda, S-Y. (1968). 'English relativization and certain related problems', *Language*, **44,** 244–66.

(1969). 'Remarks on selectional restrictions and presuppositions'. In Kiefer, F. (ed.) *Studies in Syntax and Semantics*, 138–67. Reidel.

Lakoff, G. N. (1968). 'Deep and surface grammar'. Mimeo.

(1970a). 'Repartee, or a reply to negation, conjunction and quantifiers', *Foundations of Language*, **6,** 389–422.

(1970b). *Irregularity in Syntax*. Holt, Rinehart & Winston.

(1970c). 'A note on ambiguity and vagueness', *Linguistic Inquiry*, **1,** 357–9.

(1971a). 'On generative semantics'. In Steinberg, D. D. and Jakobovits. L. A. (eds.) *Semantics*, 232–96. Cambridge University Press.

(1971b). 'Presupposition and relative well-formedness'. In Steinberg, D. D. and Jakobovits, L. A. (eds) *Semantics*, 329–40. Cambridge University Press.

(1971c). 'The role of deduction in grammar'. In Fillmore, C. J. and Langendoen, D. T. (eds.) *Studies in Linguistic Semantics*, 63–72. Holt, Rinehart & Winston.

(1972a). 'Linguistics and natural logic'. In Harman, G. and Davidson, D. (eds.) *Semantics of Natural Language*, 545–665. Reidel.

(1972b). 'Hedges: a study in meaning criteria and the logic of fuzzy concepts'. In Peranteau, P. *et al.* (eds.) *Papers from the Eighth Regional Meeting of the Chicago Linguistic Society*, 183–228. University of Chicago.

Lakoff, R. (1969). 'A syntactic argument for negative transportation'. In Binnick, R. I. *et al.* (eds.) *Papers from the Fifth Regional Meeting of the Chicago Linguistic Society*, 140–7. University of Chicago.

(1971). 'If's, and's, and but's about conjunction'. In Fillmore, C. J. and Langendoen, D. T. (eds.) *Studies in Linguistic Semantics*, 115–50. Holt, Rinehart & Winston.

(1972). 'The pragmatics of modality'. In Peranteau, P. *et al.* (eds.) *Papers from the Eighth Regional Meeting of the Chicago Linguistics Society*, 229–46. University of Chicago.

Landesman, C. (1972). *Discourse and its Presuppositions*. Yale University Press.

Langendoen, D. T. and Savin, H. B. (1971). 'The projection problem for presuppositions'. In Fillmore, C. J. and Langendoen, D. T. (eds.) *Studies in Linguistic Semantics*, 55–61. Holt, Rinehart & Winston.

Lasnik, H. B. (1972). 'A general constraint: some evidence from negation', *Quarterly Progress Report no. 101 of the Research Laboratory of Electronics MIT*, 215–7.

Leech, G. N. (1969). *Towards a Semantic Description of English*. Longman.

Lees, R. B. (1960). *The Grammar of English Nominalizations*, Mouton.

Lemmon, E. J. (1962). 'On sentences verifiable by their use', *Analysis*, **22**, 86–9.

(1966). 'Sentences, statements, and propositions'. In Williams, B. and Montefiore, A. (eds.) *British Analytical Philosophy*, 87–107. Routledge & Kegan Paul.

Lewis, D. K. (1969). *Convention: a Philosophical Study*. Harvard University Press.

(1972). 'General semantics'. In Harman, G. and Davidson, D. (eds.) *Semantics of Natural Language*, 169–218. Reidel.

Linsky, L. (1967). *Referring*. Routledge & Kegan Paul.

Lyons, J. (1968). *Introduction to Theoretical Linguistics*. Cambridge University Press.

McCawley, J. (1968a). 'The role of semantics in grammar'. In Bach, E. and Harms, R. (eds.) *Universals in Linguistic Theory*, 125–69. Holt, Rinehart & Winston.

(1968b). 'Lexical insertion in a transformational grammar without deep structure'. In Darden, B. J. *et al.* (eds.) *Papers from the Fourth Regional Meeting of the Chicago Linguistics Society*, 71–80. University of Chicago.

(1971). 'Where do noun phrases come from?'. In Steinberg, D. D. and Jakobovits, L. A. (eds.) *Semantics*, 217–31. Cambridge University Press.

MacKay, A. F. (1972). 'On Mr. Grice's theory of meaning', *Mind*, **80**, 57–66.

Martin, R. M. (1959). *Toward a Systematic Pragmatics*, North-Holland.

(1971a). *Logic, Language and Metaphysics*. New York University Press.

(1971b). 'Some thoughts on the formal approach to the philosophy of language'. In Bar-Hillel, Y. (ed.) *Pragmatics of Natural Languages*, 120–44. Reidel.

Montague, R. (1970). 'English as a formal language'. In *Linguaggi Nella Societa e Nella Tecnica*, 189–223. Edizioni di Comunita, Milan.

(1972). 'Pragmatics and intensional logic'. In Harman, G. and Davidson, D. (eds.) *Semantics of Natural Language*, 142–68. Reidel.

Morgan, J. (1969). 'On the treatment of presuppositions in transformational grammar'. In Binnick, R. I. *et al.* (eds.) *Papers from the Fifth Regional Meeting of the Chicago Linguistics Society*, 169–77. University of Chicago.

Morris, C. W. (1938). 'Foundations of the theory of signs'. In *International Encyclopaedia of Unified Science*, **1**, no. 2. University of Chicago Press.

(1946). *Signs, Language and Behavior*. Prentice-Hall.

Nerlich, G. (1965). 'Presupposition and entailment', *American Philosophical Quarterly*, **2**, 33–42.

Odegard, D. (1963). 'Unique reference and entailment', *Analysis*, **23**, 73–9.

Perlmutter, D. (1970). 'On the article in English'. In Bierwisch, M. and Heidolph, K. E. (eds.) *Progress in Linguistics*, 233–48. Mouton.

Postal, P. (1970). 'On the surface verb "remind"', *Linguistic Inquiry*, **1**, 37–120.

(1971a). *Cross-over Phenomena*. Holt, Rinehart & Winston.

(1971b). 'On coreferential complement subject deletion', *Linguistic Inquiry*, **2**, 439–500.

Prior, A. N. (1962). 'Possible worlds', *Philosophical Quarterly*, **12**, 36–43.

Quine, W. V. (1953). *From a Logical Point of View*. Harvard University Press.

(1966). *Elementary Logic*. 2nd edition. Harvard University Press.

Quirk, R. *et al.* (1972). *A Grammar of Contemporary English*. Longman.

Reichenbach, H. (1947). *Elements of Symbolic Logic*. Dover.

Rescher, N. (1968). *Topics in Philosophical Logic*. Reidel.

Robbins, B. (1968). *The Definite Article in English Transformations*. Mouton.

Roberts, G. W. (1969). 'A problem about presupposition', *Mind*, **78**, 270–1.

Rosenbaum, P. S. (1967). *The Grammar of English Predicate Complement Constructions*. MIT Press.

Ross, J. R. (1967). 'Constraints on Variables in Syntax'. Unpublished Ph.D. thesis. MIT.

(1969). 'On declarative sentences'. In Jacobs, R. A. and Rosenbaum, P. S. (eds.) *Readings in English Transformational Grammar*, 222–72. Ginn & Co.

(1972). 'Act'. In Harman, G. and Davidson, D. (eds.) *Semantics of Natural Language*, 70–126. Reidel.

Russell, B. (1905). 'On denoting', *Mind*, **14**, 479–93.

Sadock, J. M. (1970). 'Whimperatives'. In Sadock, J. M. and Vanek, A. (eds.) *Studies Presented to R. B. Lees by His Students*, 223–38. Edmonton.

(1971). 'Queclaratives'. In Adams, D. *et al.* (eds.) *Papers from the Seventh Regional Meeting of the Chicago Linguistics Society*, 223–31. University of Chicago.

(1972). 'Speech act idioms'. In Peranteau, P. *et al.* (eds.) *Papers from the Eighth Regional Meeting of the Chicago Linguistics Society*, 329–39. University of Chicago.

Schelling, T. C. (1960). *The Strategy of Conflict*. Harvard University Press.

Schiffer, S. R. (1972). *Meaning*. Clarendon Press, Oxford.

Schnitzer, M. (1971). 'Presupposition, entailment, and Russell's theory of descriptions', *Foundations of Language*, **7**, 297–9.

Searle, J. R. (1968). 'Austin on locutionary and illocutionary acts', *Philosophical Review*, **77**, 405–24.

(1969). *Speech Acts: An Essay in the Philosophy of Language*. Cambridge University Press.

Sellars, W. (1954). 'Presupposing', *Philosophical Review*, **63**, 197–215.

Smith, C. (1964). 'Determiners and relative clauses in a generative grammar of English', *Language*, **40**, 37–52.

Stalnaker, R. C. (1972). 'Pragmatics'. In Harman, G. and Davidson, D. (eds.) *Semantics of Natural Language*, 380–97. Reidel.

Stalnaker, R. C. and Thomason, R. (1973). 'A semantic theory of adverbs', *Linguistic Inquiry*, **4**, 195–220.

Stenius, E. (1967). 'Mood and language-game', *Synthese*, **17**, 254–74.

Stockwell, R. P., Schachter, P. and Hall-Partee, B. (1973). *The Major Syntactic Structures of English*. Holt, Rinehart & Winston.

Strawson, P. (1950). 'On referring', *Mind*, **59**, 320–44.

(1952). *Introduction to Logical Theory*. Methuen.

(1954). 'A reply to Mr Sellars', *Philosophical Review*, **63**, 216–31.

(1964a). 'Identifying reference and truth values', *Theoria*, **30**, 96–118.

(1964b). 'Intention and convention in speech acts', *Philosophical Review*, **73**, 439–60.

(1971a). *Logico-Linguistic Papers*. Methuen.

(1971b). 'Meaning and truth'. In Strawson, P. *Logico-Linguistic Papers*, 170–89. Methuen.

Thomason, R. (1973). 'Semantics, pragmatics, conversation, and presupposition'. Mimeo.

Van Fraassen, B. (1968). 'Presupposition, implication and self-reference', *Journal of Philosophy*, **65**, 136–52.

(1969). 'Presuppositions, super-valuations, and free logic'. In Lambert, K. (ed.) *The Logical Way of Doing Things*, 67–91. Yale University Press.

(1970). 'Truth and paradoxical consequences'. In Martin, R. L. (ed.) *The Paradox of the Liar*, 13–23. Yale University Press.

Vendler, Z. (1967a). *Linguistics in Philosophy*. Cornell University Press.

(1967b). 'Causal relations', *Journal of Philosophy*, **64**, 704–13.

Vermazen, B. (1966). 'Review of Katz, J. and Postal, P. *An Integrated Theory of Linguistic Descriptions* and Katz, J. *The Philosophy of Language*', *Synthese*, **17**, 350–65.

Weinreich, U. (1962). 'Lexicographic definition in descriptive semantics'. In Householder, F. and Saporta, S. (eds.) *Problems in Lexicography*, 25–43. Mouton.

(1966). 'Explorations in semantic theory'. In Sebeok, T. A. (ed.) *Current Trends in Linguistics* 3, 395–477. Mouton.

Wiggins, D. (1971). 'On sentence-sense, word-sense and difference of word-sense. Towards a philosophical theory of dictionaries'. In Steinberg, D. D. and Jakobovits, L. A. (eds.) *Semantics*, 14–34. Cambridge University Press.

Wilson, D. (1972). 'Presuppositions on factives', *Linguistic Inquiry*, **3**, 405–10.

(forthcoming). *Presuppositions and Non-truth-conditional Semantics*. Academic Press.

Young, J. J. (1972). 'Ifs and hooks: a defence of the orthodox view', *Analysis*, **33**, 56–63.

Index